An Environment: Twentieth-Century Britain

An Environmental History of Twentieth-Century Britain

John Sheail

palgrave

© John Sheail 2002

All rights reserved. No reproduction, copy or transmission of this publication may be made without written permission.

No paragraph of this publication may be reproduced, copied or transmitted save with written permission or in accordance with the provisions of the Copyright, Designs and Patents Act 1988, or under the terms of any licence permitting limited copying issued by the Copyright Licensing Agency, 90 Tottenham Court Road, London W1T 4LP.

Any person who does any unauthorised act in relation to this publication may be liable to criminal prosecution and civil claims for damages.

The author has asserted his right to be identified as the author of this work in accordance with the Copyright, Designs and Patents Act 1988.

First published 2002 by
PALGRAVE
Houndmills, Basingstoke, Hampshire RG21 6XS and
175 Fifth Avenue, New York, N.Y. 10010
Companies and representatives throughout the world

PALGRAVE is the new global academic imprint of St. Martin's Press LLC Scholarly and Reference Division and Palgrave Publishers Ltd (formerly Macmillan Press Ltd).

ISBN 0-333-94980-3 hardback
ISBN 0-333-94981-1 paperback

This book is printed on paper suitable for recycling and made from fully managed and sustained forest sources.

A catalogue record for this book is available from the British Library.

Library of Congress Cataloging-in-Publication Data
Sheail, John.
   An environmental history of twentieth-century Britain / John Sheail.
     p. cm.
   Includes bibliographical references and index.
   ISBN 0-333-94980-3 (cloth)
    1. Environmental policy–Great Britain. 2. Great Britain–Environmental conditions. 3. City planning–Environmental aspects–Great Britain. 4. Human ecology–Great Britain.

HC260.E5 S5 2002
333.7′0941′0904–dc21   2001053155

10 9 8 7 6 5 4 3 2 1
11 10 09 08 07 06 05 04 03 02

Printed in China

To the memory of Gordon E. Cherry, 1931–96

Contents

Preface ix

1 **Histories of Their Time** 1
  Introduction 1
  A Twentieth-Century Conspectus 5

2 **The Management of Change** 12
  Introduction 12
  Housing and Town Planning 17
  Local Planning 20
  National Planning 27
  Political Laboratories 33
  A Vision Lost 41

3 **Nature Incorporated** 46
  Introduction 46
  The Sanitary Authorities 48
  Sewering the Suburbs 56
  New Towns and Oysters 62
  The Multi-Purpose Use of Water 72

4 **New Beginnings in Forestry** 82
  Introduction 82
  The Forest Authority 90
  Forest Parks 94
  Multi-Purpose Forestry 98

5 **A Third Force** 103
  Introduction 103
  The Agricultural Context 109

National Parks   115
Nature Reserves   122
Coastal Preservation   131
The Challenge of Leisure   137

6 **Environmental Conservation**   146
Introduction   146
Agricultural Improvement   151
Arresting 'the Engine of Destruction'   158
Towards 'Creative Conservation'   165

7 **Transport and the Environment**   177
Introduction   177
'Mixed Blessing'   182
London's Third Airport   191
Commercial Pipelines   196
The Pipe-Lines Act   204
Environmental Assessment   212

8 **Environmental Hazards**   218
Introduction   218
Dereliction   227
Before 'Silent Spring'   235
Air Quality   246

9 **The Century of the Environment**   257
Introduction   257
Raising Awareness   262
'Movers and Shakers'   271

Bibliography   283
Index   301

Preface

The study of environmental history has grown apace since the 1970s. Much of the stimulus has come from contemporary concerns for the natural environment and, more particularly, the human impact on its life-giving resources. The book breaks new ground by providing illustrative accounts of how some of the most pressing concerns came to be recognised, and a response formulated. In as much as one of the most notable features of the twentieth century has been the increasing importance of government in everyday life, highly relevant insights are to be found in the further sub-field of planning history. The book makes considerable use of the archives of central and local government, business, and the professional and voluntary bodies.

Far from there being a single twentieth-century environmental history, there were many such histories that overlap and intertwine in the most intricate way. Only a few can be pursued in a book of this size, which seeks, largely through a thematic approach, to convey some sense of the skill and experience gained in coping with, if not mastering, environmental issues. Rather than exploring further the theoretical dimensions, which have already received so much attention, the book illustrates the range of situations and practices alluded to in such debate. The book sets out especially to encourage those who want to know more fully *where* and *when*, and *how* and *why*, environmental initiatives were taken, and the significance to be placed upon them. Through such closer study of the original printed material and documentation, there is the possibility of identifying more exactly the role of personalities and events in determining the course of policy-making.

I am grateful to Professor Mike Roberts, the Director of the Centre for Ecology and Hydrology, and colleagues at Monks Wood for the opportunity to write the book, and, as always, to Gillian and our family. Professor Jeremy Black and Terka Acton, my Commissioning Editor, have given much encouragement and support. It will be obvious to readers the extent of my gratitude to the Cambridge University Library, the Public Record Office (PRO) and Scottish Record Office (SRO), and the numerous record offices cited. The Confederation of British Industry and Esso UK kindly gave access to material in their keeping.

JOHN SHEAIL

Hilton
Census Night 2001

Note

References to archival sources are given in the text, both for convenience and to emphasise where such evidence has been found. The abbreviation PD refers to material in the relevant volume and columns of the published Parliamentary Debates (Hansard). PP denotes Parliamentary Papers, the full citation of which is given in the Bibliography. The measurements cited in the text are those used in the original source.

CHAPTER 1

Histories of Their Time

Introduction

Some of the most exciting research occurs where academic disciplines meet. Such meeting-points may be planned but more often than not they just evolve around a common interest – in this case what has come to be called the 'environment'. If 'environmental history' is quite literally 'a history of the environment', no wonder it has become a somewhat crowded meeting-point. There is a twofold interest. One is the intrinsic fascination of recreating the past – in answering the question, What was the Victorian, or the early-twentieth-century, environment really like? The other motive is to help explain how today's environment has come about. As Ian Simmons wrote, in his introductory text, *Environmental History,* there is no breaking point – a time when the past can be forgotten (Simmons 1993).

Historians have long moved away from political histories to write about economic and social life. An important growth-point in geography has been the historical geography of how human aspiration and activity have impacted upon, and have themselves been affected by, the physical world. With the expansion of extra-mural education and car ownership, local history became immensely popular. By emphasising how much could be learnt from the landscape, if interpreted aright, W.G. Hoskins, in his book *The Making of the English Landscape*, encouraged readers to explore and discover the town and countryside for themselves (Hoskins 1955). The rapidity of change in the 1960s and 1970s, and consequent removal of much historical evidence, encouraged two further sub-fields to emerge, namely landscape archaeology and industrial archaeology. They sought not only to catalogue but to understand how such artefacts related to one another, in what Tom Williamson called 'a particularly complex kaleidoscope of patterned creation and structured destruction' (Everson and Williamson 1998). Britain came to lead Europe in telling the history of its landscapes, and such knowledge and understanding strengthened opinion as to the need to conserve such diversity in town and countryside (Thirsk 2000).

It was no coincidence that much of the stimulus for another emerging field, historical ecology, came from naturalists and ecologists increasingly concerned with the threat to 'the natural heritage'. There was an urgent need to identify and acquire the finest examples as nature reserves. A knowledge of how the wildlife habitats were formed in the past was seen as a key to understanding their survival and significance. It was the basis for management plans for sustaining them. Where local historians were encouraged to get 'mud on their boots', as they used the evidence that was there to be studied in the landscape itself, such histories provided a framework of reference for those already with muddy boots. Such stimulus and insight nurtured 'an historical imagination amongst ecologists', at a time when practical means were being urgently sought to protect what were perceived to be 'old' woodlands and grasslands, and species-rich hedgerows, from large-scale destruction (Kirby and Watkins 1998).

There were parallel and considerably more pretentious moves to look afresh at the origins and evolution of the present-day North American landscapes. A 'round-table' organised by the *Journal of American History* in 1990 reviewed how environmental history had quickly become part of the mainstream of American history. A leading practitioner, Donald Worster, recalled how it had first taken shape in the 1970s, as conferences on the global predicament were organised and popular environmental movements gathered momentum. Environmental history was 'born out of a strong moral concern', that matured as a study of 'the role and place of nature in human life' (Worster 1990). It retained a political purpose. As the editors noted of a collection of *Essays in European*

Environmental History, highly relevant perspectives were provided on how a new type of threshold was being crossed, where the limiting factor to further economic and social growth might no longer be capital, markets or labour, but the environment itself. Environmental history emphasised how the present-day environmental difficulties were so fundamental that something more than developing an appropriate technology was required. The very nature of the economy and society had to change (Brimblecombe and Pfister 1990).

Writing of environmental history from a Scottish perspective, Christopher Smout found that despite there being several departure-points, and a range of academic interests involved, there was a common focus on the human interaction with the natural world. But what should be the ideological stance of environmental historians? Where economic historians had been accused of striking a triumphalist tone in chronicling the human conquest of nature, environmental historians remained, for the most part, full of gloom and doom, perceiving change in the natural world as always for the worse (Smout 1993). In his monumental volume, *Landscape and Memory*, Simon Schama regretted that although environmental history offered some of the most original and challenging history now being written, it seemed to repeat the same dismal tale of land being taken, exploited and exhausted. Where traditional societies lived in sacred reverence of the soil, they had been displaced by the reckless individualist – the capitalist aggressor (Schama 1995). Christopher Smout insisted it was 'no part of the job description of historians of any kind to rebuke the past', any more than it was for them to foretell the future. The 'straight political reason' for writing environmental history was to produce 'useful history'. It was neither to justify nor direct the present, but to inform it through making such history 'available' (Smout 2000).

Such debate as to the purpose of environmental history raised questions of scope and priorities. Donald Worster distinguished three conceptual levels, the first or lowest being nature, or rather the dynamics of the systems upon which all life depended. The next level in the structure were the political economies by which people lived and worked within such a dynamic world. The third or highest was of a cognitive kind – the belief systems that comprised the ideas, ethics and sentiments by which people perceived their relationship with the other two. For Worster, the priority was to discover more about how people had adapted and transformed nature to produce the food, clothing and shelter required, and of how they had in turn changed their lifestyles and social relations so as to raise that productivity further. Not only did Worster's writings have a rural focus but, in an essay, 'Doing Environmental History', he argued that it would be inappropriate to give much attention to built environments, in as much as towns and cities were so 'wholly expressive of culture' that there were no obvious linkages to nature or the 'non-human' sphere (Worster 1988).

Another American environmental historian, William Cronon, disagreed, insisting that even the least natural of landscapes merited attention (Cronon 1990). Such debate focused attention on a further growth-point during the 1960s and 70s, namely urban history. In pursuing their own economic and social goals, urban historians had already begun to highlight the many ways in which cities had impacted on the natural environment, both within or beyond the city limits, and the importance of the environment for those living and working within the city (Rosen and Tarr 1994). The innovative contribution of the American urban historian, Joel Tarr, had been to join historians of science and technology in attempting to gain a better understanding of how the 'networked city' evolved, in terms of its streets, pipes and wires, and of how pollution came to affect an ever-widening sphere of water, air and land (Tarr 1996).

It is in the context of society's response to the scale and nature of physical change, particularly in the city, that a further sub-field of planning history has become especially important. Gordon Cherry wrote one of the first planning histories, *The Evolution of British Town Planning*, as part of the celebrations of the Diamond Jubilee of the Royal Town Planning Institute. It helped explain how Britain, over the previous sixty years, had established one of the most comprehensive planning systems in the world (Cherry 1974).

But the 'new wave of self-conscious planning history' of the 1970s also corresponded with a time of economic malaise and widespread misgivings on the part of the planning profession as to its current practices. As Anthony Sutcliffe recalled later, it was a time for catching one's breath, and making 'sober appraisal' of what had happened during the previous quarter-century of frenetic change. A greater awareness of history would not, by itself, restore confidence among planners, but it might make the experience a more positive one (Sutcliffe 1981a).

Far from splintering off areas of history for separate study, planning historians perceived their role as one of contributing an essential element to the larger picture. They offered highly relevant insights into one of the twentieth century's most notable features, the increasing importance of government in everyday life. In his environmental history of the United States, Hal Rothman characterised the twentieth century as 'the regulatory century', with environmental regulation among the most pervasive in everyday American life. The relationship of people to their physical world became ever more closely defined by regulation and agency (Rothman 2000, 133–4). One of the attendant bureaucracies to be established in Britain was the regulation of land use, first at a local and then increasingly at the national scale. As Gordon Cherry wrote, histories of that planning endeavour involve more than simply tracing the sequence of building form, spatial layout and individual projects. Insights are sought into the impact of ideas, the interplay of power structures, and the currency of fashion. As well as tracing what was physically achieved, questions are raised as to why even the most powerful of movements often left their adherents disappointed, in the sense of their mission being only partly fulfilled (Cherry 1991 and 1994).

A Twentieth-Century Conspectus

How then might the ground be prepared for the environmental histories that spring from contemporary preoccupations? One model might be James Winter's study of the impact of steam technology in both threatening and enabling the Victorian environment to be sustained (Winter 1999). But it remains true, as Michael Williams remarked, that there is still no comprehensive and authoritative synthesis of the nineteenth century, whether in terms of environmental ideas or of the history of human impacts. Such a task was even harder for the twentieth century, especially as the historian came closer to the present. More happened, more was known, and many more people had a view (Williams 1998).

Where one approach may be to create some overarching framework within which to study, others have sought 'entry' through case studies. As Roy Gregory remarked, there is a good deal to be said for the view that case studies are best left to speak for themselves (Gregory 1971). Yet some conclusions have been drawn. Kimber and Richardson (1974) emphasised the political element in managing the environment. The concluding chapter of their book, *Campaigning for the Environment*, offered guidance on the tactics and strategies whereby pressure groups might achieve greater prominence. Gregory, in his volume *The Price of Amenity*, wrote similarly of how, in a complex society, nothing could change without disturbing existing arrangements and affecting someone, or some group of interests. In a much-governed country, not even public bodies could stand apart from the fray, where decisions were bound to leave a trail of aggrieved citizens. Where the late-twentieth-century systems of resource management had many shortcomings, Gregory's purpose was to demonstrate how such expressions of outrage and resentment were not so much signs of inefficiency and ineptitude, but were an inevitable outcome of any decision-making process.

Any account of the pace and direction of change is closely affected by the source material that survives and is accessible. Max Beloff claimed the inter-war years were a period of unique opportunity for the historian. Although there was unprecedented archival data on the 'strivings of the masses and of particular groups', the records were still manageable. Decision-making in government remained 'the prerogative of the few'. There were still only some 500 generalists and 50 specialists in the higher levels of the civil service in 1939 (Beloff 1975). Where most people had previously left only 'snapshots' of themselves in parish registers and census returns, the rudimentary welfare-reforms of the early 1900s led to an enormous expansion of record keeping (Vincent 1998). The Finance Act of 1910 instigated a survey of 13 million properties, whereby over 40 million items of information were collected. The wartime National Farm Survey of 1941–43 recorded some 250 pieces of information for each of 300,000 holdings in England and Wales. Both used large-scale maps (Short 1997).

The invaluable guide, *Record Repositories in Great Britain* lists those archives open to the public (Mortimer 1997). There are the national record offices, and most obviously the Public Record Office at Kew, in Surrey, and the Scottish Record Office in Edinburgh, whose records are drawn upon so heavily in this volume. The local record offices are supported by local government. A further guide, *Record Offices. How to Find Them*, includes both maps of their location and 'a code of practice' for the 'tens of thousands of people who get pleasure and fascination from using the marvellous heritage of records' (Gibson and Peskett 1998). A key objective of this book is to illustrate the use to which the environmental and planning historian might put the evidence drawn from those repositories, as well as the manuscript material preserved more widely in private archives. The latter includes the often huge collections of miscellaneous papers, sometimes found in the offices of individual businesses, professional and voluntary bodies, and in the cupboards of the individual home (Lord 1999).

Where they have been formally preserved and catalogued, such old files and papers may be kept for their insight into how policies were drawn up, precedents set, or for the primary data (administrative, technical or scientific). Such paperwork invariably represents only a tiny fraction of what once existed. Over 95 per cent of the records of central government (that accrue each year) are destroyed, yet over a mile of shelving is nevertheless filled in the Public Record Office. They constitute what Rodney Lowe called the fullest archive of 'the real evidence' of how British society has evolved. There are the papers of what political scientists call 'the core executive', namely those of the Prime Minister and Cabinet, and its Committees. It is however the 'lower-level records' of government departments that so considerably amplify, amend and corroborate what the historian might otherwise learn from the published record and personal memories. They include not only the material generated from within government, but all the other material sent in, or collected from, non-governmental sources (Lowe 1997).

Yet even where the archival material is preserved, its use is conditional. Although the Public Records Act of 1958 conferred for the first time a legal right of access to official material, the principle of the collective responsibility of ministers and officials in the decision-making of Cabinet and departments requires there to be strict limits to public access. Where such files were closed for fifty years after the date of the most recent papers within the reference, a decision was taken by the Cabinet in August 1965, and described by Richard Crossman in his controversial diaries (Crossman 1975, p. 303), to reduce the period of closure to thirty years. Such guidelines for central government are generally followed by those responsible for the archives of local government and other such repositories. They go far in explaining the heavy bias of this book, and much modern history, towards the earlier period, for which more intimate insights into the decision-making process are available.

The published record may be all that is available. Yet even where there is much relevant documentation, the printed work remains of critical value. As Philip Williamson remarked of Stanley Baldwin, one of Britain's longest-serving Prime Ministers, it would be easy, when confronted with 'the rich private evidence' of his archive, to forget how such figures came to public pre-eminence. Their right to be policy-makers, tacticians and administrators was not achieved through such private correspondence and discussion, but through the persuasive powers of their public utterances. Personal beliefs might rarely be set down in private – they are simply assumed. They emerged as the underlying and consistent themes of the speeches and publications which, in time, came to distinguish and therefore define the stature of their author

(Williamson 1999). The present volume makes illustrative use of the printed word, as to be found in books, professional and learned journals, and newspaper accounts, as well as the more specialist proceedings of parliamentary debate and its committee reports and proceedings.

The historian's source material was often so much part of the decision-making process that it never provides a coldly objective insight into what came to pass. Each published and manuscript source has to be closely scrutinised for its part in the taking and implementing of decisions. What was its original purpose? What was its status and scope to exert influence? An example may be cited. News that Arthur Greenwood, the Minister of Health in the Labour Government of 1931, intended to appoint an official Committee of Inquiry into Garden Cities, drew a sharp (and historically illuminating) commentary from the Treasury. The Minister was censured for drafting its terms of reference in a way that assumed that Garden Cities should be established. His choice of such ardent proponents as members meant the conclusions of the Committee were substantially known before it had even met. As a Treasury official wrote, a Committee of Inquiry should be 'a microcosm of the Nation and so balanced as to represent as far as possible the various interests of the Nation'. Experts and advocates of any particular course of action should be consigned to the role of witnesses. And yet the Treasury itself was hardly a disinterested party. It pressed for the abandonment of the Committee. Having failed, an official minuted in July 1932 how there was merit in letting it 'function in the present atmosphere' of a world economic recession. There would be 'no temptation to be lax on finance' (Public Record Office (PRO), T 161 660, S36496).

In a first attempt at writing a self-conscious 'environmental history' of Britain since the Industrial Revolution, B.W. Clapp wrote of how the subject-matter of such histories would only be decided by long practice and example. They would assuredly embrace pollution and the depletion of natural resources – but what else (Clapp 1994)? A major stimulus to studies made of the environment throughout the twentieth century, was the scale of squalor and, therefore, damage to the health of families and whole communities in towns and cities, where the bulk of the population was found at the turn of the century. Spurred on by philanthropic bodies, ways were urgently sought for providing adequate housing and such basic utilities as a water supply and system of waste disposal. Early chapters of this book illustrate how the status of watercourses was monitored; planning schemes devised for securing the most cost-effective way of developing land, initially at the urban edges and then wherever building was taking place. Often the first to experience such pressures for greater foresight and regulation, local authorities acted as 'political laboratories' in setting precedents for what was later taken up and generally applied.

Central government might itself innovate through such ventures as the establishment of New Towns and the support given through the Forestry Commission to large-scale afforestation or, less directly, through the financial support provided for the 'modernisation' of farming. Such ventures had often to be trimmed and adapted, so as to reduce their impacts on existing user interests in the land and watercourses affected. More positively, forms of multi-purpose resource use were devised. It was largely through such initiatives that a Third Force, alongside farming and forestry, emerged in the management of the countryside, namely the conscious stewardship of rural landscapes and the coastline for their amenity and wildlife, and the opportunities they afforded for outdoor recreation. Such ventures closely reflected the increasing opportunity of those living in cities and towns to visit and experience for themselves both the inherent variety of scenery and situation, and the large-scale changes being wrought by urban development and intensity of rural management practices and by the impact of the visitors themselves. The physical effects of this revolution in communications often drew hostile comment, most obviously in respect of such large-scale projects as motorway and airport development. Paradoxically, the comparatively inconspicuous development of another revolutionary form of transport, the underground pipeline, excited so little concern as to have passed almost unnoticed by the environmental or planning historian.

Where environmental disasters played a significant part in galvanising concern for the environment, further relevant context to the emergence of the so-called environmental movement may be found in the economic and social outlook that characterised the late 1960s and the 1970s. Those chronicling the impact on public consciousness of instances of large-scale dereliction, the side-effects of agricultural pesticides on birdlife, and endeavours to combat the increasingly global manifestations of atmospheric pollution, have emphasised the significance of a small number of writers in warning of the consequences of allowing human affluence and freedom of choice to over-exploit and devastate the natural world. Attention has been drawn to the role of both the long-standing and the new conservation bodies in exciting public concern. Environmental issues came to be seen as too important to be left to governments and their expert advisers. A mixture of altruism and self-interest caused business leaders to adopt a more constructive approach to such notions as sustainable development and the elimination of the more polluting processes. Where Britain believed it had relevant skills and experience to offer in developing the international dimension, as witnessed by the Rio Summit in 1992, such thinking as to the optimal use of its own diverse physical and human resources at the close of the century again emphasised the essential role of the local community in determining what was in store for life in the twenty-first century.

To have attempted a comprehensive review of all that was significant in the environmental history of twentieth-century Britain would have either turned a book of this length into a recitation of facts, or have required the author to impose some all-encompassing, yet severely limiting, concept of what was important. The approach has rather been to temper generalisation with down-to-earth instances, drawn in large measure from archival sources. Through such examples of probing behind the decision-making in environmental policy, it is hoped to encourage others, whether for fun, a dissertation or more ambitious purpose, to burrow into the records, both for the exhilaration of such detective work and for the greater rigour of explanation it may bring.

CHAPTER 2

The Management of Change

Introduction

Even if nothing else had happened, the changes in the number and distribution of people would have made the late nineteenth century different from what had gone before. The population doubled. Where every second English person was an urban dweller in 1851, four out of five persons lived in towns and cities in 1911. Through advances in science and technology, town and country were reshaped in both their physical appearance and social structure (Newsome 1997). Most growth occurred within and around existing industrial centres on, or near, the Pennine flanks, in the North-East of England, the West Midlands, and around the coasts of the British Isles. London was by far the largest centre, attaining a growth rate of 170 per cent in the 60-year period, 1851–1911. London was both a 'world city' in the sense of being so large (Briggs 1968), and 'an imperial city' – the capital of a formally constituted and governed empire that extended to every continent and ocean, except Antarctica. The imperial metropolis was at the heart of the largest empire the planet had ever known (Schneer 1999).

Growth may have come through the accretion of existing towns and cities, but there was little guidance as to how those populations might be sustained. An increasingly urban society was both troubled and excited by a spectrum of concern that extended from personal health, through public health, to the health of the environment generally. Europeans had never lived in large towns without poisoning themselves with their own waste products. Life had survived only through migration from a healthier countryside (Hennock 1973, p. 2).

The Management of Change

It was perhaps because of the greater prosperity and provision for public health in the late nineteenth century that the revelations as to the poor health of potential recruits during the Boer War were so sensational. The British Medical Association met in Manchester in 1902, after an interval of 25 years. As the conference handbook acknowledged, there had been striking changes, both in terms of the city's role as an industrial centre for coal, machinery and cotton goods, and in such social improvement as more regular employment, better housing, a more plentiful water supply, fever hospital and public parks, and the voluntary effort and educative role of the Manchester and Salford Sanitary Association (British Medical Association 1902). And yet it was also painfully obvious that at a time when the Boer farmers of South Africa were inflicting heavy defeat on the British army, recruiting officers were having to turn away large numbers of young men because of their poor physique and health. Of the 11,000 men examined, 8,000 were rejected as unfit for military service. Such a high proportion, as repeated in other cities, seemed to support the belief, stemming from Darwinian concepts of evolution, that the main determinant of human welfare might be the urban environment itself. Not only might moral principles afford little protection against the deleterious effects of urban conditions, but the genetic effect might become so strong as to lead to a progressive degeneration of human stock (Parliamentary Papers) (PP) 1904).

Public health came to encompass not only the prevention of disease and death, but measures to improve health generally. Among 'the images and realities' of the city and town, the 'slums' figured large. Urban historians have drawn on the many contemporary surveys and other forms of description to locate and describe those poorer housing-areas, both in physical and economic terms (Yelling 1986). And yet, more recently, Alan Mayne has claimed that such descriptions perpetuated the myth of Victorian and Edwardian slums, a myth consciously cultivated in the late nineteenth century to strengthen 'bourgeois common-sense' as to how city-culture should be fashioned. The multiplicity of forms, culture and experience found in the lives and housing of the urban poor were collapsed into 'a one-dimensional world populated by stock characters and scenery'. Social investigators and news reporters delighted in the sense of danger associated with the slums (Mayne 1993). Barry Doyle found, in a study of Edwardian Norwich, that whilst the slums were far from being a myth they often attained mythical proportions in some of the representations constructed by journalists, public health officials, and campaigners. Yet, by publishing news items in such melodramatic terms, the issue could no longer be ignored. By invoking a sense of Christian duty and moral crusade, many of the obstacles to urban reform, associated with ideology, class and commerce, might be removed (Doyle 2001).

The implications of public health for personal wellbeing were highlighted by the Bishop of Manchester, the Reverend James Moorhouse, in an address to the Jubilee Conference of the Manchester and Salford Sanitary Association, held at the Town House in Manchester, which was reported in the *Manchester Guardian* for 25 April 1902. The Association could not have wished for better testimony of the value of its attempts at sanitary reform. Moorhouse began by emphasising how the strength and character of the human race had come to depend largely on the quality of urban life. Although the death rate for Manchester had fallen from 29 to 21.6 per 1,000 over the previous twenty years, it was still far higher than that of London (12) and Nottingham (14). Whilst conditions had improved, in terms of the erection of new houses, increase in the proportion of homes with water-closets, and provision of public parks and open spaces, there remained the 'depressing influence' of the central parts of the city, which were becoming 'the poverty centre for an ever-increasing population' of migrants. It was not just a question of saving lives, but of removing from those who survived the depressing effect of air pollution, the darkness of ill-ventilated, overcrowded and close and foul alleyways, and bad and inefficient drainage.

As Moorhouse continued, the factors that might enfeeble the body, debase the soul, and rob life of its use and joy, were not only an offence against the individual person, but against the community and nation. The real wealth of a nation was to be measured not in terms of trade or the extent of the Dominions, but in the quality of its citizens. In that sense, the Boers might be poor farmers, few in number and lacking in culture, but they were rich people. Their 'manly and physical qualities' had won the respect of their enemies. They ensured the Boers would play a significant part in Africa's future. In striking contrast, there was no race that stood in greater need of 'these high moral and physical qualities than our own'. For Moorhouse, the deficiency was all the more alarming in view of the nation's responsibility not only for itself but, by Divine Providence, for almost one-fifth of the world's population. Since an Englishman was more likely to be a town dweller than not, whose physical and mental qualities would depend so largely on local sanitary conditions, the issues surrounding urban reform were immense indeed.

If so much depended on sanitary improvement, Bishop Moorhouse asked, how could the vitality and virility of the race be left simply to 'the mercy of accident' or something called 'public opinion'. From his years as an incumbent of a very poor and insanitary London parish of Paddington, Moorhouse had gained much experience in soliciting the opinion of those who suffered such evils. Time and again, he found they had no heart to complain. The very evils under which they suffered had occasioned 'a mental torpor which feared nothing so much as change and disturbance'. It was for others to think for them. It was the purpose of the Manchester and Salford Sanitary Association to help generate 'a wholesome discontent with such misery', and to give a very bad time to those who sought to profit by it, or who were merely too selfish or niggardly to assist in removing it. In the Bishop's words,

> we demand that people shall be compelled to obey the law, that no sanitary abuse shall be tolerated which the law forbids and that, if there are any abuses which the law does not yet reach, new laws shall be made to abolish them.

As it came increasingly to be accepted that poverty and deprivation were not simply a personal failing, but one in which society had a direct responsibility to intervene, so new institutions were called for. Where Whiggish assumptions had seemed to imply an inexorable expansion of 'the welfare state', historians have found increasing evidence of a more pluralistic response, in which the voluntary and philanthropic activity figured large (Hennock 1973, p. 3; Laybourn 1997). The Manchester and Salford Sanitary Association claimed to be the oldest body of its kind, with a membership comprising 'medical men, engineers, chemists, lawyers, merchants and others, associated with the promotion of sanitary reform and the general well-being of the people'. Through such persons, it claimed to have intimate knowledge of 'the environment of the working classes in a manufacturing district'. Through scientific study, lectures and publications, such knowledge was used to raise awareness among those in positions of authority and influence (Manchester City Library, M 126/1/1/1–2).

The Association was both a model for other towns and cities, and an inspiration to such affiliated bodies as the Ladies' Health Society. It was through such affiliated members that the Association acquired detailed yet comprehensive knowledge of the city. The minute book reveals that, in 1891 the Association supported the Noxious Vapours Abatement Association in convening a public meeting, as a first step in persuading the City Council to make a substantial reduction in the price of gas. If gas could be substituted for coal in cooking and heating the home, significant improvements would be effected in the quality of the atmosphere and, therefore, the health of citizens. The Gas Committee consistently refused to make such a reduction. Another affiliate was the Committee for Securing Open Spaces for Recreation. In a memorial addressed to the City Council in July 1896, the Association emphasised how two of the most urgent needs of a densely populated city like Manchester were the liberal provision of open spaces and improvements to the purity of the air supply. On those two counts, the memorial pressed for the immediate acquisition of Trafford Park. Unless that were done, all hope would be lost of converting the Park to pleasure gardens, with facilities for 'athletics, cycling, football and kindred games'. Left to itself, the proximity of the park area to the Manchester Ship Canal meant it would soon be built over, causing the prevailing winds to carry even more dense smoke and chemical fumes into the central and eastern parts of the city.

Housing and Town Planning

The writings of both environmental history and planning history are replete with heroic figures, whose innovation, whether in thinking or administrative deed, has been profound and enduring. Their biographies help flesh out what is known about their respective professions and disciplines, and of the social and institutional settings in which such movements as town planning arose. The lives and works provide a more rounded knowledge and understanding of events (Cherry 1981). For Peter Hall, most of the events impacting on world cities in the latter part of the twentieth century can be traced back to a handful of visionaries (Hall 1996). Whether planners, or for that matter ecologists and environmentalists, Muller (1999) wrote of how 'the milestones that they have embedded along the highway of history have become points of reference and orientation to the profession'.

Even in the most formal of records of a committee, council or association, it is usually possible to discern the more active members. The personality that emerges most strongly within the Manchester and Salford Sanitary Association was Thomas Coglin Horsfall, who had amassed sufficient wealth from the cotton industry that he could retire and devote the rest of his life to social reform. His daily contact with the notorious district of Ancoats, combined with his earlier travels in Europe and fascination with the writings of John Ruskin, had convinced him that a community could never enjoy 'true welfare' if ignorant of the beauty of nature. If the poor lacked the means to live in the country, ways had to be found of bringing attributes of the countryside to the cities and towns. As Horsfall discovered, neither that goal nor any other could be pursued in a compartmentalised way. There was little point in establishing gardens and parks if air pollution continued to make town life generally gloomy and destroyed any plant life introduced. The foul air, bad habits, insufficient wages, and much else, interacted so closely with one another as to make each both a cause and an effect (Harrison 1991).

The chance to put forward a more holistic remedy to the evils of urban life came with the appointment by the Government of an inter-departmental Committee on Physical Deterioration in September 1903. Members found persuasive the evidence put forward by the Medical Officer of Health that everything possible was being done to effect rapid and well-sustained improvements to the health of Manchester. Comparisons of children included in photographs taken of the slums some fifteen years ago, and at the present day, showed 'a very decided improvement in the clothing and physique'. The Committee also found Horsfall 'a very competent witness'. He accepted that the decline in health and physique might not be *intensifying*, but he warned of how it might be becoming more *extensive*. Unless suburban building was regulated, the 'squalid slums' of the city centres would soon be reproduced on the outskirts too. In its report, the Committee acknowledged that if 'judicious foresight and prudence' were shown in drawing up building plans and regulations (along the lines that Horsfall had found in Germany), there was a possibility of the newly 'urbanised' districts acquiring at least some of 'the attributes of an ideal garden city' (PP 1904; Marr 1904; Horsfall 1904).

Further publicity was given to the German experience, and its relevance to the plight of English towns, at a conference convened by the Mayor of Manchester in October 1906. Instigated by the Manchester and Salford Sanitary Association, Horsfall gave the principal address. He was supported by John C. Nettlefold, the Chairman of the Housing Committee for Birmingham Corporation, and himself the author of a book, *A Housing Policy*, published in 1905 (Cherry 1994, pp. 102–5). Before an audience of over 120 representatives of local corporations and urban district councils, both men described the dangers of allowing the conditions of the city centres to spread to the suburbs. Under existing powers, there was nothing a local authority could do to prevent this happening. The conference passed a resolution, drafted by Horsfall, calling for parliamentary powers that would enable town councils and other local authorities

> to control, by means of town extension building plans, the laying out of all land within the boundaries of the towns, or which may hereafter be incorporated. (*Manchester Guardian*, 12 October 1906)

Historians have discerned a developing dichotomy. There were those who advocated improvement through the establishment of garden cities, of the kind pioneered by Ebenezer Howard and his followers at Letchworth Garden City, in Hertfordshire, in 1904. Others sought 'town-extension planning' citing, for example, the Hampstead Garden Suburb Act of 1906, whereby powers were conferred on the Suburb Trust 'to develop and lay out lands as garden suburbs'. Of far more concern to some contemporary commentators was the risk that the two movements would distract attention from the immediate necessity of improving living conditions within the houses themselves. As the *Manchester Guardian* emphasised, in reporting the Manchester conference, this had to remain the priority. If the individual buildings remained overcrowded and, in the worst sense, a slum, a municipal plan would convey a false impression of decency (Sutcliffe 1981b).

In that context, there was considerable merit in the town-extension powers being conferred as part of a wider measure to tackle the problems arising from 'the urbanization of the people' (to quote a Section heading from the report of the Committee on Physical Deterioration). The election of a Liberal Government in December 1905, and personal interest of the Prime Minister, Henry Campbell-Bannerman, caused the National Housing Reform Council, of which Horsfall and Nettlefold were key figures, to campaign even more strongly. In the course of pressing for a new Housing Bill in November 1906, a delegation outlined the intricacies of town planning to officials of the Local Government Board for the first time. The President of the Board, John Burns, sought to incorporate such powers in a proposed Housing Bill, using clauses drafted by Nettlefold. There was further commitment to the introduction of those powers, when Campbell-Bannerman met a delegation from the Association of Municipal Bodies, convened by Nettlefold. Whilst the greatest stress continued to be laid on improving conditions within the home itself, a section of the eventual Bill sought

> to ensure, by means of schemes which may be prepared either by local authorities or landowners, that in future, land in the vicinity of towns shall be developed in such a way as to secure proper sanitary conditions, amenity and convenience in connection with the laying out of the land itself and of any neighbouring land.

The tightly drawn town-planning section aroused comparatively little comment during the Bill's passage through parliament. As well as support from the National Housing Reform Council and the Association of Municipal Corporations, even the land-owning interests seemed reconciled to a curtailment of their freedom to develop land as they wished. As Sutcliffe (1988) noted, the key to such consensus was probably the realisation that town planning might not only protect, but even enhance, the value of land. Such town-extension powers provided the most certain means of avoiding the damaging effects of slum development on neighbouring properties.

Local Planning

It is hard to perceive the first half of the twentieth century without the hindsight that comes with knowledge of the two world wars. It is all the more reason for seeking out such writers as Sidney and Beatrice Webb, who emphasised the dynamic forces at work during the Edwardian and inter-war years. Writing at the close of the Great War, they traced how Britain had become 'a very different entity' from that of the 1890s, in the growth and mobility of population, manufacturing and marketing, and the increasing speed with which knowledge and understanding could be communicated. Of all the factors encompassed by the word 'environment', the Webbs considered the most potent to be not the climate or other natural forces, but the institutions which society created for itself and by which minds and bodies were moulded. As leading socialists, the Webbs believed human control of that environment must continue to depend on further adapting such institutions. However well adapted to the needs of the previous generation, they would, by the very nature of life, be ill-suited to the next (Webb and Webb 1920).

For the historian, such pressures for adaptation, and the response of the respective authorities, provide valuable insight into the range of issues confronting a community. In his volume *The Making of Modern Yorkshire*, J.S. Fletcher wrote, in 1918, of how no private house could be built without supervision. No speculator might lay out a street or square according to his whim. Sanitation had developed into a cult where scientists were for ever experimenting. In Fletcher's words, it was the era of local government, where towns vied with one another in demolishing slums and setting standards for their street cleaning and lighting (Fletcher 1918). However exaggerated, such sentiments highlighted the burgeoning responsibilities of local government as the country emerged from the bloodiest war in history. The Webbs expected the revival of civil patriotism would lead to such local councils becoming responsible for 'the whole mental and physical environment' of the population they were appointed to serve – in town planning, in the joint organisation of the rapidly dwindling spaces between towns, elimination of hideous advertisements, and 'prevention of defilement of the ground and streams'.

Such scope for intervention and, perhaps, regulation, in the affairs and activities of those using the resources of town and countryside had to take close account of the far reaching changes taking place in both central and local government. Where it had been the President of the Local Government Board, John Burns, who had promoted the Housing, Town Planning, &c., Act of 1909, the Board was combined with the Health Insurance Commission to form the Ministry of Health in 1919. Almost every locality was affected by the far-reaching changes in the size and boundaries of local authorities, following the Local Government Act of 1929. To cite one of many hundreds of examples, the East Riding of Yorkshire County Council sought to reduce the number of rural district councils from 12 to 3. The support given by officials of the Ministry of Health to the creation of fewer, but larger, units had to be 'in great confidence'. The Minister would be required to exercise his quasi-judicial powers, following a local inquiry, as to whether such proposed changes should be upheld (East Riding of Yorkshire Record Office, Beverley, County Council, file 294). The antipathy invariably generated between local councils frequently impaired the goodwill required for such county-wide initiatives as those increasingly sought in planning.

The scope for prevarication and delay remained immense. Growth might be as much an impediment as a stimulus. The West Riding town of Doncaster was granted county borough status in 1926. As the centre of 'an important and rapidly-developing coal-mining area', it had doubled in population since 1911. Its locomotive works employed almost 5,000. British Bemberg had just opened a silk factory. And yet the Council had still not approved a town-planning scheme by the time war broke out in 1939, despite repeated admonitions from the Ministry of Health. An early impediment was the restriction of such schemes, under the 1909 Act to 'land in the course of development, or likely to be used for building purposes'. Doncaster was one of a handful of authorities to secure the precedent, under the Doncaster Corporation Act of 1931, to include the built-up area of the city centre (Doncaster Record Office, AB9/TC3, 527). Such an enabling provision was generalised to all local planning authorities, under the Town and Country Planning Act of 1932.

Although any suburb, inner urban-area, and even the remotest tract of countryside might be brought within the compass of a planning scheme, the decision remained firmly with the individual borough council, urban or rural district council. Whilst the Minister was required to scrutinise the draft scheme and perhaps hold a public inquiry, so as to assess whether it complied with the intention of the Act, central government had no powers to initiate a scheme, nor to compel local authorities to do so. Even where a local council wished to intervene, it might be severely constrained by the right of a landowner to claim compensation, where adversely affected by a planning scheme. The council had to defray the cost of such payments. In as much as property values and, therefore, the size of claims were likely to be highest where regulation was most needed, local authorities were frequently deterred from intervening. At best, it meant the preparation and implementation of a scheme was heavily dependent on the goodwill and concessions voluntarily made by those owners most likely to be affected (Sheail 1981).

Officials in both the Ministry and some local authorities sought to reassure and stimulate. A leaflet from the Ministry of Health in 1925 explained how the object of a planning scheme was to ensure that if, and when, development occurred, it advanced the welfare and prosperity of the whole community. In broad outline, a scheme simply fixed the areas that should be used for industry, business and residences, the principal roads and open spaces, and density of housing. A circular of March 1932 further emphasised how such planning schemes were 'a business proposition'. Well-planned industrial sites, conveniently situated by road, rail and, where possible, water, would reduce both direct costs and traffic congestion. Oscar Kirby, the engineer to the Doncaster Borough Council, endeavoured to explain how the city had developed historically on more or less haphazard lines, with 'an indiscriminate medley of commercial, industrial, public and residential buildings'. Without a scheme, the Council had no control of either the use of land or buildings. Although some £400,000 had been spent since 1900 on street widening and improvement, much more definite and determined action was needed (Doncaster Record Office, AB9/TC3/527).

The name most closely associated with such inter-war planning activity was Patrick Abercrombie, the Professor of Civic Design in the university of Liverpool. His pioneer textbook, *Town and Country Planning,* first published in 1932, sought to emphasise the urgent need not only for regulating building development but, more particularly, to discover the positive means by which scientific study should replace 'the self-centred interest' of speculative builders and the amateurism so commonly encountered in local government. As Abercrombie (1932) remarked, 'the practical man might say he knew his town, its history and every inch of its present extent'. In as much as he carried it in his head, there was no need for 'the cumbrous machinery of maps'. As Abercrombie often found, such a person knew no more about his town than 'his tongue does about the state of his teeth'.

It was however one thing to write textbooks, and to give exhortatory lectures, but another to be given the chance to apply such insight to actual towns and tracts of countryside. Here Abercrombie and his generation of advocates drew heavily on the opportunities afforded by a comparatively small number of local authorities, often through the good offices or, rather, the missionary zeal, of George Pepler, the Chief Town Planning Officer of the Ministry of Health. Pepler convened a conference of local authorities in the Doncaster area in January 1920, so as to emphasise the need for more orderly development in what promised to be Britain's most productive coalfield, the Yorkshire 'concealed' coalfield. The conference resolved that a Regional Planning Scheme should be prepared. The report, prepared by Abercrombie and T.H. Johnson, the architect and surveyor of the Doncaster Borough Council, was published in 1922. As the first Regional Planning Scheme of its kind, it provided a model of what might be attempted elsewhere (Abercrombie and Johnson 1922; Dix 1978).

It was the Clerk to the North Riding of Yorkshire County Council, Hubert Thornley, who provided Abercrombie with the opportunity to demonstrate the potential of regional planning in a predominantly rural area. Thornley had been appointed to the prestigious Clerkship in 1916, where he became an outstanding local-government lawyer and acknowledged authority on highway law and administration. By the 1930s, he had developed a deep sense of personal commitment to the countryside of the North Riding. Just back from a motoring holiday in Norway, he wrote of how 'the siting of the buildings, the indiscriminate building of bathing huts and bungalows on the little islands' off the Norwegian coast provided an object lesson in what could happen if development was not carefully regulated in the North Riding. Anxious 'to strike a blow in defence of the preservation of the North Riding', Thornley sought the advice of the clerks of other county councils. The Somerset County Council provided the relevant model, where the schemes were formulated in the name of the district councils, but the county council had engaged an expert, W. Harding Thompson, to draft the overall regional-plan (North Yorkshire Record Office, County Council Records, P, 1.4).

Through such personal initiative, the North Riding became an exemplar of what others might achieve through consensual planning. The County Council appointed a Town Planning and Zoning Committee in December 1932, which commissioned Abercrombie to compile a map and report as the 'basis for the preparation of more detailed schemes' covering, in aggregate, the entire Riding. Abercrombie completed his task in May 1934, and 250 copies of his report were printed and circulated. Beyond his immediate task, there was an obvious opportunity to explain directly to councillors both the necessity and practicality of such schemes. In Abercrombie's view, 'a very simple scheme' was required, neither too expensive to prepare nor disruptive of the existing ownership pattern, that would act as 'a directing force, gently and imperceptibly pushing the individual in the way in which he is persuaded he should go'. Four types of land-use planning zone were envisaged, namely free-entry building land; potential building land; open-space reservations; and agricultural zones. It was, in Abercrombie's words, a question of deciding where building was so sparse as to be an incident in the rural scene, and where building became a community affair. In the latter case, the need for utilities and other public services meant the public authorities had direct reason to intervene and say how it should be done.

By the time Abercrombie had completed his report, most district councils had agreed in principle to a planning scheme to be drawn up for the whole county. The question was Whose scheme?

Thornley asked the district councils in June 1934 to relinquish their statutory powers formally to the County Council. At a meeting of 50 representatives, it was Thornley's turn to advocate the need for, and practicality of, planning. His speech stressed the benefits of preventing ribbon and other unsuitable forms of development, minimising the cost to the utilities, and the economic advantages of preserving amenity in the coastal resorts, dales and moors. The County Council formally resolved in May 1935 to prepare a planning scheme covering the whole of the 'relinquished' areas which, by that time, included almost every district. Public inquiries 'passed off without any bother'. The Minister of Health approved the first two of the six area schemes covering the county in August 1939. Much of the credit went to the County Planning Officer, S. Lee Vincent, who had seen his priority as one of 'establishing friendly relations with developers, explaining to them the objects of a Planning Scheme and giving advice and assistance in the preparation of proposals for buildings' (Sheail 1979a).

In a paper, 'The Place of Science in Town and Country Planning', the geographer, L. Dudley Stamp, sought to put such scheme-making in context. As he emphasised, the face of Britain bore striking evidence of earlier planning, both in its rural landscapes and city streets and housing. It had been undertaken for the most part by large landowners. By the Second World War, many such estates had been broken up or impoverished. Some 5 million householders owned their property. Whilst this meant a much larger proportion of the population had a direct stake in land, there was, in Stamp's words, a need 'to learn to work together for the common good'. Town and country planning was a necessary function of a democratic state (Stamp 1946).

Not only might government be even more ambitious than the largest landowner, but there was the potential to make more positive use of the expertise to be found in the natural and social sciences. In identifying the optimal use (or rather uses) of tracts of land, closer analysis might be made of the character and causes of its present-day use. Dudley Stamp had himself directed a Land Utilisation Survey of Great Britain, which had recorded the use of every parcel of land within the period 1931–34 (Stamp 1948). Such individual analyses required synthesis as to their bearing on employment, the home and wider community, and the demand for land for farming, forestry, communications and leisure-pursuits. Considerable skills would also be required in ensuring such findings were readily comprehensible to the politicians directly responsible for the planning process. An obvious challenge, therefore, was to devise the institutional structures that enabled such knowledge and understanding of 'the scientific method' to be integrated more closely into the political process.

National Planning

Where the planning historian might perceive the town-planning measure of 1909 as a first phase, and the Town and Country Planning Act of 1932 as a second, the beginnings of a third phase can be discerned during the 1940s. The Town and Country Planning (Interim Development) Act of July 1943 extended planning control to the whole country, irrespective of whether the local authority had drawn up, or implemented, a planning scheme. Immediate enforcement action could be taken where a development was deemed prejudicial to the longer-term planning of town and country. Not only did the Town and Country Planning Act of 1947 (and another for Scotland) place the national system of planning control on a peacetime footing, but it sought to extend and complement such regulation with more positive powers to enhance the quality of town and countryside. The building of New Towns and rehabilitation of abandoned industrial areas were perceived as part of that wider movement that also included the appointment of a National Parks Commission in 1949.

Where such advances in the 1940s were consciously advocated as a new beginning, both the strategy and detail might be more convincingly portrayed as a fitting conclusion to the first half-century of statutory planning in Britain. Such wartime and immediate postwar legislation was remarkable not so much for its anticipation of the second half of the century, but for its enactment of what such figures as Patrick Abercrombie had so long advocated. The strongest underlying force of the inter-war years had continued to be technological development. The net effect was to pull Britain out of recession more quickly than many leading competitors. In the five years following 1932, real investment rose by 19 per cent, gross domestic production by 23 per cent, industrial production by nearly 46 per cent, and gross fixed investment by 47 per cent (Dewey 1997).

Yet it was the wastage of human and other resources that had haunted that inter-war generation as Britain, once 'the Workshop of the World', endeavoured to restructure. Where an 'inner core' of the Home Counties and Midlands prospered, the industrial North and West, characterised by their greater dependence on staple export-led industries, experienced almost unrelieved physical decay and social deprivation. Whereas the national average for unemployment over the period 1929 to 1936 was 16.9 per cent, it was as low as 7.8 per cent for the South-East and as high as 30.1 per cent in Wales. It was 22.7 per cent in the North-East, and just under 22 per cent in Scotland and the North-West. As Cherry (1988) noted, the fact that the Depression affected most severely the cities and towns that had undergone the most rapid and ill-conceived development in the nineteenth century exacerbated the already acute sense of deprivation, arising from a backlog of unfit housing, congestion and overcrowding.

Of all the unresolved questions of the inter-war years, two stood out, namely the extent to which there should be some kind of regional-aid policy and secondly (and with an obvious bearing on the first) how far the State should pursue a more interventionist policy. At first, the depressed areas had to exist as best they could on the dole and reliance on spontaneous recovery. It was not until 1934 that some kind of special assistance or preferential treatment can be discerned. In April of that year, investigators were appointed to report on conditions in South Wales, industrial Scotland, West Cumberland and, fourthly, Tyneside and Durham. Although the Board of Trade believed it had collected such information as was relevant, it saw political advantage in further public confirmation that Government could do no more. As anticipated, the reports from three of the depressed areas confirmed the value of existing programmes, in terms of the retraining and movement of manpower to other parts of the country, and providing social palliatives for those who remained (Ward 1988).

The Investigator's report for Tyneside and Durham went much further in recommending greater intervention by central government in the location of industry, together with more specific local and regional initiatives. As well as growing public sympathy for the plight of the depressed industries and communities, there was increasing concern on the part of business as to the severe penalties that would be incurred, both in terms of output and marketing, if the depressed areas were left to languish. There was also a strong military case for avoiding so large a proportion of industry and its workforce being located in the most vulnerable part of the country, namely the South-East. On the premise the bomber would always get through, it made sense to distribute such assets at least more evenly through the country. The Cabinet compromised by appointing a Commissioner for the depressed areas of England and Wales, and another for Scotland. The House of Lords substituted the title 'Special Areas' for 'Depressed Areas' (PP 1936–37).

Perhaps the most significant decision was to appoint Sir Malcolm Stewart as the Commissioner for England and Wales. A successful businessman, in the brick and cement industries, he personified, in Steven Ward's words, the progressive business opinion that had become so important in the advocacy of a shift towards regional policies and economic planning. Stewart pressed the obvious constraints of his office to the limit (Booth 1978; Ward 1988). From very hesitant beginnings, Stewart began to develop a partnership between central and local agencies. New, corporate-style agencies were formed to spearhead fresh industrial development, and most famously the new trading estates in the Teme valley near Gateshead, Treforest in Pontypridd, and Hillington, Glasgow. Individually, and when taken together, they were a symbol of a qualitative change in State intervention. But as anticipated by Government, their impact on the employment situation was minimal (Ward 1988, pp. 227–31).

By the mid-1930s it was clear that the massive dislocation of heavy industry was no temporary aberration of the British and world economies. As the middle and professional classes came also to feel insecure, increasing interest was taken in the concept of a planned economy, as developed by the Roosevelt 'New Deal' and Soviet Five Year Plans. In his capacity as Special Commissioner, Stewart urged the introduction of curbs on the growth of Greater London as a means of securing a 'more evenly distributed' pattern of regional prosperity (Pearson 1939). Where the Cabinet's instinct had been to appoint a Royal Commission on the growth of Greater London and other large cities, it was announced in July 1937 that, under Sir Montague Barlow, its purpose was 'to inquire into the causes which have influenced the present geographical distribution of the industrial population of Great Britain'. In their deliberations, the Commissioners soon confirmed that a large-scale drift of industrial population was taking place from the depressed regions of England, Scotland and Wales, into a central coffin-shaped area between South Lancashire and the Home Counties. The Commission believed the only way to secure the necessary national response was to end the prevailing administrative confusion by appointing a new central authority, which would help secure the redevelopment of congested urban areas and the decentralisation or dispersal of industries, and industrial population, from these areas (Public Record Office (PRO), HLG 68, 50; PP 1939–40).

Dissension occurred when the Royal Commission turned to defining the executive powers and status of the new central authority. Besides appointing a new central authority with research, advisory and publicity functions, the majority of members believed it should have executive powers to regulate additional industrial building in London and the Home Counties. Three of these members pressed for such positive inducements for locating industries outside the London area. In a Minority Report, a further three members (who included Patrick Abercrombie) claimed the need for executive action on a national scale was so urgent that the new central authority should be invested with the executive powers of a ministry.

The Reports were not published until January 1940. The Minister of Health, Walter Elliot, warned of how 'it is no use pretending that, merely by the device of setting up a new Minister, we shall get away from the difficulties of deciding where industries should be located or continued'. In the same House of Commons debate, Ernest D. Simon, a leading figure in local government and economic planning, spoke of how war had 'reunified democracy'. There was determination to build a new civilisation where expediency gave way to resolute action (Scottish Record Office, DD 10, 304; Parliamentary Debates (PD), Commons, 359, 1026–94). Almost every official engaged in statutory planning had been transferred to more immediate wartime duties. It was another minister, in another department, who secured a revival of interest. Appointed to the post of Minister of Works, Lord Reith obtained personal responsibility for the 'physical' planning of post-war reconstruction. Although by that time out of office, he had achieved sufficient progress for the Ministry to have absorbed the statutory planning responsibilities of the Ministry of Health, and to have been restyled the Ministry of Works and Planning. This in turn became the Ministry of Town and Country Planning in March 1943, charged with securing 'consistency and continuity in the framing and execution of a national policy with respect to the use and development of land throughout England and Wales'. Similar powers were vested in the Secretary of State for Scotland. A memorandum published by the Ministry in December 1943 warned of how 'the waging of peace and the production of the munitions of peace demanded a single strategy no less than do the requirements of war' (Cullingworth 1975, pp. 98–9).

A more pro-active stance to land-use planning was seen as essential in breaking away from what was increasingly perceived as the static approach of the inter-war years. There were, however, two things that darkened counsels. As F. Blaise Gillie, an Assistant Secretary first in the Ministry of Health and then Ministry of Town and Country Planning, recalled later, there was little appreciation of the immense problems of a more 'positive' intervention in land-use development. It would not only be hugely demanding of manpower, but there would be even greater risk of treading on the toes of other interested parties. In assessing what was feasible within the resources available to local and central government, the further major deficiency had to be addressed, namely that of the calibre of those required to work the system. And secondly, even the Treasury came to accept that statutory planning could never achieve its goal of bringing order to land use, until a solution was found to the twin problems of compensation for restrictions on land use and the collection of betterment where planning consent was given. Whilst those living in the blitzed and blighted parts of cities could not be re-housed immediately, it was important to scotch the activities of speculators, rumoured to be buying up bombed sites in the expectation of making rich pickings after the war. To that end, Lord Reith appointed what Schaffer (1974) later called a small 'think tank', the Uthwatt Committee on Compensation and Betterment. Its report of June 1941 eschewed the even more contentious question of land-ownership by seeking fundamental changes to the system by which land was valued (PP 1941–42) . A White Paper of May 1944, *The Control of Land Use*, followed the report closely in proposing that a betterment charge should be levied on all planning permissions. Compensation for a refusal should be limited to any development value residing in the land on 31 March 1939. Both the betterment charge and compensation were to be administered by a single Government organisation. Compulsory purchase powers would be used where necessary to secure properly planned development (PP 1943–44b).

A further Town and Country Planning Bill of 1944, based on these principles, taxed the consensus of the Wartime Coalition Government to the limit. In the teeth of strenuous opposition from propertied and *laissez-faire* elements (as represented by right-wing elements in the parliamentary Conservative Party), its scope had to be limited to the immediate needs of the inner cities. The 'Blitz and Blight Bill' (as it came to be called) permitted local authorities to buy, in the simplest and most expeditious way, those built-up areas extensively damaged by bombing, or blighted by bad layout and obsolete development, with a view to the comprehensive redevelopment of those city and town centres. The sweeping powers conferred by the Act provided invaluable experience for ministers and officials in drafting the Town and Country Planning Bill of 1947, that was intended comprehensively to set the scene for post-war planning.

In his 'official' Peacetime History of reconstruction and land-use planning between 1939 and 1947, Cullingworth (1975, pp. xi–xv) illustrated the value of looking not only at the minister's speeches, and the parliamentary debates over individual pieces of legislation, but at the discussions in Cabinet Committees and, perhaps more particularly, to the memoranda and minutes of meetings held at both a departmental and inter-departmental level. The historian is impressed not so much by the excitement as by the apparent multiplicity and complexity of the issues confronting ministers and officials alike. Few persons could have fully grasped the implications of what was being discussed and decided. Far from being a strident response to the land-use issues of the period, the reality behind the rhetoric appears to have been more one of uncertainty and deference.

Political Laboratories

Given the considerable involvement of many members of the Cabinet in local government, the post-war Labour Government was especially conscious of how local authorities were more than simply recipients and interpreters of central-government policy. Indeed, Aneurin Bevan moved a motion in the House of Commons, in November 1929, to make it easier and cheaper for local authorities to promote Local Bills. Both central and local government had to be 'elastic and responsive' to changing needs. Since those changes invariably affected different parts of the country unevenly, Bevan believed local authorities should have every opportunity to modify general legislation so as to bring it more closely into line with local needs. Often the first to be 'exposed' to changing economic and social conditions, they might act as 'political laboratories', where 'the small powers' granted by parliament under Local and Private Bills frequently became the basis for national legislation (Parliamentary Debates (PD), Commons, 231, 2125–38).

Local and Private Bill records are far more numerous than Public and General Bills, namely those promoted by ministers, in the records of parliament. Historically, they had developed as a petition for extraordinary powers to carry out an activity otherwise impossible or impracticable under existing statutory law. Taken together, they were the means by which much of the infrastructure of nineteenth- and early-twentieth-century Britain was developed, most obviously in the form of the railways, dock and harbour development, the gas and water utilities, and civic improvement generally. Whilst the first drafts were usually drawn up by the Clerk and senior officials of the council, parliamentary agents played an essential part in identifying precedents for the powers in previous Local Bills, and in ensuring the new Bill accorded with the Standing Orders of Parliament (House of Lords 1997). The measure had to pass one of the Houses of Parliament and then, if passed, be separately scrutinised by the other. It was not debated, unless challenged on a basic point of principle. The decision as to whether the Bill should pass, with or without amendment, was essentially taken by a Committee in each House, comprising of up to six of the most experienced members of that House. They considered petitions from both the promoters and any opponents of the Bill. Where the Bill or individual clauses were contested, the Committees heard evidence from policy and expert witnesses for the various parties, as presented and cross-examined, through legal counsel. The petitions, opening and closing speeches of counsel, and minutes of evidence, taken before Opposed Bill Committees, provide the historian with voluminous accounts as to how local authorities sought, on behalf of their ratepayers, to enlarge their field of governance.

Although the role of the Minister and his officials was essentially advisory, such parliamentary Committees took close note of any views expressed. A review found that the Ministry of Health had reported on 58 of the 99 Local Bills deposited in the session

1929–30, and 37 of the 68 Bills of the following year (PRO, HLG 54, 445). Some Bills were of immense length and complexity. The Brighton Corporation Bill, which received the Royal Assent in September 1931, comprised 587 clauses and 12 schedules. As the first part of the Preamble explained, its overriding purpose was 'to consolidate with amendments the local Acts and Orders (already) in force within the Borough of Brighton'. The 29 parts of the new Bill covered such topics as boundary extensions; the provision of water supplies and sewerage; the tramway and electricity undertakings; the regulation of food sales, slaughter houses, hackney carriages, burial grounds, and employment agencies; the management of public buildings and parks, the Royal Pavilion, aquarium, libraries, museums and art galleries, and finally the borrowing powers and other financial matters of the Corporation (Brighton Corporation Act, 1931, 21 and 22 George V, c. cix).

One of the more novel pressures on local government was the provision of recreational facilities. The Holidays with Pay Act of 1938 gave formal notice of the increase in leisure time, and of disposable income for holidays spent away from home. All statutory bodies responsible for enforcing minimum wages were to provide a paid holiday of at least one week in each year. By the end of the year, some 9 million people enjoyed such holidays with pay, of which 4.5 million were covered by such collective agreements (Pimlott 1947). An article published in *Better Health*, the journal of the Central Council for Health Education, emphasised the importance of 'weaving' the concept of holidays with pay into the industrial fabric. It was written by Ernest Bevin, the General Secretary of the Transport and General Workers' Union. The intensification of production methods and increasing wear-and-tear on modern life made such holidays imperative for both working families and industry. Just as the general standard of living was advancing, so too did the conception of holidays. Not only did the 'rising generation' have definite ideas of its own, but there had to be more 'scientific consideration' of the facilities required. Far from being an imposition on the holiday resorts, Bevin (1937) saw such pressures as an outstanding opportunity for municipal enterprise. It might not only provide the leisure facilities required, but accommodation where guest and boarding houses could not cope.

The implications of such recreational development went even wider. As Ernest Bevin pointed out, there was little point in improving such facilities within resorts, if the adjacent coastline and countryside were spoilt. Building development, for whatever purpose, had to be strictly controlled. The challenge to local authorities was illustrated by an article, on the front page of the *Hull Daily Mail*, for 15 November 1933, under the headline, 'King's Counsel scathing indictment of Primrose Valley Shacks'. It recounted how the Filey Urban District had shown foresight by acquiring the foreshore round Hunmanby Gap, but the backlands fell within the Bridlington Rural District. The Council was accordingly powerless to stop the charm of Filey Bay from being ruined by holiday development, where a tent today might become a hut tomorrow, and a permanent shack the next week. With only the most primitive sanitation, it would not be long before the epidemics that broke out among the huts brought the entire area into disrepute. The occasion for the remarks was a public inquiry, at which the Legal Counsel defended the recommendations of the East Riding of Yorkshire County Council that the boundaries of the Filey Urban District should be extended to include the area of the Primrose Valley shacks.

It was the practice of parliament to refer even uncontested Bills to an Opposed Bill Committee, where 'novel and important principles' were being established. One such example was the Lindsey County Council (Sandhills) Bill of 1931. As was explained to the two parliamentary committees, the Lincolnshire Sandhills were the longest length of sand dunes in Britain. Although the owners of the adjacent 'inlands' claimed ownership of the sandhills, the Court of Appeal concluded that, in adjudicating a dispute over title at Mablethorpe in 1918, that there was no automatic right of ownership. A possessory title could, however, be established by any person exercising acts of ownership over a 12-year period. The judgement encouraged many to establish a possessory title as quickly as possible, by such acts as erecting fences and buildings on the dunes. The hills were popular for holiday making. The motor cycle and car made it easier to penetrate beyond the traditional resort and its railway station. There were increasing profits to be made from hiring out holiday homes and camping sites (Sheail 1977). Not only did the increasing number of enclosures prevent direct access to the beach, but many of the 'holiday homes' were 'eyesores and abominations'. As the *Lincolnshire Standard* of 29 November 1930 remarked, they had no other merit than that visitors could be induced to pay good rents for them during the holiday season.

Although a further set of squatters established a possessory title each year, there was no public body with the powers to regulate such an anarchical situation. The small staff of the Spilsby Rural District Council had difficulty enough in keeping the increasing number of caravans, bus bodies, shacks and tents under surveillance. About 50 circular, corrugated iron-huts were let, for example, as furnished homes at Bohemia, near Sutton on Sea. The *Louth Standard*, of 1 August 1931, described them as 'rusty pork pies on the top of the dunes'. The County Medical Officer of Health warned of how the earth closets and poor drainage were a hazard to public health. The Clerk to the County Council, Eric Scorer, expressed alarm from an even wider perspective. Largely through his initiative, the Lindsey County Council resolved in November 1930 to promote a parliamentary Bill granting it powers to preserve all the sandhills and beaches as public open-space and, secondly, to regulate their future development. Although all petitions against the Bill were eventually withdrawn, and both the Home Office and Ministry of Health were sympathetic as to its objectives, there was profound concern as to the important precedents set by the measure.

The most obvious solution was for the County Council to be given powers of compulsory acquisition over the entire sandhills and 'to purchase them lock, stock and barrel'. Not only was this well beyond practical politics, but also beyond the financial reserves of the county. Instead, a two-staged procedure was proposed, whereby the County Council would first assume control over development and, at a later date, decide what limited parts of the dunes to acquire, if necessary by compulsion. Not only would there be greater flexibility in responding to the uncertain development of the holiday-making industry, but there would be no commitment to large-scale expenditure. All future costs in regulating or purchasing the hills would be discretionary – a vital factor in winning the support of members of the County Council and Government departments at a time when the nation was in the throes of a financial crisis (House of Lords Record Office, Minutes of Evidence of Select Committee of Houses of Commons and Lords, Lindsey County Council (Sandhills) Bill, 1931–32 Session).

The Lindsey County Council (Sandhills) Bill was given the Royal Assent in July 1932, and most of its powers were delegated to a Sandhills Sub-Committee. As envisaged, the designation of controlled areas proceeded in stages, and the seventeenth and last area was included in 1937. By vesting day, settlements for compensation had been agreed for 12 miles of the coastline, and no compensation was claimed for some other parts. The Sandhills Sub-Committee claimed, as early as 1935, that

> the effect had undoubtedly been to stop a lot of very undesirable development and has prevented the Sandhills from being spoiled by numbers of unsightly erections.

More generally, the promotion and enactment of the Bill provides an outstanding example for the inter-war period of how local initiative could be taken, within the parameters laid down by parliament and Government departments. Far from being impotent in the face of large-scale environmental change, some local authorities showed considerable prescience in meeting potential conflicts in land use and management. In doing so, they often prepared the ground for more general legislation as the environmental pressures came to be recognised, and demanded resolution in other parts of the country.

Even where Local Bills, or crucial clauses of those Bills, were lost, the parliamentary process might still have a considerable impact on the perception of a problem. An outstanding example was the West Sussex County Council (Lancing and Shoreham Beaches, &c.) Bill of 1946. Instead of flowing directly into the English Channel, the river Adur was deflected by a bank of sand and shingle, upon which accommodation for some 3,500 people had been built before the war. Most of the structures were 'the very poorest possible'. The smallest of the 700 plots were only just large enough for a converted railway-carriage or wooden shack. Used as a battle-training ground, the Beaches became even more of a 'scene of abomination and dereliction' (Hardy and Ward 1985).

Whilst over half the 400 property-owners indicated their intention of rebuilding or repairing the beach homes, the County Council and district councils saw 'a unique opportunity' to replace the unsightly inter-war development with 'a good class of residential estate' and more orderly holiday development. The Minister of Town and County Planning in the post-war Labour Government, Lewis Silkin, visited the beaches in February 1946, and endorsed his Department's view that the County Council should promote a Local Bill to acquire the freehold of the entire beach, by compulsion where necessary. The Bill was heard before an Opposed Bill Committee of the House of Lords in May–June 1946. Rather than redevelop the beaches themselves, the County and District Councils would lease the area to a development corporation for 999 years, which would in turn sub-lease plots for development, according to a scheme prepared by the County Council, in consultation with the Ministry. The ground rent paid by the corporation would offset the loan charges incurred by the Council on the capital required to compensate the dispossessed freeholders on the beaches. As legal counsel for the County Council emphasised, the scheme would help to relieve the severe housing shortage. There would be a substantial rise in rateable income, at no immediate cost to ratepayers (House of Lords Record Office, Committee of the House of Lords, West Sussex County Council (Shoreham and Lancing Beaches, &c.) Bill; PRO, HLG 79, 734; West Sussex Record Office, Acc 249, West Sussex County Council, TCP 95D and OC/CM 94/4/1, and UD/SH 3/3/8 and UD/SH 21/1/7).

Somewhat unusually, the Chairman of the House of Lords Committee, Lord Mersey, also visited the Beaches. On the one hand, he agreed it was beyond the resources of any private individual or body to restore the entire area. Without the intervention of some public authority with sufficient powers and resources to do so, there was a grave risk of the same kind of haphazardous development taking place as before the war. On the other hand, Lord Mersey realised that not all the beach was devastated. About 300 of the original 733 buildings were still habitable. He warned of how the Committee would be 'loath to expropriate' these freeholds, particularly at a time of housing shortages. Thus, whilst acknowledging how the preservation of such existing buildings would make comprehensive redevelopment considerably harder, the Committee felt its greatest sympathy should be shown for 'the little man who had been quite content perhaps to live in a railway carriage', but is now threatened by a Council that believes he should live in a superior (and more expensive) building. As Lord Mersey observed, 'the principle that affects the minds of the Committee is that a man should not be compelled to go and live in a better class of house than he wants if his own house is a reasonable one'.

The Bill had encountered formidable opposition from the Beachowners' Association. Its legal counsel described the Bill as both arrogant and unnecessary. Not only were owners keen to rebuild, but local planning authorities already had the powers to impose conditions as to density, layout, size and design. As the legal counsel for the County Council pointed out, these were essentially negative powers. The planning authority could not compel owners to develop according to any desired plan. Refused consent for their choice of development, they might simply leave the land in its present 'abominable and derelict state'. A 'gappy' or 'pepper-pot' type of development would evolve, with 'certain types of building on larger, better plots' intermingled with smaller plots, 'left unoccupied to go to wrack and ruin'. The Bill was the only way to avert such a situation. Not only was there compensation for the occasional personal hardship, but it would be a small price to pay for enhancing the life and appearance of the entire beach area.

At this stage in the proceedings, the Select Committee took a short adjournment and then announced that the clauses of the Bill relating to the beachlands had been rejected. Although Lord Mersey followed the custom of not giving reasons, an official of the Ministry of Town and Country Planning attributed the failure of the clause to the Committee's continued suspicion of the proposed development corporation, and belief that existing planning powers were adequate.

Beyond the beachlands, how significant was the rebuff to the County Council? Were the members of the Lords' Committee completely out of touch with prevailing sentiment, or were they more attuned to shifts taking place in public opinion? Officials of the West Sussex County Council believed the mutilation of their Bill caused the Minister, Lewis Silkin, to be even more determined in securing the strongest powers possible for his Town and Country Planning Bill of 1947. The attitude of Lord Mersey and his Committee indicated there was no other way of ensuring adequate control over land use, and of redevelopment being achieved on the scale required. Whatever the grounds for such speculation, the kind of antipathy revealed by the proceedings on the West Sussex Bill reinforced the need to define as clearly as possible where the primary responsibility should rest for drafting and implementing the planning schemes required as part of the postwar reconstruction of town and countryside.

A Vision Lost

In his volume *The Politics of Town Planning*, Gordon Cherry perceived planning as a culturally driven activity. It was a twentieth-century response to the undesirable effects of industrialisation and urbanisation. Whether as visionaries or as local-government officers, planners strove to tidy up the detritus of economic growth. They articulated and imposed standards of civilised living. They absorbed the sunshine of full employment and rising wealth, and shared the disillusionment that came from both the relative decline of Britain's standing in the world and a slump of confidence in society's experts and leaders (Cherry 1982).

Political support for planning had been given on the basis of what Cherry (1982) called its twin promises of 'social pacification and economic efficiency'. In the sense of its not being overtly radical, land-use planning could be accommodated within the political system. Where such early figures as Ebenezer Howard and the Garden City Association were essentially reformist, the Town Planning Institute, founded in 1913, followed the classic strategy of other professionals in the town hall and Whitehall, namely of developing a more technical, non-political stance (Blowers and Evans 1997, pp. 1–4). Such a 'classical' approach to town planning was perhaps best exemplified by Lewis Keeble's textbook of 1952. Town planning was 'the art and science of ordering the use of land and the character and arrangement of buildings so as to secure the maximum practicable degree of economy, convenience and beauty'. Without such an orderly approach, there would be even more instances of traffic jams in town centres, ribbons of suburban growth, and Peacehaven-type development at every vantage point on the coast. These and 'many other anarchic messes' remained as legacies of the inter-war period. Nor was it enough simply to prevent harmful development taking place. Rather than 'a form of mild censorship', planning must become a more 'positive dynamic force'. The 'proper arrangement' of the physical environment of a modern, complex society required 'the intervention of some impartial public agency armed with legal powers to co-ordinate and harmonise the diverse aims of various developers' (Keeble 1952, pp. 8–10).

And yet, as early as his textbook of 1952, Lewis Keeble expressed concern at the gap remaining between the legal powers of the various planning agencies, and their political willingness and financial ability to use them. Such was the fratricidal strife common between local authorities, and confused division of responsibilities between central and local government, there was a real danger of the planning process becoming largely stifled (Keeble 1952, p. 2). It had all become so very different from the immediate post-war euphoria. Although priority had been given to the 'socialisation' of coal and other basic industries and utilities, and the further advance of 'the welfare state', a Town and Country Planning Bill was enacted as early as 1947. The ten-part Bill for England and Wales (there was another for Scotland) was intended to be more flexible and positive in its regulation and direction of development in every part of town and country. Where the planning schemes of the earlier 1932 Act had pre-defined the use of each area of land, so as to inform developers of what was permitted, it had also prevented there being any amendment to suit changing circumstances. Under the 1947 Act, the Development Plan became essentially a statement of intent. Developers had to seek permission, even where their proposals seemed in harmony with the Development Plan. Unlike the pre-war 'operative schemes', permissions could be withheld.

The intention of the 1947 Act was not so much to shift responsibility from local to central government, but to enable *both* to become more assertive in determining the optimal use of land. Evelyn Sharp had spent almost her entire career in the statutory planning sector of the Ministry of Health and successor departments, before becoming the first woman Permanent Secretary of any department in 1955. Brought up to believe passionately in local government as the foundation of democracy, she remained committed to 'a really strong system of local government where, at least in the larger authorities, the real job of the Clerk was to be that of general manager' (Sharp 1960). It was the purpose of the 1947 Act to enhance that managerial role. Where the 1,441 district and borough councils had been the primary planning agencies under the 1932 Act, such powers were transferred to the 145 county councils and county borough councils. Each was to operate a simplified decision-making process, whereby planning consent was required for any prescribed development, or change in use. Compensation was only payable where there was infringement of previously granted rights.

Whilst the broad outlines of the system proved remarkably robust, their survival owed more to pragmatism than to conviction. On the one hand, the system of development control was no longer distorted by the bogey of compensation. The concept of publicly controlled development rights survived and, in time, was strengthened. The support for green-belts became an effective bulwark against further urban sprawl. On the other hand, much of the idealism and fervour that had instigated and shaped the system were quickly lost. The preparation of Development Plans and guidance given through day-to-day development control soon developed into a full regulatory routine. Much that had promised to be bold and imaginative turned out to be sterile and couched in professional mumbo-jumbo (Cherry 1982, pp. 46–50). It was hardly surprising, therefore, that the betterment charge, which had provoked such controversy and opposition from propertied interests, should be abolished by the first post-war Conservative Government in its 'bonfire of controls' (Schaffer 1974).

Some fifty years later, Barry Cullingworth recalled the vision that had given the Act such priority in the legislative timetable as 'a dream too far'. Although so ephemeral, that vision had however been widely shared. A broad framework was put in place for land-use planning. Its retention, however, owed more to fear of the administrative and political consequences of overhauling such a framework, than to any accuracy in foreseeing the challenges ahead. As Peter Hall remarked, the British might be obsessed with urban growth, but the policy was one of containment rather than dynamic change (Hall *et al.* 1973). The Act anticipated stability where problems of a redistributive kind could be dealt with as if a game of chess. People would move from overcrowded cities to new and expanded towns beyond the green-belt. Economic activities would be constrained in the Home Counties, and directed to the North, Scotland and Wales. Such containment and redistribution prevented much that was deplorable but, as Cullingworth (1996) asserted, it took little account of the structural changes that arose as post-war austerity ended and new technologies spread.

As a Discussion Document on the South-East expressed it in February 1964, the post-war projections had correctly anticipated the major preoccupations of housing and employment, and had made good use of the data then available, but had failed to take account of the possibility of a rise in the birth rate or, more particularly, household formation. The population of England and Wales had risen by over 2.5 million, of which 2 million was by natural increase. There were expected to be at least 3.5 million additional people living in South-East England by 1981 (Ministry of Housing and Local Government 1964). Not only did car ownership double in the 1950s, but an unprecedented range of land-using activities grew up, and continued to develop, over town and country as a whole. Few recognised, let alone knew how to manage, such fluid, complex and interactive forces, and thereby plan their land-use implications. As Cullingworth (1999) put it, such vision required a far more positivist and interventionist form of planning than had become politically acceptable, let alone administratively possible, in the second half of the century. The succeeding chapters focus on a range of the principal activities to impact on land and more generally the environment, beginning with the earliest of major preoccupations for local government, namely that of how to make greater use of the natural environment in disposing of the wastes arising from an urban style of living.

CHAPTER 3

Nature Incorporated

Introduction

In a study of nineteenth-century industrialisation in New England, Theodore Steinberg wrote that, whilst Nature had been there all along, historians have largely neglected its role. He accordingly adopted the title *Nature Incorporated* to emphasise how New England's productive output had expanded as new technologies were manipulated and applied to the region's available natural resources. The 'commodification' of the water bodies had called for particular management skills. Where land might be fenced off 'into discrete bundles of commodities', there was almost invariably complaint from other user-interests of the water being depleted or fouled. Close study and prescription were called for, if such water bodies were to be sustained and the maximum productive value therefore realised (Steinberg 1991).

The demand for a larger-scale and more reliable water supply arose, for the most part, from industry. However pressing the demand for improvements in the availability and qualities of drinking-water, the overriding consideration was economic, namely for water as an industrial raw-material and for the purposes of fire-fighting. But once provided, there was both a ready supply for domestic use and for the removal of both trade and domestic wastes. The purpose of a sewerage system had originally been to remove the rainwater that fell as rain on streets, courts and rooftops. Its discharge into open ditches had little impact – at least for as long as houses had privies with ashpits. The plentiful provision of water meant, however, that it became increasingly feasible to instal water closets – subject to their greater volume of waste being instantly removed from the premises by what became an essentially integrated water-supply and drainage system. The greater the progress made in that direction, the more pressing became the need to find ways of mitigating the polluting effect on local watercourses (Sheail 1996). The solution, as many urban authorities came to acknowledge, was to construct a series of low-level, large capacity, sewers, that followed the line of the local river and thence conveyed the intercepted flows to a common outlet, and perhaps treatment works, on the river bank. Such a scheme for Manchester was approved by the Local Government Board in 1889. The treatment and disposal works at Davyhulme, on the river Irwell, were commissioned in 1894 (Read 1997).

None doubted the efficacy of land treatment, where the sanitary authorities had sufficient land for adequate filtration through the soil of a sewage farm. There was however increasing pressure from those authorities which had run out of land. For them, the obvious course was to build 'artificial' treatment works. It was also realised that the changes wrought by passing sewage through the soil arose not so much from filtration, but from the decomposition caused by the action of microscopic organisms. Such observations had already encouraged the County Boroughs of Leeds and Sheffield to experiment with a cheap filler for artificial filters, which would encourage such organisms, and a mode of operation that ensured there was a sufficient period of rest for the oxidising properties to be renewed (Sheail 1997a).

From the evidence submitted to the Royal Commission on Sewage Disposal, appointed in 1898, and its own investigations, Commissioners concluded that land treatment and artificial filters were essentially the same process, and were equally capable of purifying sewage to the degree required. The Local Government Board indicated, in its annual report for 1901–2, that, whilst artificial processes must still be regarded as experimental, it would be possible to sanction in certain cases the treatment of sewage by 'artificial' processes alone (PP 1902a). Although the smaller sanitary authorities were likely to continue with land treatment, there was every reason for the larger authorities to invest in the new methods. Whilst Leeds might otherwise have had to convey its entire sewage output some 17 miles downriver, to the nearest site large enough for conventional land-treatment, it was possible to accommodate the much smaller demands of biological filtration within the immediate vicinity of the borough.

The Rivers Prevention of Pollution Act of 1876 had required sewage to be rendered harmless before being discharged to a stream. Such an absolute standard had impaired progress, in the sense that sanitary authorities had no difficulty in proving the impossibility of meeting such a goal, both technically and financially. They simply claimed exemption from that part of the Act. As sanitary engineers emphasised, the most important consideration, in any case, was the state of the river, once the discharge had been mixed with its water. It was in that larger context that guidelines were sought as to the scientific criteria by which such evolving case-by-case, standards might be set. The Royal Commission, in its eighth report of November 1912, found, from survey and experiment, that the commonly used criterion of the organic content of the effluent was too unreliable as an index to the impact on the stream. It was also necessary to establish the rate and degree of absorption of dissolved oxygen by the mixture of the effluent and water. It accordingly recommended that effluent should not normally contain more than 3 parts of suspended matter per 100,000. It should not take up more than 2 parts of dissolved oxygen per 100,000 over 5 days at 65 degrees F in temperature. Although the criteria were never given statutory effect, their widespread adoption signified for many the beginnings of a modern approach to waste management in Britain's watercourses (PP 1912–13; Sidwick 1976).

The Sanitary Authorities

The water-carriage system, by which piped-in water conveyed, cleansed and dispersed trade and domestic wastes, represented an early form of urban planning (Peterson 1979). With its economies of scale and centralised administration, sewage technology was a key factor in both consolidating and extending the urban area. Once adopted, it demanded managerial expertise and a local bureaucracy. By the same token, technology and the administrative process might set one community against another. The health benefits, in terms of the complete and rapid removal of one town's wastes, might carry a heavy cost for communities downstream (Tarr *et al*. 1984). Whatever the standards recommended by the Royal Commission on Sewage Disposal, the whole notion of water quality was also shaped by the value perspectives of the individual authorities and the credence given by parliamentary Select Committees to the evidence of policy and expert witnesses. As Hamlin (1990) expressed it, science was 'a rich and expressive idiom', seeking a natural truth yet so flexible as to be capable of supporting almost any argument one wished to advance.

It is therefore as much within the 'workings' of such authorities, as any advice given by the civil engineer, that the location, timing and nature of sanitary improvement can be traced. Central government 'experts' played an increasing role in drawing up standards, most obviously through the statutory requirement, on the part of the sanitary authorities, that they should obtain the approval of the Local Government Board, prior to raising loans to meet their capital costs. Such requirements as that every authority should appoint a medical officer of health led in time to the emergence of a range of national professions. Through their annual meetings, and the formal presentation of papers and informal conversation, there was abundant opportunity to exchange firsthand experiences. Originally mere servants of their respective authority, such officials came increasingly to see themselves as local representatives of a national profession (Hennock 1982).

In exploring the rapport between elected members and their respective officials in local and central government, much may be learned from the career paths of individual officials. Arthur Newsholme rose from being a part-time Medical Officer of Health in a London vestry to become, for twenty years, a full-time Medical Officer of Health for Brighton. He was appointed, in 1908, the Medical Officer of Health for the Local Government Board, at a time when most of the social-welfare initiatives taken by the pre-war Liberal Government were enacted (Eyler 1997). And yet, in reflecting on his career, Newsholme believed it was as a local government officer that he exerted the greater influence. Although an 'expert' might contribute through written minutes and conferences, there was no systematic pooling of knowledge and experience in a central-government department, such as the Local Government Board. The technical input was soon 'snowed' under as an 'ascending series of officials' came to consider it, before reference to a minister. In Newsholme's judgement, there was much greater opportunity for officials 'to educate their masters' in local government. Proposals would first be considered by a relevant committee and if accepted, albeit in modified form, they went to the full council. They might be scrutinised by the press and made the subject of public agitation. Whatever the outcome, the council official would have received a good hearing, with the fate of the proposals decided by a majority vote (Newsholme 1936).

The complex interplay of relationships between one sanitary authority and another, and with central government, and the opportunism displayed by elected members and officials, may be highlighted by the inter-war experience of the Nottinghamshire County Council, a pioneer in such environmental matters. The immediate stimulus to the appointment of its Rivers Pollution Sub-Committee was the prospect of intervention by the Ministry of Agriculture and Fisheries in local watercourse management. A Salmon and Freshwater Fisheries Bill of 1923 had strengthened the powers of riparian owners and fishery boards. The Salmon and Trout Association pressed the Minister to appoint an *executive* body to provide the leadership required in making full use of such powers in tackling 'the deplorable position of the fisheries in relation to river pollution'. The Minister agreed to form a small *advisory* committee, representative of fisheries interests and the Federation of British Industries. A Standing Committee on River Pollution (SCORP) was appointed, with the Fisheries Minister himself as Chairman. Through its initiative, a one-day survey of the river Trent took place, at 24 locations, some of which were in

Nottinghamshire. From such data, the Ministry's chemist identified lengths of the river that fell below the standards recommended by the Royal Commission on Sewage Disposal. Technical officers from the participating authorities agreed a procedure for an annual series of hydrographical surveys (Sheail 1993a).

Although never formally opposing the principle of such collaboration, or indeed the formation of an *ad hoc* River Board for the entire length of the Trent, the Nottinghamshire County Council believed it could fulfil the same objectives for the administrative county, at half the cost. The Council's Public Health and Housing Committee appointed a Rivers Pollution Prevention Sub-Committee in July 1923. It was to ascertain the condition of every watercourse and the sources of any pollution, prevent further pollution, and thirdly to collect and analyse samples, wherever pollution was suspected. As the Medical Officer of Health, Dr A.C. Tibbits, wrote, the County Council soon became 'the readily-acknowledged Rivers Authority'. A full-time Rivers Pollution Officer was appointed in May 1927. Although public health remained the primary concern, a much wider constituency of interests was served. As Tibbits remarked, the watercourses were an essential amenity to housing along their banks. Their waters might offer 'the really glorious forms of recreation – angling, swimming, rowing and sailing' (Nottinghamshire Record Office, Nottingham, CC3/13/1/4–6, CC/HE/1/6/1–2, and CC4/1/19–26, 33–9, 42, 45, 48 and 51).

The Sub-Committee's quinquennial report for the years 1928–32 described the best rivers as being very good indeed, with the worst experiencing some improvement. Most samples were analysed for oxygen absorption and nitrates in the County Laboratory. The Erewash remained the most heavily industrialised tributary – the worst pollution coming from the premises of the Notts and Derby Coke and By-Products Company at Pinxton, on the Derbyshire side. As Tibbits remarked, the problem was entirely a scientific one. Although the company was willing to try any remedy, so long as it was effective and practical, none had been found. A further quinquennial report of 1937 recorded how, over the ten years, the number of sewage works had risen from 71 to 84. Twenty-four were newly built, 32 had been so extended and modernised as to be essentially new, and 11 had been abandoned. The Minister of Health had given statutory consent to nearly all the 52 applications for loan sanction, following a Local Inquiry. With the installation of electrically driven pumps at the Retford sewage works in early 1933, the river Idle was at last free of untreated sewage. Within only a few months of improvements made at the pumping plant at Worksop, the very thick growths of sewage fungus had begun to disappear.

The Rivers Pollution Sub-Committee was in no doubt as to the wisdom of adopting a policy of persuasion, assistance and encouragement. As well as identifying sources of pollution, every effort was made to suggest a remedy. Information was provided on suitable plant. Not all schemes, however, brought the desired results. Although the works at Annesley had been designed and constructed on modern lines, the effluent proved so disappointing that a finer medium was sought for the top layers of the filters. The report for 1927–32 expressed surprise and disappointment at the short-sightedness of some authorities. Despite spending thousands of pounds on 'delicate' plant, they entrusted its management to anything but skilled hands. Whilst pollution occurred in its starkest form in towns and cities, few watercourses, even in the agricultural eastern part of the county, were entirely free from untreated sewage. The stream at the end of the garden was often the most convenient way of disposing of the contents of pail closets. Pollution was worst on washing days. It often changed colour on 'slaughtering' days.

It was often the combination of different types of pollution, and the threat of worse to come, that forced improvements to be made. The most usual incentive in the 1930s was the extension of mains-water supply to rural districts. The quinquennial reports emphasised the importance of anticipating the greater volumes of sewage. The Council responsible for the Sutton-in-Ashfield disposal works was congratulated. Although its works had been reconstructed only five years previously, it had applied for loan consent for an extension to cope with the new housing estates and conversion of older properties to the water-closet system. Not all authorities were so responsive. News that piped-water was to be brought to Bingham caused the Medical Officer of Health to write urgently to the District Council, in the autumn of 1932, stressing the need to install a sewage disposal works. In his response, the Surveyor wrote of how

> the Council are of opinion that the existing arrangements are satisfactory, but they will have the matter in mind and give it further consideration as and when developments due to the water supply may render it necessary.

In his reply, Tibbits expressed astonishment that the Council should wait until householders had installed water-closets and baths.

It called for great tact in seeking improvements in trade effluents. As the Rivers Pollution Officer wrote, manufacturers could hardly be expected to rush into improvements that would cost them so much but yielded so little profit. Some intervention by an outside authority was necessary. He was nevertheless surprised by the generally positive response elicited. Of the nine gas-works in Nottinghamshire, six belonged to local authorities. Five had already been connected to public sewers by 1933. The discovery that the Mansfield gas-works was discharging ammoniacal liquor into the nearby watercourse led to urgent steps being taken in the spring of 1927 to divert all the liquor to the Corporation's sewers. The 'devil liquor' was however so damaging to the normal operations of the sewage disposal works that within a short time it had again to be diverted to the stream. Although the manager of the gas-works and the British Union of Gas Engineers claimed trials were under way, a satisfactory solution had not yet been found. There was still a 'distinct gas-liquor smell' as the water passed over the weirs. It was not until the replacement of the gas-works in 1935 that all noxious discharges ceased.

The county's six chemical works gave rise to a very wide range of effluents. There was no mistaking their enormous 'avidity' to absorb the oxygen of the river water, in addition to promoting fungal growth. Whilst the most effective treatment was to mix the effluents with large quantities of domestic sewage, preliminary treatment was often required. The local authority greatly extended its sewage disposal works at Beeston and Stapleford in 1933 so as to provide adequate treatment for the increasing volumes of complex waste from Boots, the manufacturing chemists. Even so, almost all the samples taken of effluents between 1933 and 1936 were 'unsatisfactory', or 'bad'. Two settling tanks, four percolating filters and three humus tanks were added in 1937, together with facilities for using additional chemical precipitants.

A search for the source of oil, frequently found on the surface of the river Idle, in 1925, revealed the railway-engine washing-sheds at Retford to be the culprit. The solution was to fit suitably sized scum boards, and to enlarge and clean out the catch-pits. There was nothing, however, that the Sub-Committee could do to reduce the quantities of oil washed into the Trent, both directly from road surfaces and from the increasing number of public and private garages to be found in modern towns. Not only was there no attempt on the part of manufacturers to reduce the substantial amounts of oil dropped onto surfaces by standing cars but, to be effective, any regulatory scheme would have to cover a wide area beyond the river banks.

Agriculturally-based industries might pose a threat, especially where they came to be concentrated in a small number of large-scale works (Sheail 1993b). The waste waters from the wheat-washing process at the East Caudwell flour mills contained large amounts of suspended matter of a putrefactive nature. The washings of the cheese cloths and floors from a cheese factory led to a profuse growth of sewage fungus below Colston Bassett, on the river Smite. The sausage-casing works in Mansfield Woodhouse discharged a particularly objectionable effluent. Perhaps the most dramatic form of rural industrial development was the establishment of two beet-sugar factories on the banks of the river Trent, at Colwick and Kelham, in the early 1920s. In his quarterly report of January 1928,

Tibbits described how both factories were making serious attempts to improve the quality of their effluents. It was relatively easy to screen and settle-out the wastes from cleaning the beet. It was far harder to treat the liquids from the refining process. Although piecemeal improvements were welcomed, any longer-term solution required the conversion of the works to a continuous diffusion process that eliminated the need for any kind of waste product. The managers of both Nottinghamshire factories protested that, even if found to be practicable, such conversion would cost many thousands of pounds. Valuable machinery would have to be scrapped.

However dramatic the impact of the beet-sugar factories on local watercourses, the most widespread industrial threat to the county's streams and rivers arose from coal mining. It was not until the 1920s that the middle and lower reaches of the river Maun were significantly polluted, following the opening of collieries and growth of villages along its banks. The increasingly stringent requirements for high-grade steam coal meant even more washing-plant had to be installed to separate the mined coal from its impurities. Although the wash-water might be used many times over, there was heavy pollution when eventually released. The 'gritty, irritating and turbid mixture' turned even the loveliest of watercourses 'into drab and murky courses between black-slimey-banks and ravished foliage'.

Tribute was paid to the colliery companies which, without exception, had tackled the problem 'in a generous and able manner'. For its own part, the Rivers Pollution Prevention Sub-Committee maintained a 'friendly' relationship, whilst 'pressing home in as persuasive a manner as possible the imperative need for adjustment and extension'. In practice, there were three courses of action open to the companies by the mid-1930s. Seven coal pits had constructed lagoons. Ten had built settling tanks. There was always a risk of pollution when cleaned out. Six collieries took the further precaution of passing the top-water through a series of final tanks, cinder barriers or shallow lagoons. By 1936, seven mines used flocculation and filter plant. The deposited solids could be burnt in the colliery's boilers.

Whilst the discharge of slack-washing waters posed the greatest threat, pollution might also arise from other sources. Once a week, some 30,000 gallons of almost boiling, brownish liquid was discharged from the boilers of Bentinck colliery into the Erewash, over a 30-minute period. A tank was installed in late 1929 of sufficient capacity to hold the entire discharge until it had cooled sufficiently, and some settlement had taken place. Pit-head baths accommodating up to 2,000 men at a time were installed at Harworth and Bilsthorpe pits in 1931, and at the Manton and Linby collieries in 1932. Of the 19 built or under construction by 1937, 14 were connected to public sewers. The volume of sewage from each shift was so large that it had to be stored so as to 'equalise' the effect over a 24-hour day.

And with such rapid and large-scale development of the Nottinghamshire coalfield, there was considerable housing activity. The sewerage scheme under construction for the parishes of Calverton and Golham had to be further expanded, so as to cope with the 500 additional houses required at Calverton, following the decision to sink another mine shaft. The large settling tank had hardly coped with the needs of the village of Shireoaks. An extra 200 houses were planned for the new colliery village of Rhodesia. The District Council and Butterley Colliery Company negotiated an agreement, whereby the cost was borne by the Company, until such times as the rateable income from the development enabled the Council to raise a loan from public funds.

Sewering the Suburbs

For some, environmental history offers abundant opportunity to chronicle the ineptness with which the natural environment has been used and managed. The files related to large-scale sewerage schemes would seem to offer rich pickings. But the same files might also emphasise the foresight and tenacity required on the part of both elected members and officials, and their 'expert' advisers, in developing the infrastructure required by a rapidly developing community over the long term, within the constraints set by the physical and social environments (Holland and Stewart 1998).

As Gordon Cherry recalled, in his volume *Cities and Plans*, it was the squalor and unhealthiness of the northern manufacturing towns, as much as the condition of London's 'rookeries', that had led to measures of sanitary regulation and housing improvement in Victorian and Edwardian times. By the inter-war period, it was no longer sufficient to 'retrofit' urban development. There was also need to keep abreast of, and to anticipate, the rapid expansion taking place in the more affluent areas and, most obviously, the Home Counties (Cherry 1988). The population of London rose from 7.5 million in 1921 to 8.7 million by 1939. Over 60 per cent of that total was due to natural increase, an excess of births over deaths. There was also considerable movement of population, as families moved from the inner London streets to the suburban fringe. Speculative developers took advantage of the new light industries and the greater access afforded by the railways, bus, motor-cycle and car. Estates of small, three-bedroomed, semi-detached houses spread across the hitherto open landscape. There was soon a crisis in the management of local rivers and streams (Sheail 1993c).

Far from there being a unified response to the challenge, Young and Garside (1982) found, in their study of the politics of inter-war London, considerable conflict between local authorities. There was great apprehension as to the increasing influence of the London County Council. A Royal Commission on the Local Government of Greater London was appointed in October 1921. Whilst its report of February 1923 was far from unanimous, and gave short shrift to the ambitions of the London County Council, there was consensus that some kind of unified service was urgently required to administer the drainage needs of the area. In response to further deputations, the Minister of Health arranged for a technical inquiry to be carried out by his Chief Engineering Inspector and the Chief Engineer of the London County Council. Their report, eventually completed in August 1934, recounted how, as communities spread and joined with one another, the capacity of individual sewage works was outstripped. Occupants of housing estates, that were built ever-closer to the previously remote works, complained of the smell and fly-nuisance. Two solutions were put forward. The cheaper course, in terms of operational costs, was to discharge the largely untreated sewage directly into the sea. The cheaper, in capital outlay, was to devise regional schemes that together covered the Greater London area. As well as the existing London Main Drainage system, which served the City and County of London, a West Middlesex drainage scheme was then under construction (Ministry of Health 1935).

Suburban development had become so extensive in West Middlesex by the late 1920s that the Rivers Committee of the Middlesex County Council had concluded that the only realistic way of protecting the watercourses was for the County Council itself to take the initiative. Expenditure of £500 was authorised for commissioning the consultant engineer, John D. Watson, to carry out a preliminary survey. Through his wealth of expertise and experience, gained first as the Chief Engineer of the Birmingham, Tame and Rea District Drainage Board, and thereafter through his own engineering consultancy, Watson was well placed to highlight the deficiencies of the existing works, in both a technical and administrative sense, and to draw up a comprehensive scheme of the most ambitious kind. He recommended that the entire output of the existing 28 sewage works, then operated by the 22 local authorities in West Middlesex, should be diverted, by intercepting sewers, to a single purification works. There were obvious economies of scale. A single large scheme would attract a commensurately higher level of rateable income. It would be easier to raise loans for capital investment and provide sufficient revenue to maintain the works to a high standard, and employ highly trained staff. Through the combination of closer supervision and scope to conduct experiments, the works might be at the very forefront in developing new techniques (Sheail 1993d).

The Middlesex County Council Bill received the Royal Assent in June 1931. As the Chief Engineer of the Drainage Department, C.B. Townend, later recalled, it was an outstanding opportunity to apply the latest technical advances. The most notable was the activated sludge process (London Metropolitan Archives (LMA), MCC/CL MD 5). Watson's proposals had provided for both biological filtration and the activated sludge process. There was however insufficient space at the site at Mogden, in Isleworth, for all the filters required to treat the sewage from an eventual population of 2 million. The decision was therefore taken during construction to rely solely on the activated sludge process, which took up much less room. The entire works was brought into operation in May 1936. A network of intercepting sewers conveyed the sewage from the entire catchment to the Mogden works. Any smell to the nearby housing estates was minimised by pumping the sludge to Perry Oaks, a distance of 7 miles, where land was both cheap and more readily available. Not only was purification on such a scale outstandingly successful, but there seemed every prospect that (what was intended to be) the first phase of the works would suffice in meeting the anticipated increases in sewage and trade effluent.

Attention had already turned to the drainage of the other half of the county, East Middlesex. The Ministry of Health pressed for its extension to include the whole of the lower Lee Valley. At the instigation of the County Council, the Principal Assistant Secretary in the Ministry, I.G. Gibbon, took the chair at a conference of the relevant authorities. He secured the consent of the Middlesex, Hertfordshire and Essex County Councils to their meeting the cost of a consultative report. That report was completed by Watson in December 1934. Watson again perceived such a feasibility study of the technical aspects of the scheme as an essential part of the wider educative and confidence-building process. He began by describing how one of the most outstanding features of local government over the previous decade had been the growing realisation that planning had to be on broad lines. Some town-planning schemes extended to whole counties. Ambitious schemes were being drawn up for transport, electricity, water supply and mains drainage. Administrators of vision now recognised that it was only through such planning that pleasant and healthy living-conditions could be protected from haphazard speculative development. With such a declaration for pro-active local government, Watson turned to the immediate challenge and how it could be met. For most of its course, the river Lee acted as a source for London's water supply and a conduit for sewage and trade effluent. An average of 70 million gallons a day (mgd) was abstracted, and a further 15 mgd pumped from wells in the catchment, for water supply. Some 3 mgd of sewage effluent were currently discharged into the river above the intakes of drinking water – an average that would rise to 39 mgd when the area was fully developed for housing (LMA, MCC/CL.L/EMD 1, 20–23 and 42).

Watson's report focused on that part of the Lee Valley where the population had already risen by a quarter in ten years. The boundaries of the 28 boroughs, and urban and rural districts, bore little relationship to natural drainage. Finchley straddled the watershed of the rivers Brent and Lee. The disposal works of 4 local authorities occurred within one mile of the council offices of Friern Barnet. Although some works had been modernised, and the improvement of others was planned, the best course by far was to replace all of them with a single comprehensive scheme. Watson recommended that each of the existing 36 disposal works, which together occupied over 1,000 acres, should be replaced with a single purification works of some 100 acres, using the most modern techniques. As anticipated, there was a considerable outcry as to its cost, especially in the light of the Government announcement of the end of its unemployment relief scheme that had so considerably helped the West Middlesex project. As instructed, Watson hastily prepared a much smaller scheme in January 1936 for East Middlesex and the local authorities of Barnet and East Barnet in Hertfordshire. The existing 6 disposal works, covering 525 acres, would be reduced to one. The estimated capital cost would be £1.79 million. The annual cost of £143,000 represented a rate of 7 shillings per head of the estimated population.

A leading councillor, Sir William Prescott, acknowledged from the chair, at a meeting in July 1936, how the question of costs must 'be uppermost in the minds of public representatives, especially in these days'. However great the savings in the longer term, there were bound to be worries as to the immediate increase in the rates. Although Enfield stood to gain most from the scheme, it was also the most highly rated authority in Middlesex. Friern Barnet had already invested £50,000 in new works. So as to forestall the outright rejection of even the revised scheme, the Clerk to the Council suggested that an application should be made to the Ministry of Health that the loan (required to undertake the scheme) should be extended from the usual 30 years to 40 years. It would considerably reduce the initial costs. The Minister agreed, and at a reconvened meeting the Ministry's Chief Engineer emphasised the many advantages already being gained from the West Middlesex Drainage Scheme. It had been 'a great blessing'. The meeting approved a motion allocating £1,000 for the preparatory work. The East Middlesex Drainage Committee of the Middlesex County Council resolved in June 1937 that a Parliamentary Bill should be drafted, in accordance with Watson's 'basic scheme'. The precedents of the West Middlesex Drainage Scheme should be followed, with control vested in the County Council, working through a special committee.

Under the Middlesex County Council (Sewerage) Act of July 1938, the Council obtained powers to include in a single scheme 8 districts in Middlesex, 4 in Hertfordshire and 2 in Essex. An intercepting sewer, some 24 miles long, was to be built, conveying the sewage from an area of 100 square miles, to the disposal works at Deephams, in east Edmonton, from where the effluent was to be discharged into Salmon Brook, a tributary of the river Lee, and the sludge conveyed to Rammey Marsh in Enfield. Earlier, in February 1938, the East Middlesex Drainage Committee had hired a motor coach to tour the sites of the proposed works and then the Mogden works of the West Middlesex Drainage Scheme. Reporting the visit, the *Edmonton Citizen* described how the first thing to catch the eye at the Mogden works was a high grass-embankment, planted with shrubs. Inside the gate, one might have been in a public park, had it not been for the large expanse of water in the purifying bed. Members were told of how property values near the works had actually risen.

New Towns and Oysters

Writing from the perspective of a planning historian, Gordon Cherry described the post-war New Towns as the most obvious expression of a nation, where the State was the wise, beneficent steersman to a nobler future. 'As jewels in planning's crown', New Towns were perceived as civilised, attractive, agreeable places in which to live, with all the richness of community life that the new social order would bring (Cherry 1988, pp. 157–62). As Minister of Town and Country Planning, Lewis Silkin played a pivotal role both in promoting and in implementing the opportunities that stemmed from the New Towns Act of 1946. As he later recalled, they were intended to shake free from 'the soulless suburbia, ribbon development, single-industry towns, and one-class housing estates' that characterised so much of the development of the 1930s. In his words,

> our big cities need not forever go on expanding until all their people were engulfed in a sea of bricks and mortar, cut off from the open countryside.

The 'obsolete, overcrowded, slum-ridden, and bomb-stricken towns could be thinned out and transformed from their Victorian squalor into decent centres of living', in which Britain could take some pride (Silkin 1972; Ward 1992).

In recalling that endeavour, Lewis Silkin was at pains to emphasise the scale of the challenge. Despite the pioneering work of Ebenezer Howard and the models provided by Letchworth Garden City and, from 1919 onwards, Welwyn Garden City, there was no real knowledge of the organisation and materials required, nor of the social problems that might arise. Not only did decisions have to be taken quickly, but each of the post-war New Towns threw up its own set of problems. The solutions had to be tailor-made to meet the needs of the intended population. There has however been much unevenness in recounting how those solutions were found. The volume, *The New Towns: The Answer to Megalopis* by Frederic J. Osborn and Arnold Whittick, appraised the achievement of the first 19 New Towns, but only from an aesthetic perspective. The more material considerations are hardly mentioned (Osborn and Whittick 1963). For some insight into the more mundane aspects of 'inserting' such New Towns into their respective parts of the UK, one must turn to Frank Schaffer's volume, *The New Town Story*, in which a few paragraphs are devoted to the provision of an infrastructure . Schaffer himself was an Under-Secretary in the Ministry of Town and Country Planning, for seven years in charge of the New Towns Division (Schaffer 1972).

The designation of four New Towns, Stevenage, Harlow, Hatfield and Welwyn Garden City, within the catchment of the river Lee, was always likely to raise difficulties. The river provided not only 20 per cent of London's water supply, but was heavily polluted by the effluent of existing settlements. One of the reasons cited for the court action brought by local residents against the Minister's designation of Stevenage New Town, was the lack of consideration given to such aspects as sewerage. Although the action was overturned in the Court of Appeal, on the grounds that a technical solution could be found, the judgement took little account of the cost of such a regional sewerage scheme. Even Schaffer's account gives little intimation of the acrimony that arose between the Government, Development Corporations and local authorities as to how the eventual cost of the scheme was to be apportioned. Although the Government was prepared to advance the monies, the Treasury insisted they must be repaid. The local authorities accepted that their ratepayers had derived some benefit, but insisted the regional drainage scheme would never have been needed if it had not been for the Minister's decision to designate the New Towns in the same catchment, as part of a larger strategy to improve living conditions within London (Sheail 1995a).

The word 'sewerage' does not appear in the index of Osborn and Whittick's volume, and yet it was the greatest challenge to the building of Basildon, another of London's New Towns of those formative years. Schaffer (1972, pp. 150–1) writes only cursorily of how 'an anguished howl' went up when it was first proposed to discharge its sewage and trade effluent into the river Crouch. He remarked on how, as a result of what he called 'a formidable opposition' mounted by the Ministry of Agriculture and Fisheries, the interests of the oyster industry of the river Crouch were put before those of the 80,000 future inhabitants of Basildon. The Development Corporation was forced, at great cost, to divert the whole of its drainage to the river Thames. Perhaps more accurately, the whole episode might be described as an outstanding example of how the resolution of one environmental problem threatened to create another.

The remainder of this section illustrates how, through study of the contemporary documentation of the relevant Government departments, namely the Treasury, Ministry of Town and Country Planning, and Ministry of Agriculture and Fisheries (which fought almost single-handedly for the protection of the oyster fishery), a fuller picture begins to emerge of the nature and consequences of the decision to establish a New Town of Basildon. Far from detracting from the 'New Town story', it highlights the achievement embodied in realising the concept with so little disruption to the wider, already heavily utilised urban and rural environments of South-East England. It takes cognisance not only of the pioneering role of the New Town visionaries, but of the positive contribution made by other interested parties. The overall effect was an even broader perception of planning issues, as post-war society strove consciously to learn from the past in designing environments for the future (PRO, MAF 209, 846 and HLG 91, 124, 328 and 346–7).

By March 1948, officials of the Ministry of Town and Country Planning (MTCP) were ready to put before the Minister 'firm' proposals for a New Town in the Pitsea–Laindon area of south Essex, of about 25,000 inhabitants. The priority had been to decide the location and layout of the streets and housing. The drainage system and possible threat to the nearby oyster industry were at first treated as 'two relatively minor matters'. The Ministry of Agriculture and Fisheries saw things very differently, intimating its concern in a letter addressed to the Ministry of Health in December 1947. Within the Ministry, officials and their expert adviser, Dr H.A. Cole, the Principal Naturalist of the Ministry's Fisheries Experimental Station at Conway, Caernarvonshire, concluded there would be no alternative but 'uncompromising opposition'. There were already far too many bankrupt and derelict grounds on the East and South Coasts, as a result of accepting the claim of some local-government official that the damage would be less serious than supposed. In nearly every case, pollution had dealt the *coup de grâce*. The number of productive oyster beds in the British isles had fallen from 50 at the turn of the century to less than 10. Not only was the Crouch fishery the most important of those to survive, but the Ministry had just established an experimental station at Burnham-on-Crouch, to study ways of increasing productivity of oyster beds generally.

The Draft Designation Order for the New Town confirmed that an outfall into the Crouch was the most economic form of drainage, but acknowledged there were anxieties as to the impact on the fisheries. At the Public Inquiry into the Order, in October 1948, the Ministry's representative emphasised how there would be the fullest consultation before any works were carried out. As preliminary works for the New Town of Basildon (as it had come to be called) got under way, tension mounted. The MTCP sought the guidance of the Ministry of Health in November 1950, emphasising how the point of discharge was fundamental to the design of the whole drainage system. In the same month, Cole pressed for high-level discussions. It was wrong, in principle, 'to set down a new town in a rural area and let loose a torrent of sewage on to the oyster beds, when a reasonable alternative was available'.

At an interdepartmental meeting of December 1950, Fisheries representatives correctly surmised that they had made 'a definite impression'. Whilst their annual value was currently £15,000, the oyster beds were recognised to be worth potentially much more. As an official of the New Towns Division of the MTCP privately minuted, if the question resolved simply around the sewage aspect, 'we should be prepared to urge the Corporation' to go to the Pitsea Marshes, on the Thames estuary. But for both Ministries, the really 'disturbing' factor was the disposal of surface-water. On the basis of a 40 per cent run off, as opposed to an existing level of 5 per cent, a discharge of 100 million gallons per day might be anticipated from the New Town. It would be prohibitively expensive to divert this to the Thames. Since its total effect might be at least as polluting as foul sewage effluent, the Development Corporation argued that any diversion of flows was pointless. Cole continued to oppose any compromise regarding foul sewage. An acceptable arrangement for the surface-water was, however, possible. The Essex Rivers Catchment Board (which was similarly concerned at the prospect of large-scale flooding down-river of the existing Shotgate sewage-treatment works) recommended that the surface-waters should be diverted in times of high rainfall into a suitable combination of washlands and lagoons, within the designated area of the New Town. Not only was agreement reached as to the location of these works, but there was evidence that such earthworks might help to reduce the risk of winter flooding generally.

At a further meeting, in February 1951, which was intended to reach a final settlement, officials of the MTCP emphasised how the Minister, Hugh Dalton, was determined that building in the northern part of Basildon should start immediately. An interim drainage scheme was therefore required that would double the dry weather flow from the Shotgate works. It was hoped a system of recirculation within the works, with double filtration, would maintain a high standard of effluent. Fisheries representatives agreed to both the interim arrangements, and longer-term discharge of surface-water into the Crouch, but rejected the proposed longer-term scheme for foul sewage. Whilst a diversion of sewage to the Thames would be expensive, they insisted it should be seen in the context of the total expenditure on New Towns and the savings in compensation payments to the oyster companies.

Fisheries representatives were, however, shocked to discover that even if the threat of the New Town effluent were removed there was a further source of pollution to be considered, namely the impact of the increase of 15,000 in the population of Billericay–Wickford, recently approved under an Expanded Town Order. Over 15 years, discharge into the upper Crouch was expected to rise by 750,000 gallons a day. There was clearly no point in protecting the Crouch from the New Town, if other settlements in the catchment were to pollute its waters. As an official in the MTCP, M.M. Dobbie, observed,

> I am myself very fond of oysters and have nothing but tenderness for the welfare of the infant oyster, but if the most that we can achieve at considerable extra expense would be to keep the oyster nursery going for another fifteen years, I find it very hard to see any justification in doing so.

To make matters worse, the revelation exposed even more clearly the greatest weakness in the Fisheries' case, namely the inability to say specifically what amount of sewage could be accepted into the Crouch without damaging the fishery. So many factors were involved. The tolerance of the oyster might reflect its stages of growth from larvae to maturity. Account had to be taken of the volume and nature of the pollution. At most, Cole could only make general comparisons with what had happened in other estuaries. The fishery in the Upper Fal was not seriously harmed by the untreated sewage from the city of Truro, of 13,000 inhabitants, whereas great difficulties had been experienced in the fishery below Colchester, with a population of 57,000. The fishery on the Orwell had been obliterated by the discharge of some 100,000 people living in Ipswich. Given the topography and particular vulnerability of the breeding grounds, Cole warned of how the tolerance of the Crouch might be as low as 20,000. In a letter of March 1951, the Ministry of Agriculture and Fisheries indicated that if the Thames scheme were completed quickly, and the Shotgate works closed, it should be possible for the fishery to survive an additional discharge from Billericay–Wickford.

A further consideration of those negotiating a compromise was the restructuring of Government departments in January 1951. The achievements of W.S. Morrison in the wartime Coalition Government, and of his successor, Lewis Silkin, had been remarkable, given that, as Minister of Town and Country Planning, they did not have Cabinet rank. Their actions were severely circumscribed by much larger and longer-established Departments. Not only did the Ministry of Town and Country Planning survive, but it further absorbed the responsibilities of the Ministry of Health for housing, local government, water supply and sewerage in early 1951, when its name changed to that of the Ministry of Local Government and Planning (MLGP). The new Minister, Hugh Dalton, was a senior politician with Cabinet rank, but he had a long-standing personal interest in the Department's subject field. The Ministry acquired the further new title following the election of a Conservative Government in October. It became the Ministry of Housing and Local Government (PP 1955–56; PRO, HLG 91, 124; Dalton 1962; Pimlott 1985). Where once 'a wretched little backwater', the Ministry became one of the most important administrative departments within Whitehall.

It seemed increasingly likely that the whole question of the Crouch fisheries would require Cabinet decision, and that Dalton would prevail. From his perspective, the Ministry's additional responsibilities provided a golden opportunity to accelerate housebuilding. Sewerage problems, which had previously 'wobbled' to and fro, could now be settled speedily within the same Ministry. The New Towns Division, and Water and Sewerage Division, could now speak with a single, and therefore strengthened, voice. Convinced that the Crouch was the right choice, Dalton enquired anxiously in February 1951 whether he should first raise 'the oyster problem' with the Minister of Agriculture and Fisheries.

Although Fisheries officials feared the worst, there were increasing misgivings in Dalton's own Ministry. As one official minuted in May 1951, the Development Corporation would have to prove at the Local Inquiry into the designation of the New Town, that there was no feasible alternative to discharge into the Crouch. To do that, it would have to demonstrate that all possibilities had been examined, including the comparative costs of discharge into the Thames. Without that, opponents would have grounds to seek a Court Injunction. It was only after the most senior official in the Ministry, the Permanent Secretary, had spoken at length with the

Chairman of the Development Council, Sir Launcelot Keay, that the Corporation commissioned a study of alternative schemes on both the Crouch and the Thames. It was found that where it would cost up to £1 million in capital works, and £67,285 in annual costs, to develop a scheme for the Crouch, an outfall at Vange Creek on the Thames, with a similar full treatment of the sewage, would cost as much as £1.3 million and £77,120 respectively. To the Development Corporation, the studies simply added detail to what was already known. For officials of the MLGP, they confirmed what had been suspected, namely that the savings were too small to justify the Ministry trying to force the Crouch scheme through the Cabinet. More importantly, the Corporation had still not considered the full range of options. As guidance to the Corporation, in deciding 'which scheme they might profitably pursue', prior to making a formal proposal, officials of the Ministry of Health had previously explored the possibility of discharging the untreated sewage directly into the main channel of the Thames, thus avoiding the cost of a treatment works. Given that the river at that point was over a mile wide and opening into the sea, it was most unlikely to create 'offensive conditions'.

Patience with the Development Corporation finally snapped in May 1951, when the General Manager accused the MLGP of causing unnecessary delay. One official demanded that 'someone should send the fool a stinker *and do it quickly*'. Another minuted that the fault lay with Keay, who was well known for having all the faults of a 'problem child', including 'a shocking temper'. At a 'quite friendly meeting', it was explained how the Ministry was simply striving to ensure that the scheme, eventually submitted for formal approval, was one which the Minister, on the face of it, could approve, whatever the strength of opposition at a Local Inquiry. Whilst appreciating the point, Keay complained of being placed in the impossible position where houses had to be built as rapidly as possible, without any assurance of there being the sewerage arrangements on which development depended.

Given the pressure to build houses, Keay protested, at a meeting of July 1951, of how it would take 16 months longer to complete the

Thames scheme. However true in a technical sense, Ministry officials claimed it would nevertheless be commissioned long before the opposition, and possible litigation, against the Crouch scheme had been overcome. It was agreed the Ministry should draft a memorandum describing the two schemes and the differences between the Department and Corporation, so that Dalton could decide which scheme to advise the Corporation to take to a Local Inquiry. Since the Minister would have to give a quasi-judicial decision, after the Inquiry, the Corporation was asked to treat the memorandum as being entirely informal and confidential. Together with the technical, cost and construction details, the memorandum explained how opposition to the Thames outfall would be minimal, even if there was only partial treatment. Even with the highest standards of purification, there was bound to be objection to the use of the Crouch, of 'a kind which sewerage authorities are warned in public health and river pollution law, to take very seriously'. Even if the Corporation obtained the Minister's approval to the Crouch scheme, it would remain in peril of Common Law actions. On the basis of this memorandum, Dalton decided that the Corporation should be advised to prepare a scheme for the Thames.

For the Ministry of Agriculture and Fisheries, news that the Corporation was seeking to buy land for a sewage disposal works, in September 1951, was the first tangible evidence that 'the battle of the Crouch' had been won. It would be a valuable precedent in tackling pollution problems in other areas, such as West Mersea and Whitstable. Much as the Ministry disliked the idea of putting 6 million gallons per day of crude sewage into that part of the Thames, it was at least better than the almost certain destruction of the Crouch industry. There was therefore the greatest consternation when Fisheries officials learned that their colleagues, concerned with the 'land-use angle', had objected to the disposal works being located on some of the best farmland in the area. Predictably officials of the New Towns Division of the MLGP protested at the further cost of funding an alternative site. The local authorities were already up in arms. The agricultural objection was hastily withdrawn.

The conflict that had encompassed issues of both public and environmental health had run its course. As invariably happened, each party looked back on it with misgivings. For the Ministry of Agriculture and Fisheries, there were anxieties of two kinds. Negotiations had been conducted on a confidential basis. Whilst it suited officials to handle the matter singlehandedly and behind closed doors, they were nevertheless astonished and disturbed to find that the Kent and Essex Fisheries Committee, the supposed 'watchdogs of inshore fishermen', remained either unaware or unconcerned at the threat to its most important fishery. At least as worrying was the weakness of the fisheries interest in as much as so little was known about the effects of different volumes and types of pollution on oysters and their breeding grounds at different stages in the life cycle and seasons of the year. Such ignorance severely limited the scope for accommodation between unrestrained pollution and a complete ban on any form of discharge.

There was frustration too among those responsible for local government and planning. The Billericay Urban District Council had remained unaware of the abandonment of the Crouch scheme until it received formal notice, in January 1952, of the Local Inquiry required to hear an application for a Compulsory Purchase Order to acquire the site of the disposal works. Both then, and at the Local Inquiry held in April, the Council complained bitterly at its 'shabby treatment'. It demanded compensation for the substantially higher costs that would fall on ratepayers. It was not until the publication of the Minister's decision to grant the Order that officials were able to say publicly why a Thames outfall had been chosen. In the meantime, there was every opportunity for critics to convey the impression that the Government was bent on imposing expensive civil-engineering schemes on local people, without any thought of how the cost might be borne. Not only did the Development Corporation appear to enjoy the Ministry's obvious embarrassment but, much to the annoyance of officials of the Water and Sewerage Division, it had bought off local opposition to the location of the sewage disposal works by agreeing to full treatment. Apart from the considerably higher operating costs, officials feared it would encourage pressure for similarly high standards, both on the Thames and other badly polluted estuaries. There was, however, no alternative but to concede. In a letter of July 1952, the Minister approved the location of the main sewerage works at Frampton's Farm, from where the effluent would be piped to Pitsea Creek, at a total cost of £1,182,200.

More generally, an obvious conclusion from the case study is the need for the historian to range beyond the published word, say in proceedings and various submissions made to a Local Inquiry, and to look more closely at the discussion and correspondence that accompanied such decision-making. Only then might due weight be given to the respective institutions, and such professions as the planner and scientist, in judging how particular lines of argument came to prevail.

The Multi-Purpose Use of Water

The transfer of water from remote areas of the country to cities and towns has always received close scrutiny from parliament. The relatively unchanging Local and Private Bill procedures accordingly provide a valuable insight into the changing perceptions of town and countryside. By the late nineteenth century, an increasing number of urban authorities found themselves committed to civil-engineering schemes of ever-larger scale and complexity – and to resolving 'the problems of environmental control' that arose from their construction and operation (Fraser 1982; Hassan 1998). The ensuing acrimony frequently called into question the efficacy of the procedures followed in adjudicating between the contending parties. Paradoxically, both government and parliament were so concerned as to the enormity of the consequences of making any false move, that there was every temptation to take refuge in the practice and precedents established by water management in the past.

Such concerns as to the 'sweeping powers' sought by water-undertakers were considerably magnified where the water of one catchment was transferred to another. One of the first major clashes occurred when, in 1878, Manchester Corporation turned to the Lake District and, more specifically, sought to enlarge and impound Thirlmere. When the Corporation sought, by a further Bill of 1919, to impound and raise the level of Haweswater, the Lancashire County challenged its right to take precedence over the needs of other undertakers in the North-West of England. In the words of its petition, it was time such upland catchments were 'treated in the character of a national trust'. The Select Committee responded by stipulating that the Corporation must supply water (without deriving profit) to those localities through which the aqueduct from Haweswater to Manchester passed, and to those in the vicinity of Manchester, 'which are not able to go to distant sources for themselves'. It had become the practice to stipulate that about one-third of the stream water should be left as 'compensation water' for the industrial and other interests downstream of any new reservoir (Sheail 1984). Such was the opposition of fisheries interests to the Haweswater scheme that the further precedent was set whereby a proportion of the residual flow was to be released in the form of freshets, or spates, so as to assist the salmon and river trout in swimming up the river during the breeding season (House of Lords Record Office (HLRO), Commons and Lords Select Committees, Manchester Corporation Bill, 1919, minutes of evidence; Manchester Corporation Act, 1919, 9 & 10 George V, ch. cxix).

Both the accelerating per capita consumption, and enlargement of its water-distribution area, caused the Manchester Corporation to promote, in the autumn of 1961, a Bill to abstract water from Ullswater and to create a reservoir in Bannisdale. It was met by a massive outcry from amenity groups and almost every statutory and local authority. Perceived as the first stage of a much larger project, opponents sought, by rejecting the proposals root and branch, to prevent Manchester from ever returning to the Lake District (Dolbey 1974). Lord Lonsdale, a considerable landowner in the Ullswater area, persuaded Lord Birkett, the famous barrister and former President of the Friends of the Lake District, to move a motion, and thereby force a debate on the Second Reading, to omit the waterworks clauses from the Corporation's Bill. Although such a thing had been done only seven times before, Birkett argued that this was a Bill where 'the point of principle was so grave' that it should be for the whole House to consider the matter. Birkett's motion was carried by 70 to 26 votes (PD, Lords, 237, 209–354).

Manchester's need for water remained. The Ministry of Housing and Local Government convened in February 1962 a conference of the relevant local authorities and statutory bodies which, a year later, both confirmed that need and identified possible sources. The Corporation announced in the spring of 1964 its intention of seeking permission to abstract from Ullswater and Windermere. The more modest proposals fell within the scope of a draft Order, under the Water Act of 1945. It meant everything now hinged on gaining the consent of the Minister. At the Public Inquiry, opponents generally conceded Manchester's need for more water. The Corporation justified its proposals on the basis of how quickly they could be implemented. There would be scarcely any difference to lake levels. Public access would be retained. The Inspector's report of September 1965 confirmed that the additional water was both needed and could be provided without damage to the lakes.

Richard Crossman, the Minister of Housing and Local Government, wrote in his diary of December 1965, of how his initial intention had been to accept the 'first-rate report'. The Chief Whip, Edward Short, had however been a leading opponent. His family had lived near Ullswater for generations. Crossman's loan of the report, whilst it was still confidential, brought forth 'a powerful letter', insisting that not 'a drop of Ullswater' should be taken. Crossman (1975, p. 405) sought compromise. A visit made 'very secretly' with the Inspector in April 1966 convinced him that 'a marvellous solution' had been found. Manchester obtained its water but further concessions were made to amenity, including the stipulation that a water-treatment works should be built, thereby further removing any need to restrict public access. But as Crossman conceded, in his diary, he only just scraped a majority for his compromise in the Cabinet's Home Affairs Committee. Rather than risk the embarrassment of announcing his decision to approve the scheme in the House of Commons, with 'my own Chief Whip sitting beside me' and the Conservative Chief Whip, William Whitelaw (the Member for Penrith) opposite, Crossman held a press conference. Although Crossman (1975, pp. 503 and 512) believed everything possible had been done for amenity, he remained concerned as to whether Manchester had been treated too harshly. The Water Order was formally approved in February 1967.

Where typically such long-distance schemes transferred water from upland gathering-grounds to industrial and urban markets in the valleys and on the coasts, there was increasing need for water storage and transfer schemes within the lowlands themselves. A priority of the Water Resources Board, established under the Water Resources Act of 1963, was to assess and plan for the needs of South-East England. Not only were living standards rising, but the population was expected to rise by 3.5 million over 20 years. Some half of that figure would have to be accommodated in new and expanded towns. *The South East Study*, published in 1964, saw no overriding obstacle to meeting demand, provided there was adequate planning and capital investment. A pumped-storage scheme was already under construction at Diddington in Huntingdonshire (Ministry of Housing and Local Government 1964, pp. 105–12). Known as Graffham Water, it was the largest artificial water-body in England, when commissioned in 1967.

Water-resource planning became more skilled. The various water-undertakers were merged. Central government played a larger role, and yet there was still conflict as to the location, timing and character of the individual schemes. A sense of the frustration and disillusionment felt by both undertakers and those affected by such schemes can be discerned in the debates on a Bill promoted in 1969 for the construction of what became known as Rutland Water. Its purpose was to authorise the Welland and Nene River Authority to acquire land and to construct a pumped-storage reservoir of 3,114 acres on the upper waters of the river Gwash in Rutland, and to enable the Mid-Northamptonshire Water Board to abstract water from a point upstream of the town of Stamford, when the flow of the river Welland exceeded 8 million gallons a day (mgd) and from above Peterborough when the flow of the river Nene was over 30 mgd. Although some water would be taken directly from the reservoir, most would be returned to the rivers during periods of low flow for abstraction and use by the Water Board at those downriver points. Opposition was so strong that the House of Commons (the first House) divided on the Bill at its Second Reading, before its referral to a Select Committee. Opponents focused on four questions. Was more water needed? If so, how much? Over what kind of period? And fourthly, were there reasonable alternatives to a reservoir so near to the village of Empingham on the Gwash? (HLRO, Welland and Nene (Empingham Reservoir) and Mid-Northamptonshire Water Bill, 1969, minutes of evidence).

A technical study by the Water Resources Board had identified 'a deficiency zone'. Extending from Northamptonshire in the north to the London Basin in the south it included four major town-expansion schemes, namely at Daventry, Northampton, Corby and Wellingborough, as well as Peterborough to the east. It seemed likely that the present supply of 27 mgd would be outstripped by 1974. The deficit would increase to 20.37 mgd by 1981 and 50.22 mgd by 1991. Both policy and expert witnesses warned of how any failure to make up such deficits would jeopardise the development of not only town-expansion schemes, but the future prosperity of other market towns and villages. There would be little or no chance of those 'living in the blackest slums of London and Birmingham' moving to the area, let alone to houses with water closets, baths and running water.

The proposed reservoir was second only in size to Windermere, the largest natural lake in England. The Member of Parliament, Kenneth Lewis, asserted that his constituents in Rutland did not want their county (the smallest in England) 'to be a kind of towpath round a lake'. Other Members were concerned as to the wider implications for the countryside. Angus Maude observed:

> What worries people in rural areas more than anything ... is the way in which large areas of first-class land and the environment of hundreds of people are gradually eroded or destroyed as a kind of reflex from urban development which has often been planned with no long-term thought about the secondary implications in terms of water demand and other things.

Angus Maude continued:

> All too often, the country dweller gets the impression that somebody plans development first and then we are presented with a *fait accompli* in the form of the flooding of another 2,000 or 3,000 acres of agricultural land comparatively remote from the areas where the development is to take place.

Other Members, in the course of a Third Reading on the Bill, were at pains to deny there was an urban/rural conflict. The rural county of Rutland needed water just as much as the expanded towns. The demand arose not only from urban development but from the fact that rural areas were now being provided with a piped-water supply, where hitherto 'they probably had to go off with a bucket and draw it from the nearest well' (PD, Commons, 781, 554–618 and 786, 313–44).

In attacking the Bill as being Victorian in concept, Kenneth Lewis warned that, 'when history comes to be written', it would be said that

> we clung to the old-fashioned methods at increased cost, rather than going forward with more modern, innovative methods that come to us through our modern technology, and which in the early stages might be expensive but in the long run would provide us with cheaper water, just as we now have cheaper oil and gas.

The Water Resources Board insisted a reservoir was the only way of guaranteeing there was sufficient water from the mid-1970s until the late 1980s. Although both Select Committees found the case for the Bill overwhelming, there was considerable concern as to the lack of alternative forms of water supply. After a hearing of 8 days, the Commons Committee took the exceptional step of issuing a special report and of sending a letter to the Prime Minister, emphasising the need to embark on a feasibility study of a Wash Barrage with minimal delay. During the Third Reading debate, a Member spoke of the need to throw out the Bill, as a way of making 'the water boards get cracking on developing other sources'. As it was, the Bill obtained a relatively narrow majority of 75 to 65 votes. The Bill received the Royal Assent in 1970, and the scheme was commissioned in 1977 at a capital cost of £29 million and annual running cost of £500,000.

Most critics of the scheme had sought compromise, rather than outright rejection. As legal counsel for the petitioners conceded in the course of the Commons Select Committee, a reservoir was 'a deplorable and regrettable necessity'. An obvious compromise was to be found in the more sensitive treatment of what was being built. Speaking as an expert witness for the promoters, the leading landscape architect, Sylvia Crowe, described her preliminary landscaping proposals to both Select Committees. Such a water-body might be alien to the Rutland landscape, but her experience in creating such a lake in the Australian capital of Canberra had shown how water was 'an extraordinarily accommodating feature in any landscape'. The earth-dam would be turfed and merged with the natural contours. It was intended to regrade and reclaim the more shallow parts so as to create a shoreline of banks and higher ground. The visual effects of an annual draw-down of an average 7 feet would be further improved by the planting of such grass species as *Agrostis stolonifera aquatica*, together with willows at or just below the waterline. As well as the planting of shrubs and saplings, Silvia Crowe emphasised how the adjacent areas should be 'very carefully maintained and managed on an ecological basis', so as to prevent their becoming 'a tangled wilderness' or a formal garden. They should be properly managed as 'a good piece of countryside'.

The Bill's promoters were required to strike a balance between those wanting to exploit the recreational potential to the fullest, and those who censured any encouragement of visitors. As one Member of Parliament argued, it was bad enough for farmers to lose their land, but even worse if the surrounding area were to be turned into 'an urban tourist resort'. Sylvia Crowe recommended that only water-based sports, such as sailing and fishing, should be encouraged. A nature reserve should be designated along those parts of the shoreline where wildfowl congregated. In the event, parking for 3,000 vehicles was provided at four picnic areas, and a bridleway constructed around most of the water's edge. A 350-acre nature reserve was managed by the Leicestershire and Rutland Trust for Nature Conservation. With a planned capacity of a thousand craft, a sailing club was built, and the lake well-stocked with trout from the Authority's own hatchery.

It seemed that as one impounding scheme was approved an even larger one was being prepared. Where the Rutland Water had drawn heavily on the experience of Graffham Water, Keilder Water marked the climax of large-scale, twentieth-century reservoir construction. There had been a series of increasingly controversial schemes for the provision of water to the industrial North-East of England. The Tees Valley and Cleveland Water Board had suddenly been faced, in the summer of 1964, with the need to double supplies, following the decision of the Imperial Chemical Industries (ICI) to construct two of the largest ammonia plants in the world. The only feasible course was to construct another river-regulating reservoir. The Water Resources Board confirmed that a reservoir of 770 acres, at Cow Green, would be the cheapest and quickest site to develop. A letter to *The Times* in February 1965, signed by 14 eminent botanists, drew attention to the unique assemblages of rare plant species. A joint petition, mounted by almost every amenity and naturalists' society of any standing, insisted that, however great the need of industry for water, nothing could justify the destruction of 'so splendid a heritage'. Upper Teesdale was 'an irreplaceable open air laboratory, containing unparalleled scientific riches which include a remarkable complex of plant communities'. The offer of £100,000 on the part of ICI for a 'crash' programme of research, prior to flooding, overlooked the long-term nature of experiments and the continued improvement of research techniques (HLRO, Commons' Select Committee, Private Bills, 1966, printed evidence, vol. III).

The opposition to the destruction of such plant communities caused the Bill to be debated in both Houses of Parliament. As Roy Gregory remarked, 'it was emotion and sentiment, rather than a cool and open-minded approach to the issues involved, that dictated the attitude of most MPs'. The Select Committee of the House of Lords came to a similar decision as that of the Commons, namely that, in view of the pressing need for the water, and that only 20 acres of the plant community would be inundated, it would be unreasonable to prevent the reservoir being built. The Bill received the Royal Assent in March 1967 (Gregory 1971). The immediate feeling for naturalists and ecologists was one of acute disappointment. It was poor consolation to know that things could never be quite the same again – the promoters of civil-engineering schemes would have to take greater account of ecological considerations if they were to avoid prolonged argument and adverse publicity.

There was in any case need for a fundamental reappraisal of strategy in the North-East. A feasibility study of 38 sites in 1969 identified two approaches. One was to build further reservoirs on the highest sections of the three east-flowing rivers, the Tyne, Wear and Tees. The potential of the Tees was, however, not only exhausted, but the Wear was too small to support any additional reservoirs. The alternative was therefore to build one or more reservoirs on the northern uplands, and to transport the water southwards across the region. The North Tyne valley had a higher potential than the Irthing valley of Cumbria. A public inquiry held at Newcastle in March 1972 heard 191 objections. Further alternative schemes were considered at a reconvened hearing in June–July 1973. The site eventually chosen enabled the dam to be built at one of the narrowest points in the North Tyne valley. The sparsely-populated valley above the dam had already been considerably affected by large-scale afforestation.

The scheme was completed in 1982 as Britain's first example of a regional water grid. Water from the Keilder reservoir was used both to maintain minimum flow levels on the Tyne, Derwent, Wear and Tees at times of low natural rainfall, and to allow additional flows to be released for water-supply purposes. Keilder Water became the largest lake in northern Europe, located within the most extensive forest in the UK. Both the new road round Keilder Water and a toll road through the forest (the longest in Britain) provided both easy access and many vantage points from which to look across the Border Forest Park. The eighteenth-century hunting lodge of Keilder Castle was converted to a visitor centre. A Civic Trust Award for 1984 cited the scheme's 'outstanding contribution to the quality and appearance of the environment' of that previously remote and little-visited part of Northumberland.

CHAPTER 4

New Beginnings in Forestry

Introduction

A doubling of the woodland area of the UK within a century might seem like planning history writ large. The campaign was centrally directed, closely focused, and sustained. It was driven at least initially by a conscious desire to learn from the lessons of history, namely that the nation must never again run short of timber during a military crisis. Of the European nations, only Portugal had proportionately less woodland cover at the turn of the century. High-quality timber could be imported so easily from Scandinavia, Russia and North America that even where woodlands existed they tended to be managed for game and amenity, rather than for timber. Reflecting the generally low standards of husbandry, home-grown timber acquired a poor reputation for its quality (Scottish Record Office (SRO), AF 79, 1). Some 95 per cent of the woodlands were privately owned – the principal exception being the Crown Estate.

There was no shortage of appeals, in the early twentieth century, for greater investment in softwood timber production. Britain imported more than 90 per cent of its requirements (more than any other country). Imports had risen fivefold since 1850. A Departmental Committee, appointed by the Board of Agriculture in 1903, emphasised how it was not only wasteful, in as much as properly managed plantations were capable of meeting a much greater part of the nation's needs at competitive prices, but it was highly imprudent in view of the likely shortage, if not dearth, of world supplies. Not only was consumption per head of population rising, but the yield of the world's forests was thought to be

New Beginnings in Forestry

declining. By 1913, Russia supplied half of Britain's needs – the only large reserves within the Empire were those of Canada, which were being 'rapidly depleted by fire' (PP 1902b; SRO, AF 43, 529).

Historians have recounted how the First World War demonstrated, in the most graphic way, the vulnerability of a nation so dependent on the import of bulky raw materials, essential not only for 'purely war purposes' but, in the case of timber, for the coal mines (Ryle 1969). Forest histories have described how in July 1916 the Prime Minister invited the Parliamentary Secretary to the Board of Agriculture, Sir Francis Dyke Acland, to become Chairman of a Forestry Sub-Committee of the Reconstruction Committee of the Ministry of Reconstruction to consider

> the best means of conserving and developing the woodland and forest resources of the UK having regard to the experiences gained during the War.

Its unanimous report of May 1917 recommended the afforestation of 1,770,000 acres by the end of the century. By bringing the existing woodland area of 2 million acres to a high state of production, the Sub-Committee believed the combined yield would be sufficient to sustain the country through a further war of up to three years (PP 1917–18). After further consideration by a Committee, consisting of Lords Curzon and Milner, and a Treasury official, the report's findings were accepted by the War Cabinet in late 1918. An informal Committee was appointed, under Acland, which quickly assumed the status of an Interim Forest Authority, its main task being to draft a Forestry Bill. This was enacted within only two months of its introduction, in July 1919. A Forestry Commission was appointed in November 1919, charged with

> the general duty of promoting the interests of forestry, the development of afforestation and the production and supply of timber in the UK.

The immediate goal was to build up an adequate reserve of pit-timber as rapidly as possible. The Crown woodlands were transferred to the Commission, under the Forestry (Transfer of Woods) Act of 1923, the Commission having already been made responsible for their management.

Such an outline history typically emphasises how few lessons were learnt by those in charge of forestry policy in the inter-war years. Although the Forestry Commission survived 'the Geddes axe' over public expenditure of 1921, its activities were severely curtailed (Pearson 1933). Despite a doubling of the Forestry Fund in 1928, a further round of economies followed. In his presidential address to the Society of Foresters in 1938, an Assistant Commissioner, William L. Taylor, described British forestry as 'a sorry picture of waste and indifference'. No more than a quarter of the 450,000 acres of woodland felled in the Great War had been replanted. Whereas the Acland Sub-Committee had estimated the yield of existing woodlands to be only one-third of their potential, W.L. Hiley believed the proportion had dropped to one-fifth in 1939 (Taylor 1939; Hiley 1939a).

The Second World War is generally portrayed as a period of renewed hope for forestry. The transfer of the operational aspects of home-timber production to the Ministry of Supply in the early stages of the war meant the Forestry Commissioners themselves had greater opportunity to plan for post-war reconstruction. Their report, *Post-War Forest Policy*, was published as a White Paper in June 1943. It pressed with renewed vigour for a national forest of 5 million acres by the end of the century. Whilst it was impracticable to aim for national self-sufficiency, the Commission believed it was feasible to build up and maintain a stock of inexhaustible timber, on the principle of sustained yield, that would in time reduce imports substantially, support a saw-milling and wood industry, and help maintain settlement in the remoter parts of the countryside (PP 1942–43).

Reference to rural settlement, in a report ostensibly setting out to capitalise on the strategic concerns of a nation at war, provides a broad hint of how policy-making for the countryside was rarely simple. There is need to probe more deeply. Afforestation had long been advocated as a means of increasing rural employment and, therefore, of sustaining the communities of the upland and remoter parts of the country. It was for those reasons that the terms of reference and membership of a Royal Commission on Coastal Erosion were extended in 1908. Under the additional warrant, the Royal Commission was to assess

> whether in connection with reclaimed land or otherwise; it is desirable to make an experiment in afforestation as a means of increasing employment during periods of depression in the labour market, and if so by what authority and under what conditions such experiments should be conducted. (PP 1909)

If pursued on an adequate scale and in accordance with well-recognised scientific principles, the Commissioners believed the afforestation of suitable areas would be 'a sound and remunerative investment'. Records of the Board of Agriculture indicated that there were 1 million acres of poor tillage-land that might be more profitably used for forestry. Of the 2.8 million acres of land identified as 'mountain and moorland' in the annual Agricultural Census, at an altitude of less than 1,500 feet, 1.5 million might be suitable for afforestation. Not only did these lands produce relatively little meat but, as the Royal Commission emphasised, sheep farming provided less than one-tenth of the permanent employment that might be afforded by 'the maintenance of a similar area of land under forest'. The Commissioners believed the most effective way of establishing such a national forest was to entrust the task to special forest commissioners. Under their auspices, employment might be provided by the plantations themselves , and from associated farm-holdings. Local wood-using industries might be established, and areas set aside for public recreation. In the words of the report,

> money expended in afforestation differs in kind from other calls on the national purse. It is productive investment of capital. To provide this capital sum out of taxes would be an act of unprecedented generosity on the part of the present generation of taxpayers in favour of their pos-

terity. No stronger justification for proceeding by loan than a reproductive outlay exists.

The weight given to the relief of rural unemployment, by the Acland Sub-Committee, has generally been attributed to Sir Francis Acland, himself a major landowner, and to J.D. Sutherland, a member of the Board of Agriculture for Scotland and its Commissioner for Small Holdings. Acland's political stance was revealed in a short piece he wrote on 'Land and Agriculture', as a contribution to a Liberal Party document on post-war reconstruction, published in 1918. There should be bold town-planning work in country districts, large-scale afforestation, and the extensive reclamation of moors and estuaries. Returning soldiers and sailors should be given the chance to establish 'co-operative colonies' on the land. For all these things to be possible, Acland (1918) wrote of how there had to be cheap and easy access to land.

The Acland report emphasised how the districts most likely to benefit from afforestation were the poorest and most backward, namely the hilly regions of northern England, Wales and Ireland, and the Border Country and, most importantly, the Highlands of Scotland. The productivity of the sheep runs and deer forests was so low that any improvements would be prohibitively expensive without other forms of industry to help bear the preliminary outlay on roads and bridges, and to provide other forms of employment, especially in winter, for the farmer and his family. Whilst local sea-fishing, and mines and quarries, might help, forestry and its associated industries provided the only realistic alternative. The Acland Committee went on to calculate that a thousand acres of hill grazing might require no more than two shepherds, and that an acre of even the best land might produce less than 10 lbs of mutton and 2 lbs of wool in a year. Under silviculture, the same area might employ ten men, besides those in the nurseries and associated industries. Where plantations of several thousand acres were laid out, it would be worth providing not only for roads, railways and the telegraph, but for schools, shops and many of the other comforts and amenities of civilisation, beyond the reach of the solitary crofter (PP 1917–18).

Whilst the value of forestry in sustaining a nation at war might be further strengthened by its role in sustaining rural communities in peacetime, something more is needed to explain why it was given such priority in the Government's legislative programme. What caused ministers to appoint the Acland Sub-Committee in the first place, and then to establish a Forestry Commission with unprecedented powers to change the use and appearance of so large a part of the countryside? Here again, some deeper probing of the surviving documentation is required.

The appointment of the Forestry Commission in 1919 was by no means the first attempt on the part of Government to promote silviculture. In his famous budget of 1909, Lloyd George had gathered together, under a single Development Grant, all the existing schemes, whereby modest grants could be made towards such ventures as light railways and harbours. The Grant was to be extended and greatly enhanced, so as to cover such ventures as afforestation. The moneys would be disbursed by Development Commissioners, appointed under the Development and Road Improvement Fund Act (Rogers 1999). The Board of Agriculture appointed an Advisory Committee on Forestry. There was another for Scotland, following the establishment of a separate Board of Agriculture for Scotland in 1912. Both were charged with identifying how and where demonstration forests might be established, and silviculture generally promoted, having due regard to 'the interests of other rural industries'. The landowner Sir John Stirling Maxwell was appointed Chairman of the Scottish Committee, whose members included Lord Lovat (himself the owner of an estate of 181,800 acres) and J.D. Sutherland.

It proved to be something of a false dawn. Whilst grudgingly agreeing to the appointment of a salaried 'expert' adviser to the Scottish Committee, the Scottish Secretary, T. Mckinnon Wood, perceived the primary duty of the Board to be that of establishing smallholdings. Since moneys were limited, any funding of forestry should be sought from the Development Commission. After protracted correspondence, the Development Commissioners concluded that they did not have powers to advance funds for afforestation to private owners. Whilst agreeing that the Board might lease land for afforestation, the conditions on which those leases might be negotiated proved so unacceptable to landowners that little planting was achieved (SRO, AF 43, 533).

It was against this shortfall in expectations that the President of the Board of Agriculture, Lord Selborne, convened in March 1916 an informal meeting of leading figures in forestry to discuss frankly the kind of policy he might put before the Government at the end of the war. The immediate pretext was correspondence from Stirling Maxwell and Lord de Veici (in Ireland), emphasising the need to begin replanting the felled woodlands. Selborne sought guidance as to whether this should be undertaken by the State or private owners. If the latter, how far might the State go in assisting or compelling owners (SRO, AF 43, 529)? The record of the ensuing discussion reveals how many of the findings of the Acland Sub-Committee had begun to emerge long before it was formally appointed, let alone held its first meeting.

Acland warned the meeting of how parliament would be extremely reluctant to pass legislation for the replanting and extension of woodlands, without the Government first deciding what its post-war timber policy should be. An official of the Board of Agriculture, T.H. Middleton, suggested the aim should be to reduce imports by some 20 per cent of domestic needs, and plan for a future war of no more than three years. War might consume 15 times the peacetime rate of felling. Assuming each year of war would require the cutting of 100,000 acres of timber, an additional 1.5 million acres were needed on a 70-year rotation. Of this, 300,000 acres should be planted as quickly as possible.

Acland recounted how, having spoken to some 30 to 40 proprietors, he was highly sceptical of whether private owners would make any significant contribution. Most declared quite openly that they would never plant again. J.D. Sutherland pressed for landowners to be paid bonuses, say £1 per acre. Acland thought that was far too little to change an owner's mind. Parliament would, in any case, never agree to large sums being spent, without guarantee of the most suitable sites being replanted, and such prob-

New Beginnings in Forestry

lems as pest control being adequately tackled. Lord Selborne conceded that he had always regarded the capital costs as the most formidable obstacle to afforestation. The Duke of Buccleuch thought more could be done to convince individual proprietors that forestry was profitable. Acland insisted that it was the very fact that no such assurance could be given that justified the State in offering exceptional levels of assistance. From his experience, and the small use made of loans under the Improvement of Land Acts, Stirling Maxwell was convinced that planting on an adequate scale would only be achieved through a combination of State assistance and compulsory purchase. The meeting agreed it was the only way of securing the greater part of the land required.

From a political point of view, Acland thought parliament was much more likely to agree to large sums of assistance if owners were confronted by a choice of afforestation or losing their land. Lord Lovat agreed, but said that the first step must be to give as much publicity as possible to the basis on which assistance would be given. Without that, even the present low level of private enterprise would be stifled. Middleton emphasised how a measure of discrimination would be required in dealing with large and small landowners. Even if it were politically possible, the State would be reluctant to confiscate woodlands of, perhaps, less than 50 or 100 acres. Not only were the replanting and management costs of small woodlands so disproportionately high but, as the Permanent Secretary of the Board of Agriculture pointed out, it might be far better for such woodland-owners to invest their limited capital in farming. Acland agreed that such woodlands were best omitted from any large-scale scheme for afforestation.

In the course of discussion, Acland referred to discussions among ministers on the twin issues of 'national safety and employment' after the war. The forest industry must secure both an early chapter in the 'Peace Book' and a pledge as to its recommendations being carried out. Acland feared that if the case for afforestation rested solely on national safety, any consideration might be postponed until after the war, when it could be examined alongside all the other factors with a bearing on the country's readiness for war.

Afforestation would be accorded a much higher priority if it was *also* promoted as a means of providing employment for the large numbers of people who would otherwise be thrown out of work at the end of the war. The Prime Minister, Herbert Asquith, was known to be seriously concerned with the difficulties that were bound to arise in finding sufficient industrial employment.

The Forest Authority

Those attending the meeting convened by Lord Selborne, in March 1916, were determined that a forestry authority should be given unfettered responsibility for afforestation, with direct access to the requisite resources. A single forest authority, covering the whole of the British Isles, seemed the only way of making 'a definite break with the past', and of escaping both 'the welter of conflicting authorities' and arena of party politics (SRO, AF 43, 529).

Following what Lord Lovat later described as a fierce battle to keep forestry out of the clutches of any Government department, the concept of a central forest authority was accepted and enacted as an agreed measure by the three political parties. A Member of Parliament, who was also a Forestry Commissioner, would answer any Parliamentary Questions, and reply to debates in the House of Commons. Rather than returning any balances of unspent moneys to the Treasury, they might be held over in the Forestry Fund for the following year. It seemed a hollow victory. Within only two years, the whole future of State forestry was thrown into 'the melting pot'. A note inserted in the Second Annual Report of the Forestry Commission apologised for its late appearance. The Commissioners had been required to devote all their energies to arguing afresh the national need for a forestry policy.

The crisis had been brought about by the failure of a Committee on National Expenditure, under Lord Geddes, to grasp the essential reasons for large-scale afforestation. The surviving files of the Scottish Office make abundantly clear the important part played by socio-economic arguments, both within Government and in the wider pressures brought to bear on ministers by outside interests.

In memoranda to the Prime Minister, the Highland Reconstruction Committee and Home Timber Merchants' Association warned of how the abolition of the Commission would render 'futile' the large sums already expended on establishing smallholdings in the Highlands. People would only be tempted to return to the land if there was some kind of subsidiary employment. Not only did forestry provide that employment in winter, but a large part of the wages was spent locally (SRO, AF 79, 3).

Although the Commission survived, the savings of £200,000 sought over the following two years emphasised how the Government still did not understand the need for continuity as the key to successful forestry (PP 1923). In a parliamentary debate on unemployment, in May 1924, J. Ramsay MacDonald, the Prime Minister of the first Labour Government, gave what was, in effect, a personal endorsement of forestry. In calling for a much greater effort to plant both people and trees on the land, he emphasised how the forests must be planted quickly, so as to be ready for the time when 'we shall have got people settled on the land'. The Commission was given a supplementary budget of £275,000 to establish what were intended to be the first of many forest-workers' holdings. As the Commission's Seventh Annual Report indicated, this more permanent form of unemployment relief offered workers a minimum of 150 days' employment in the forests, mainly in winter (PP 1927).

With increasing pressures on public expenditure, successive Annual Reports emphasised the economies to be derived from an expansive forestry programme. The first object was to increase home supplies, so as to avoid 'the anxiety and waste caused by reliance on imported timber during a war'. An adequate reserve should, secondly, be husbanded for the time when 'the exhaustion of the virgin forests of the world' began to be felt acutely. And thirdly, afforestation was often the only way of increasing employment and productivity on poor pasture and wasteland. As an illustration, the Commission's Fifth Annual Report described how considerable tracts of almost derelict land had been acquired in Norfolk, Suffolk, Surrey, Dorset and Hampshire. The largest continuous stretch, the Thetford area of Breckland, was being turned into a forest of 20,000 acres, comparable in size with the New Forest (PP 1924–25).

The original intention had been to establish a Forestry Fund of £3.5 million, to be spent by the Forestry Commission on purposes specified in the Bill. The effect of the Forestry Act of 1919 was, however, to place the Fund under Treasury control. The almost invariably negative stance of the Treasury made the Commissioners even more determined to retain as much autonomy as possible. The *Post-War Forest Policy* paper of 1943 strongly argued for the Forestry Commission being directly answerable to parliament, rather than a government department. Both ministers and the forestry associations disagreed, claiming that if the Commission was to be given greater powers and resources, it was only reasonable that there should be greater safeguards (PRO, HLG 71, 948; Robertson 1943). As reconstituted under the Forestry Act of 1945, the Commission was required to 'comply with such directions as may be given' by the Scottish Secretary and Minister of Agriculture. With that assurance, the Chancellor of the Exchequer announced in November that the Forestry Fund would be replenished by £20 million over the 5-year period 1946–50, with the object of meeting the first 5-year quota of the White Paper, for the afforestation and replanting of 365,000 acres, and secondly for meeting such needs as forest training, research and housing needs.

The Commission's most daunting challenge was recognised to be that of encouraging private forestry to play a more active part. The challenge took two forms. First, as the Chairman of the Commission, Roy L. Robinson, emphasised in an address to the Institute of Chartered Surveyors in January 1938, the industry was poised on the edge of revolutionary change. There was an increasing range of demand for softwood, most obviously as pulp in the paper-making industry (Robinson 1938). Secondly, the Commission's own sense of purpose, in the management of its own estates, had to be extended to private forestry, with its distinctive problems of rehabilitating devastated woodlands and converting scrub and unproductive coppice to forest. A campaign by the Royal

English Forestry Society in 1937 had met with modest success, but the most fundamental problem remained, namely a lack of confidence on the part of owners.

Whilst grants would encourage those willing and able to plant, they would have no impact on those who simply refused to plant more trees. The forestry societies reported growing support among 'more far-seeing landowners' for the selective use of compulsory powers. R.S. Troup, the Professor of Forestry at Oxford, saw no alternative to some form of State supervision. In his volume *Forestry and State Control*, published in 1938, he cited numerous examples of such control in Europe (Troup 1938). Others disagreed. Rather than depriving owners of an interest and authority in their woodlands, W.L. Hiley called for better advice and practical guidance (Hiley 1939b). One of the tangible outcomes of a conference on private forestry, held in February 1938, was an offer by the Forestry Commission to start an advisory service on an experimental scale, and to launch a propaganda campaign to educate landowners and others on the national importance of proper management of woodlands. The White Paper of 1943 proposed that landowners should be given substantial financial aid where they were prepared to dedicate, or permanently set aside, their woodlands for approved forms of forestry (PP 1942–43). A further White Paper of January 1944, dealing explicitly with private woodlands, reported a generally favourable response from landowners and private forestry interests (PP 1943–44a). The Forestry Act of 1947 conferred the requisite statutory powers.

Having placed the Commission 'under new management', and introduced schemes to assist the more progressive private foresters, the Government turned its attention to what was essentially the third dimension in setting out a comprehensive legislative code, namely to ensure that, whatever the outlook and resources of the individual owners, felled woodland must be replanted. The White Paper of 1943 had recommended the continuance of the wartime system of felling licences. Under the Forestry Act of 1951, and subject to a series of safeguards, no person could fell any growing tree without a licence granted by the Commission. A licence might stipulate the need to replant. The Commission might also issue felling directions, where it seemed expedient to fell 'backgrowing' trees, or undertake thinning.

Forest Parks

Strategic and employment considerations were soon joined by a third, once the Commission began to lay out its first forests. There was need to retain the support not only of the Government, parliament and those who owned or lived in the affected areas, but also of the increasing number of visitors from town and city. The provision of access to the forests, and such facilities as camping sites, might 'go a long way to popularising the national programme of afforestation'.

The Deputy Surveyor for the Forest of Dean, David W. Young, wrote in November 1928 of how 'it would be a mistake to attempt to exclude the public from the Commission's forest areas' – but there was no denying the attendant difficulties. Extra fire patrols had to be mounted on public holidays and the local early-closing days. Of 504 fires investigated in 1930, a third were started by the public, whether carelessly or through malicious intent. Warning notices were posted around plantations. There were press notices and broadcast warnings, and lessons in local schools as to the dangers of starting forest fires. Forests were subdivided into rides. Fire traces were made and maintained alongside roads. Experience indicated, however, that the most subtle and effective forms of protection was actually to encourage visitors onto the Commission's properties. By doing so, it was easier to keep them away from the most vulnerable areas (PRO, F 19, 23 and MAF 50, 17; Long, 1926; Taylor 1930).

To succeed in that objective, and in the larger challenge of securing support for the Commission's planting programme, close attention had to be paid to the expectations and perceptions of the visitors themselves. A District Officer in Scotland, Frank Oliver, wrote that whilst the Treasury might insist on the Commission proceeding on strictly utilitarian lines, the holiday-makers who came by charabanc and motor car gave no thought to the economic side of planting. They did, however, have strong views as to what appealed to their aesthetic senses. However inarticulately expressed, Oliver (1931) warned of how State forestry ignored those views at its peril. Whilst the plantations might yield little income from timber sales for some 60 years, there was more immediate income to be gained from tourism and the increasing length of the holiday season. The visitors might furthermore have a powerful and favourable political effect long before the accounts of the Commission moved into surplus. To achieve these dividends, much more thought had to be given to the appearance of forests. However convenient the large, regular blocks of dark conifers might be for the forester, they made poor propaganda for the Commission. From experience in the Highlands, the remedy appeared to be in the forester's own hands. It was remarkable how a few clumps of birch or larch could lighten up a 500-acre block of pure Scots pine or spruce. Such groups need only be one-tenth of an acre, occupying perhaps a basin of 'bad' peat. Whilst beech might not be a timber-tree in the north, clumps might be grown for their appearance. If planted along roads, such species as larch might help relieve the sense of passing through a dark tunnel on a winter's afternoon.

The most famous clash occurred in the Lake District, following the Commission's purchase of 7,243 acres between the rivers Esk and Duddon, in 1934. Although the Commission soon discovered that 5,140 acres of the open fell were unsuitable for planting, it proceeded with a more modest planting programme of 740 acres of upper Eskdale. Even this was vigorously opposed by the Friends of the Lake District, who not only suggested alternative sites, but offered to buy Eskdale from the Commission at the purchase price. This was refused, lest it broke faith with the original vendor. The Commissioners offered, in turn, to leave a further 440 acres of upper Eskdale unplanted if the voluntary bodies compensated the Commission at the rate of £2 per acre, namely the difference between the revenue from forest and open land. The remainder of the land would be planted as 'a model forest'. The Friends of the

Lake District rejected the compromise, arguing that the real issue was the preservation of the open fell. The estate was 'in the very heart of the Lake District'. The plantable portions formed the foreground to one of the finest mountain ampitheatres – Crinkle Crags, Bow Fell, Esk Pike and Scafell. A petition of 12,000 signatures called upon the Commission to reconsider the position, and gave rise to a motion in the House of Lords in April 1936 proposing a parliamentary Select Committee to investigate the activities of the Commission. The Commissioners warned of how their target for afforestation could never be met if planting were banned over so large an area as the Lake District. Lord Zetland, a Government minister and President of the National Trust, rejected the call for a Select Committee, arguing that it would be much better if the advocates of afforestation and of the preservation of the countryside could reach a compromise by means of direct and informal discussion (PRO, F 19, 21 and 22; Cambridge University Library, Baldwin manuscripts, 25D, 3 and 9; PD, Lords, 100, 363–405; Sheail 1981, 172–5).

Although convinced of the correctness of the Commissioners' case, the Chairman, Roy L. Robinson, saw the chance to capitalise on the existence of a joint committee, which had already been set up with the Council for the Preservation of Rural England (CPRE), to examine ways of 'making plantations more acceptable from the point of view of amenity'. As Lord Zetland informed parliament, the joint committee had already begun to review 'the whole question of future planting in the Lake District so as to ensure that no land is acquired in parts where afforestation may be undesirable'. John Dower, the Secretary of the Standing Committee on National Parks, prepared a map which indicated the area where the CPRE wanted to ban planting. It included Eskdale and Dunnerdale. The Commission responded by proposing a much smaller area of 220 square miles. After prolonged debate, it was eventually agreed to exclude afforestation from a central zone of 300 square miles. A further area , including Eskdale and Dunnerdale, was designated as a 'special area'. Here, the Commission would seek alternative sites and consult with the

CPRE, whenever planting was being carried out. The agreement was published in July 1936, the Commission stressing its voluntary nature and the CPRE representatives continuing to protest at the exclusion of the 'special area' from the central 'protected' zone (PRO, F 18, 289; Forestry Commission 1955).

It was a compromise that satisfied no one, and in December 1937 the House of Commons accepted a motion drawing attention to 'the anxiety that exists with respect to the activities of the Forestry Commission in the Lake District and other areas of great natural beauty'. The Commissioners increasingly deflected criticism by arguing that they were under an explicit instruction to promote afforestation in Special Areas for the relief of unemployment (see page 29). Almost the whole of the Lake District was within, or up to 15 miles of, the West Cumberland Special Area. Alarmed at being drawn so explicitly into controversy, Treasury officials informed the Commissioners that West Cumberland had been designated a Special Area before any large-scale planting was envisaged. As a member of the Treasury observed, 'I do not think that the Treasury could object to a halt being called in the Lake District provided that the unique qualities and associations of that part of the country are recognised to have made it an exceptional case.' Robinson thought the Commission had compromised enough. Like new buildings or a planted garden, the appearance of young plantations would improve with time. The way ahead was not to resist changes otherwise required in the national interest, but to carry them through 'in the best possible way'. Within that strategy, the National Forest Parks being established by the Forestry Commission on an experimental basis were of the utmost importance as a device for combining economic timber production with the provision of recreational facilities and protection of amenity (PD, Commons, 330, 477–534; PRO, T 161, 1069, S40611; Sheail, 1981, pp. 175–81).

Following protracted negotiations with the Treasury for this more positive approach, approval was given in 1935 for the expenditure of £5,000 for 'fitting out' a National Forest Park of 35,000 acres in Argyllshire, comprising the unplantable areas of the

Forests of Ardgarten, Glenfinart, Benmore and Glenbranter. It was an immediate success. The number of people staying overnight rose from 20,419 in 1937 to 30,870 in 1938. Although hesitant about setting up further parks before gaining some experience, the increasing stridency in some quarters for a series of national parks caused the Commissioners to appraise all acquisitions and planting programmes, with an eye to their future as national forest parks. When Plynlimon was acquired in 1937, Robinson directed that 'unusual care should be taken in the layout and amenity treatment' of the plantations. A National Forest Park of 23,000 acres was opened in the Forest of Dean in 1939, and another in Snowdonia in 1940. By doing so, the Commission had become the most important statutory body for the provision of facilities for outdoor recreation (PRO, F 18, 217 and F 19, 23; Sheail 1981, pp. 181–92).

Multi-Purpose Forestry

The first Annual Report of the Forestry Commission summarised four phases in the early history of modern forestry. Many woodlands in the nineteenth century were simply cut over and left. By the early 1900s, the demand for timber, especially good-quality timber, completely outstripped home supply. There followed much enquiry and debate as to the need for a national forest authority. It took the Great War to secure both approval and resources for that authority (PP 1921). One might discern two further phases, namely the uncertain support given to forestry (and agriculture) between the wars, and the unprecedented levels of patronage enjoyed after the Second World War.

The Second World War came too soon for the Commission's plantations to provide any succour. By the mid-1950s, the Cabinet's Natural Resources (Technical) Committee was highly sceptical of whether such timber reserves would be of any strategic help, even when mature, particularly now that nuclear weapons had been developed. At most, they might be 'an important asset when the time came to repair the devastation of large urban centres and thousands of acres of dwellings' (Lord President of the Council

1957). Nor were the arguments for forestry assisting the settlement of the countryside any stronger. As the Forestry Commission's 60th Annual Report emphasised, every aspect of forestry work had undergone technological change. Although the average planting rate in the post-war years was three times that of the inter-war years, and timber output had doubled, large-scale mechanisation meant there were far fewer opportunities for employment. The Commission's workforce fell from 13,220 in September 1950 to 8,129 in March 1980. It was only in areas of extensive sheep and cattle grazing that forestry employed more labour per unit area than agriculture (Forestry Commission 1980).

If the forest industry (and farming for that matter) seemed self-assertive and unyielding in their purpose, such arrogance may have stemmed not so much from the unprecedented levels of government support after the Second World War, but from an acute awareness of the fragility of such patronage. In his Presidential Address, in 1952, marking the first quarter-century of the Society of Foresters, H.M. Steven warned that, despite the country having to learn the lessons of the Great War a second time over, influential voices were already questioning the need for so high a level of tree planting. Even if the Commission were no longer regarded as a supernumerary infant in the straitened financial circumstances of post-war recovery, it was now chastised as 'a large and menacing Giant shutting out the sun' (Steven 1952). Salvation did not lie in tactical withdrawal, but rather, in Robinson's words, in pressing on, so as to ensure there were even 'more goods in the shop window' of forestry (Robinson 1952). It was an approach that seemed, at least in the short term, only to confirm the worst fears of the industry's critics.

There was evidence of the Government's increasing awareness of the Commission's multi-purpose role, following doubts expressed by the Scottish Lord Advocate in July 1966 as to the statutory basis on which the Forestry Commission operated caravan and camping sites. The Scottish Secretary sought immediate action to remove such doubts. Advantage was taken of the Countryside (Scotland) Bill currently being drafted for the promotion of outdoor recreation and protection of amenity (page 145). A clause was introduced whereby the Forestry Commission might promote such facilities as part of the development of its forest estate. The Ministry of Housing and Local Government wanted to take full advantage of the Commission's expertise and regional organisation in its own Countryside Bill for England and Wales. The Commission should be empowered to acquire, plant and manage for amenity sites anywhere in the countryside. The Treasury argued that the Commission's purpose was to produce and supply timber on a long-term, commercial basis. To go further would be to introduce an entirely new principle. Appalled by such a narrowness of outlook, the Forestry Commission joined officials of the Ministry of Housing and Local Government in drafting 'a suitable refutation'. It succeeded to the extent that the Treasury agreed in June 1967 that such wider initiatives could be pursued where there was no obvious alternative to the Forestry Commission acquiring and managing the properties, and that there would be no material effect on the level of economic return. The Treasury's prior consent must be obtained, and assurance given that such outlay could be found within the Commission's annual planting programme. Where the Forestry Commission accepted the compromise, the Parliamentary Secretary to the Ministry of Housing, Arthur Skeffington, regarded the Treasury conditions as unduly and unnecessarily restrictive. Although the timber yield from amenity woodlands might not cover their management costs, very substantial sums were earned from tourism. Such visitors came to see the beauties of the countryside – not bare desolate fields. Negotiations had however run their course. The Treasury's terms were accepted, subject to their not being interpreted too rigidly (PRO, HLG 29, 739).

By March 1966, the Forestry Commission had sufficient confidence to publish a highly illustrated booklet, *Forestry in the Landscape*. It drew on the insights and experience gained by Sylvia Crowe, acting as landscape consultant to the Commission. However grudgingly the Commission may have first employed her, it quickly came to benefit from 'her constructive thought on the meaning of landscape' and her outstanding position amongst landscape architects. She was a Past-President of the Institute of Landscape Architects. An industry which had attracted so much censure became one of the leading patrons of such landscape enhancement. The booklet provided a set of general principles as to how such forests might be designed and laid out. The essential point was that each forest had to be considered on its merits, taking close account of such factors as the configuration of the ground and scale of variation, existing types and pattern of vegetation and land use, and the prevailing colour of the rock, soil and structures. The scale of the landscape was perhaps the most important consideration, varying say from the large-scale, rolling hills of Keilder in Northumberland, which could accept great areas of unbroken conifer forest, to the other extreme of the Lake District and parts of North Wales, where every plantation must be treated individually and fitted into the intricate pattern of small-scale contracts in landform and delicately modelled hills. As well as providing examples of the optimal shape and species-composition of planted areas, according to the variation in soil and topography, the booklet emphasised how a landscape in balance with itself, and its surroundings, looked right and made for sustained fertility and 'a healthy ecological environment' (Crowe 1966).

However halting and closely constrained such attempts to extend the practice of multi-purpose forestry, sufficient was achieved by the 1990s for visitors and the public generally to associate the Forestry Commission with the provision of outdoor recreational facilities. It was a further reason why in July 1994 the Conservative Government abandoned its long-expressed desire to privatise what had become the largest landed estate in the UK. The Forestry Commission was to remain in the public sector. As the Scottish Secretary, as Forestry Minister, emphasised, there were two principal considerations. In as much as the forests were not yet fully mature, their sale would raise only £750 million, compared with a book value of £1.7 billion. The second factor was the concern to preserve their value for recreation and public access. As revealed by an earlier Parliamentary Question, there had been some 3,000 letters and representations from 300 interest groups. The Ramblers Association attacked the potential loss of public access over so large an area of land. The Director-General of the National Trust paid tribute to how the Commission in developing its policy of multi-purpose management had made

> an important contribution to the protection of wildlife habitats, archaeology and water quality, as well as to the natural beauty of its woods and the provision of public access.

Such expressions of support gave notice of the extent to which the scale of the forest estate had become not so much a liability but the key factor in attracting public esteem. By adopting such a multi-purpose approach to the management of its properties, the Forestry Commission remained a public body. It could not be assumed that private ownership would maintain the standards of stewardship that had come to be so closely associated with its forest estate (PD, Commons, 247, 177–91; *National Trust Magazine*, 72, Summer 1994).

CHAPTER 5

A Third Force

Introduction

Gilbert White had been dead for a hundred years. The editor of a further edition of his late-eighteenth-century journals, the *Natural History and Antiquities of Selborne*, found it hard to explain its continued popularity. Gilbert White's village of Selborne in Hampshire seemed so remote from the 'stern reality' of the 1890s. And yet, in another sense, the spread of the factory system, and consequent growth of huge towns, had strengthened, rather than weakened, the love of things rural. Where once the country had been simply 'home', Warde Fowler (1893) wrote of how 'we pine for the pure air, for the sight of growing grass, for the footpath across the meadow', without first having to pass through 'grimy suburbs'. There was now 'a touch of self-consciousness in our passion for it, which finds expression in a multitude of books'.

In a study of 'the countryside idea', as developed on both sides of the Atlantic, Michael Bunce attributed such images of landscape to a three-part relationship. First, there were the historical forces through which 'the countryside idea' was formed; second, were the symbolic meanings given to particular landscapes; and third, the deliberate reinforcement of those meanings to create what were, in effect, cultural landscapes. The evolving social structures, political economy and cultural ferment of those years of industrial and urban growth could not have created a more conducive climate for nostalgia towards the countryside. The catalyst for what Bunce (1994) called 'the armchair countryside' was the rise of a middle class, attracted as much by the comfortable imagery of books and paintings as by direct exposure to the countryside itself. The publication of such books was encouraged by the rapid advances in printing and skills in marketing.

One such writer catering for 'the arm-chair traveller' was C.J. Cornish. A collection of his articles in *The Spectator* was published in 1895 under the title *Wild England of to-day and the wild life in it*. He described for the most part an unchanging countryside from the 'Southern Cliffs' to the 'Yorkshire Fen'. The wild character of the Culver Cliffs, and their plant and animal life, were for the most part self-protected. Christchurch harbour and the other estuaries of the South Coast were so attractive that their birdlife was loathe to forsake them, despite disturbance. The depression in arable farming had caused 'The Great White Horse' country to become even more thinly populated. Much building was taking place, however, in 'the pine and heather country' that extended from 'the Bay of Bournemouth to Ascot Heath' (Cornish 1895). Some seven years later, Cornish urged, in a further book, the protection of the river Thames, the only large *natural* feature left in the Greater London area. He wrote of how it was no use complaining of the loss to the local economy, once boating and fishing had been destroyed by the disfigurement of the banks and pollution of the waters. To Cornish (1902) it was scandalous that no one was responsible for preserving such 'a national property'. The river Thames or, for that matter, the New Forest, was as precious as the British Museum. They should be regarded as 'national Trusts', governed by trustees of similar standing and probity.

In terms of a twentieth-century perspective, a significant move had been made in the founding of the National Trust for Places of Historic Interest or Natural Beauty in 1895. By its Memorandum of Association, it was

> to promote the permanent preservation, for the benefit of the Nation, of lands and tenements (including buildings) of beauty or historic interest; and as regards lands, to preserve (so far as practicable) their natural aspect, features, and animal and plant life.

Perhaps more significantly, parliament passed a Private Bill in

1907, granting the Council of the National Trust unique powers to declare inalienable those of its properties held for 'preservation for the benefit of the nation'. The schedule to the Act included 28 inalienable properties. As well as the Trust's earliest properties of the cliff of Dinas-o-leu, at Barmouth in Merionethshire, and the Old Clergy House at Alfriston in Sussex, there were castles, some 4 acres of Wicken Fen, the Gowbarrow Deer Park and Aira Force of 750 acres, and Brandlehow Park of 108 acres on Derwentwater, in Cumberland. The Trust had acquired some 13 properties of value for their wildlife by 1910.

Beyond amenity and wildlife, the third and perhaps most important element was outdoor recreation. Lord Bryce had been for many years a leading advocate of greater public access to the countryside. His letter to *The Times* of 6 June 1919 illustrated both the pressures on the countryside and, perhaps most strikingly, the conflict that might arise between the different forms of recreational development. The immediate purpose of the letter was to register his opposition to a motor road from Borrowdale to Wasdale, over the Styhead Pass in the Lake District. Apart from the difficulties of building and keeping such a road in repair, where the gradients were so steep and storms so violent, no one speeding along it could appreciate the scenery of lofty summits, whose grandeur was unequalled in England. Again, the question was raised by Bryce as to

> what can be done to preserve for our people the charms of this lovely mountain region . . . this uniquely beautiful district, the favourite resort of the industrial workers of the North, a district associated with some of the greatest names in our poetic literature.

Lord Bryce proposed 'a special permanent Commission', charged with 'the duty of preventing the construction of any work calculated to inflict grave injury upon natural beauties which we owe it to posterity to preserve, because once lost they are irreplaceable'.

Of the initiatives taken after the Great War, the most significant proved to be that by the architect and town planner, Patrick

Abercrombie. From his earliest Merseyside days, when he lived at Oxton and took long walks in the Wirral and sometimes North Wales, he had realised how such countryside was affected by rapid and damaging change, from which it might take a generation or more to recover. Of Abercrombie's 16 regional planning schemes prepared collaboratively between 1923 and 1935, his proposals for the East Kent coalfield attracted the most attention, in the sense that their priority was not to improve an area already largely spoiled, but to prevent such a thing from happening. As Dix (1978) expressed it, they sought to use preventive medicine in place of surgery. It made him even more conscious of the need to protect the countryside and coast (Abercrombie and Archibald 1925). In an essay published in the *Town Planning Review*, Abercrombie (1926) advocated the setting up of a National League for the Preservation of Rural England, which might take the form of a strong joint committee representing a wide range of propagandist, learned and voluntary bodies. Where that League could make a single, simple and direct appeal, it would be for the constituent societies, and more particularly their branches, to undertake the detailed executive action required. A Council for the Preservation of Rural England (CPRE) was formally constituted, made up of 22 constituent members and a large number of affiliated bodies. An Association for the Preservation of Rural Scotland was founded on similar lines in 1927, and a Council for the Preservation of Rural Wales in 1928.

Where the Earl of Crawford and Balcarres, Sir Guy Dawber and Abercrombie were the acknowledged co-founders of the CPRE, a pivotal role was played by George L. Pepler, the Chief Town Planning Inspector in the Ministry of Health. He was one of a number of inter-war civil servants to exert powerful influence, both through his office and less formally. Such insight and patronage was especially important in the early confidence-building stages. Thus, Pepler 'jotted down a sort of statement' in October 1926 as to the aims of the CPRE. The object should be to encourage the preservation of 'all things of true value and beauty, and the scientific and orderly development of all local resources'.

This should be done not in a 'spirit of hostility to the large industrial and commercial centres', but by providing 'the country man' with 'a considered point of view when meeting their representatives in friendly conference'. A 'record and understanding of local resources' would be built up through local and regional surveys (Reading University, CPRE archive, Pepler file).

No less important at such a formative stage was the influence of ministers, both formally and through expressions of their personal interest. In an address to the inaugural meeting of the CPRE in December 1926, Neville Chamberlain, as Minister of Health, welcomed the Council's decision to concentrate attention on those evils which should be prevented, those things which should be protected, and thirdly on educating public opinion. He particularly welcomed the dropping of a fourth objective, namely of harrying the Government. Rather than flying to Government, the best remedy was often to be found in the hands of the people themselves. The biggest obstacle was convincing public opinion that something was worth preserving. By achieving that goal, the CPRE would render legislation unnecessary. The speech found resonance among leading figures in the CPRE. As the Council's Secretary, Herbert Griffin, remarked, in 1929, there was simply no point in attacking the Ministry of Health, or the Ministry of Transport, on their failure to prevent 'ribbon development' along arterial roads. They were bound to ask for solutions, where in truth there were none that everyone would accept. As Griffin warned, it would 'be unwise to try and legislate in front of public opinion' (Reading University, CPRE archive, Legal and Parliamentary Sub-Committee, 1927–41 and Pepler file).

An educative mission was necessarily long-term. The CPRE also needed a more immediate and tangible measure of its success. One of its earliest initiatives was to submit a memorandum to Ramsay MacDonald, the Prime Minister of the new Labour Government, pressing for a series of national parks. An inter-departmental committee was appointed in September 1929, under the Parliamentary Secretary of the Ministry of Agriculture, Christopher Addison. It was to investigate the need for one or more parks for the 'preservation of the natural characteristics, including flora and fauna', and 'the improvement of recreational facilities for the people'. Where Abercrombie in his evidence believed large numbers of tourists would cause little damage, provided several parks were created right from the start, the Committee concluded there was no alternative but to create two kinds of park, one primarily for outdoor recreation situated near large urban centres, and the other for the preservation of scenery and wildlife. The central question for the Committee, in its report of April 1931, was the cost of acquiring the land needed for such parks. Where the more remote areas would be cheaper to acquire, they would have correspondingly fewer visitors. The scale and cost of land purchase might be minimised through a system of regional planning, where a local-authority committee would be given exceptional powers to control development in such a 'geographical unit' as the Lake District (PP 1930–31).

Although the CPRE had won support from the Government for the principle of national parks, none was established. As the Minister of Health, Arthur Greenwood, informed Ramsay MacDonald, he accepted the Committee's recommendation that a national parks authority should be appointed for England and Wales, and another for Scotland, to help designate the park areas and to provide the regional committees with grants and expertise. But although Greenwood intended to recommend to the Treasury an outlay of £100,000 over five years, priority had first to be given to his Town and Country Planning Bill that would, in many ways, help prepare the way for such national parks legislation. By the time the Planning Bill was enacted in 1932 (see page 22), the country was in the throes of a severe financial crisis. As the economy improved, so too did the number of planning schemes. It became increasingly difficult politically to transfer the recently awarded planning powers from the local authorities to an *ad hoc* national parks authority (Sheail 1975).

The priority was to keep the national parks issue alive. The Association for the Preservation of Rural Scotland appointed a National Parks Committee. The CPRE, with the Council for the Preservation of Rural Wales, formed a Standing Committee on

National Parks. Officials within the Ministry of Health (Pepler among them) were ambivalent. On the one hand, they warned of how

> the Government will be exposed to serious criticism and discredit if a purely negative reply continues to be given to the large body of opinion in favour of definite action for the preservation of the countryside. The National Parks appear to provide the best opportunity of making a gesture to indicate the reality of the Government's interest in the problem of preservation, applied to that portion of the problem in which the national interest is greatest and the opportunity of finding an alternative solution the most remote. (PRO, HLG 68, 56)

Yet the same officials saw dangers when Neville Chamberlain (now Chancellor of the Exchequer) offered in May 1937 to consider sympathetically any application for support from voluntary bodies towards the preservation of scenery and buildings. There was an obvious opening for the Minister of Health to apply for such assistance in preserving and enhancing two or three potential park areas. But as officials explored the ramifications, so they warned of how any announcement of Treasury assistance might throw many of the planning schemes 'back into the melting pot'. Many landowners had voluntarily foregone their rights to claim compensation for loss of right to develop their land, under such schemes. They might now demand heavy recompense. A quite substantial amount of Exchequer money might find its way into 'the pockets of landowners without any appreciable result in securing *further* preservation'. Such fears caused any grant aid to be postponed by a year, by which time the claims of the rearmament programme precluded any further consideration by the Treasury (Sheail 1981, pp. 115–22).

The Agricultural Context

The twentieth century is a story in two halves. Whilst farming was generally depressed, the countryside of the first half of the century was typically diverse, beautiful and rich in wildlife. Farming boomed in the second half of the century, as those concerned with the conservation of amenity and wildlife, and promotion of outdoor recreation, came close to despair. As the expectation of farmers rose as their aspirations for security and prosperity were met, so the burgeoning demands of other user-interests came to be focused on an ever-shrinking resource (Barber 1988).

Agricultural historians have drawn heavily on the exceedingly pessimistic evidence given to the Royal Commission on the Depressed Condition of the Agricultural Interest, which sat between 1894 and 1897. The Survey Branch of the Board of Agriculture calculated that the area of permanent grass in England and Wales rose from 12.2 million acres in 1875 to 15.3 million acres in 1900, and to 16.1 million acres in 1914. Some 13 per cent of the total area of south Essex reverted to grassland in the 15 years prior to the Royal Commission. As one witness remarked, the only consolation for landowners was that of knowing that the greater area of their estates was in 'a savings bank', accumulating fertility for future use (PP 1894).

If the pre-war years provided such an outstanding example of market-driven agricultural 'set-aside', the Great War offered instructive insight into how that 'savings bank' might be drawn upon, in bringing about perhaps the most dramatic change in rural land-use ever previously achieved. With an ever-increasing proportion of food imports sunk by enemy submarines, the Board of Agriculture formed a Food Production Department in late 1916, charged with raising the area of corn and potatoes as quickly as possible. In furtherance of the Board's campaign, 'Back to the Seventies – and Better', every County War Executive Committee was instructed to issue cultivation orders and, where necessary, take the land into possession, so as to reinstate at least three-quarters of the 4 million acres of arable land in England and Wales that had reverted to grassland. In an attempt to meet the quota of 85,000 acres set for Essex, heavy reliance was placed on local knowledge in identifying those pastures which occupied previously good arable land (Sheail 1976a).

A White Paper on agricultural policy, published by the Minister of Agriculture in February 1926, re-emphasised the need for land to be used to its highest economic potential, whilst providing a reasonable livelihood for those employed. There was however no agreement as to how that might be achieved. The low level of cereal prices prevented there being a larger acreage and, therefore, greater workforce. Tariff protection was opposed by all political parties. As the Minister reasoned, subsidies would require close regulation and, if persisted in, the complete nationalisation of farming. The Government believed agriculture was the least adapted of industries for such drastic intervention on the part of the State in peacetime. The priority should be to stimulate private enterprise, most obviously through agricultural education and research, and by improved credit facilities and marketing arrangements, disease control and land drainage (PP 1926).

The industry responded in two ways. One was to publicise its parlous state, most obviously through the visual evidence of neglect and abandonment. By 1937, crops grown for human consumption covered only 18 per cent of the total area of Essex – an area even smaller than that occupied by housing. Half the county produced animal food, with fodder crops occupying over a third of what little was under cultivation (Scarfe 1942). But it was another kind of response, namely that of mechanisation, which caused Viscount Astor and B. Seebohm Rowntree to write of the inter-war years as a time of 'Agricultural Revolution'. Not only did the number of tractors increase between the wars, but they were more powerful and efficient. Combine harvesters and milking machines were increasingly used, as were oil and petrol engines in farm buildings. Machinery was not only permeating almost every branch of farming, but 'off-farm' trucks and lorries were increasingly used to collect produce for market and distribute the farmers' needs to their holdings (Astor and Rowntree 1935).

The speed and scale with which farming was reappraised in the early years of the Second World War arose from two considerations, namely the urgent need for a dramatic increase in home-food production and the extent to which this depended on farmers being assured of some continuity of policy after the war. So as to inspire confidence and therefore stimulate production, the Minister of Agriculture, R. (Rob) S. Hudson, announced in November 1940 that the wartime system of guaranteed prices and markets would be further extended until at least one year after hostilities ended. He emphasised that the Government, representing a coalition of the major political parties, recognised the importance of maintaining in peacetime 'a healthy and well-balanced agriculture as an essential and permanent feature of national policy' (PD, Commons, 367, 91–5). 'The Pledge', as it came to be regarded by the farming industry, was renewed at intervals during the war.

The Town and Country Planning Association, at its annual conference in March 1942, sought to identify a set of principles whereby the movement of industry and people out of the congested and overgrown cities might be reconciled with the needs of farming and rural life. The rapporteur, Frederic J. Osborn, found little consensus. Where Sir Daniel Hall (formerly Chief Scientific Adviser to the Ministry) saw farming as a competitive industry, which must adapt itself to world prices, most other representatives of farming saw it as a 'way of life' – as an essential socio-political element in 'the national balance'. The gulf was deep. Where Hall derided the 'retail structure' of contemporary farming, L.F. Easterbrook (the agricultural correspondent of the *News Chronicle*) was scornful of the 'factory farm concept' (Osborn 1942).

Such discussion had been prompted by the appointment of a Committee under Lord Justice Scott to assess the implications of the report of the Royal Commission on the Distribution of the Industrial Population (see page 30) for rural land-use. Through correspondence and meetings, H.G. Vincent, the Principal Assistant Secretary in Lord Reith's Ministry of Works, had secured the consent of the Ministry of Agriculture to such an enquiry (PRO, HLG 81, 1 and MAF 48, 474; Sheail 1997b). As Cherry and Rogers (1996) noted, it was the Scott report that brought together, for the first time in a formal and authoritative manner, the separate strands of land-use policy and the requirements of agriculture. It did so by arguing that the most certain way of protecting the wellbeing of rural communities and enhancing the amenity and recreational value of the countryside was to retain the existing area of farmland, which still made up over three-quarters of the UK land-area, in productive and profitable use. The geographer, L. Dudley Stamp, had been appointed Vice-Chairman. The other dominant figure was Sidney R. Dennison, the Professor of Economics in the university of Swansea. Whilst later commentators portrayed him as the most far-sighted member of the Committee, Engholm (1985) characterised him as 'an economist of the pre-war school of thought', that found renewed vigour in a campaign being waged by *The Economist* for a 'small' agriculture. If farming was to pay its way after the war, without any form of subsidy, it should be cut ruthlessly to a size that was appropriate for the production of only those foods which could be grown more cheaply at home than imported from abroad (PRO, MAF 48, 475).

The Ministry of Agriculture had acknowledged, in its evidence to the Committee, how circumstances might arise where productive land must be released for development. Each case should be carefully weighed with due regard to 'the overriding national interest'. That philosophy provided what Scott described as 'the bedrock of the Majority Report'. As Scott reaffirmed, in a critique of Dennison's Minority Report,

> permanent change to constructional use should not be allowed *unless*, after taking into consideration *every* element of national interest or value, whether ponderable or imponderable, whether capable of expression in economic terms, or only in social, spiritual or aesthetic terms; whether measurable in figures of output or only in degrees and kinds of human happiness, the deciding authority is satisfied that it is, *on balance*, in the national interest that the particular land under consideration by it should be so utilised. (PRO, MAF 48, 475)

As Scott explained, 'onus of proof' did not imply a 'right of priority', whatever the circumstances. In considering the 'proof' as to whether farming should retain the land, the Committee recognised the fundamental difference between agriculture and other forms of industry, such as manufacturing. Whereas it was practically impossible for a manufacturer to adopt a long-term policy for the location of his plant, given the uncertainties of international trade, agriculture had to adopt a necessarily long-term interest in all land which it presently occupied. In as much as land, once developed for other purposes, could never be returned to farming, the nation had an obligation to hand it on to the next generation in good condition, unless there was a comparably permanent advantage to the nation (or some exigent force like military defence), which made the case for immediate change unanswerable.

From the circulation of the first drafts of what became the Town and Country Planning Bill of 1947, it was clear that farming had secured the best of both worlds. On the one hand, the Bill emphasised how agriculture was a factor to be taken into account in preparing Development Plans. On the other hand, the fact that agriculture was not classed as 'development' meant a farmer did not require the consent of a local planning authority in changing the agricultural use of land. In sharp contrast to the bitter controversy over land-use planning in urban areas, Hudson and his successor as Minister could press the primacy of food production in Cabinet in the knowledge that he spoke for 'a firm and coherent policy community'. A meeting convened by the Royal Agricultural Society of representatives of the leading 11 agricultural and landed organisations, and a group of Members of the House of Lords, in the spring of 1944, endorsed a policy of increased food output through price support, grant aid and credit guarantees, on the basis that the industry would be required by the State to make the most efficient use of the resources provided (Courthope 1944).

With such support for 'a productive and expansionist agriculture', the Ministry had neither the inclination nor resources to address any wider requirements of the rural and urban community. Dudley Stamp had been appointed the Chief Adviser to the Ministry on Rural Land Use. Having toured the Lake District and Pennines, he warned in the autumn of 1942 how the greater threat to the prospective national parks was not from building development, afforestation or the activities of water undertakers, but from the impact of tens of thousands of visitors. There would be impossible congestion on the few roads and clamour for non-existent accommodation (PRO, MAF 48, 478).

The memorandum prompted Basil Engholm (a Principal in the Ministry and a Secretary to the Scott Committee) to write an internal memorandum in October 1942, warning of the inevitability of demands for greater public access. It was a further instance of how the Ministry of Agriculture should concern itself with all rural matters, and not just the technical aspects of farming. By developing the concept of the Scott Report that there was 'a community of interests between agriculture and amenity', the Ministry might create a large body of urban opinion 'in favour of a strong and progressive agricultural policy'. By its taking a more active part in amenity issues, the Ministry would be better placed to ensure 'the activities of the urban use of the countryside did not interfere with efficient farming'. In the margin of Engholm's memorandum, an Assistant Secretary, A.R. Manktelow, insisted that nothing should be done to deflect the Ministry from its central task. It was already overstretched in producing the food required to sustain a country at war. The overriding priority after the war would be to establish 'a sound and progressive policy' for farming (PRO, MAF 48, 665).

National Parks

'A Third Force' in the countryside, alongside farming and forestry, had begun to emerge, namely a self-conscious concern to preserve amenity and wildlife and, perhaps most important of all, the opportunities for outdoor recreation. In his volume *Landscape and Englishness*, David Matless wrote of how the leading advocates of that movement sought to ally protection with progress, tradition with modernity, and country with the city. The intention was not so much to wage some kind of conservative resistance against change, but rather to secure a landscape that was simultaneously historic and modern. Not only might such an amalgam bring greater assurance of the various goals being achieved through consensus, but a role was assured for a particular kind of 'expert' authority. That authority might be the CPRE itself but, more particularly, those who had come to play a leading role in what Matless (1998) called 'preservationist planning'. Many of those personalities were to draw heavily on the expertise and experience gained in the inter-war years in occupying positions of considerable cultural and political influence during and after the Second World War.

Such commentary provides highly relevant context to an appreciation of the contribution of John Dower, the 'Father of National Parks in Britain'. Having read history at Cambridge, he became an architect's assistant and passed his examinations of the Royal Institute of British Architects (RIBA) through self-tuition. By the late 1930s, he was an architect on his own account, with an 'almost accidental tendency to specialize in housing and town planning'. There was nothing backward-looking, or obsessively rural, about Dower. A pioneer in the design of aerodrome buildings, he experimented with the use of steel and other new materials as a means of improving standards of housing. His involvement in rural planning developed through a partnership with the architect and planner, W. Harding Thompson, and more particularly extensive surveys of South-West England for local branches of the CPRE and Somerset County Council. As an active member of the Town Planning Institute and of the pressure group, Political and Economic Planning (PEP), Dower became increasingly involved in discussions as to the extent and nature of national planning.

There were connections of a more personal nature too. Where Dower was remembered as a sociable man-about-town, little interested in public affairs, his brother Arthur recalled how all that changed, following marriage to Pauline Trevelyan in 1929. Her father Charles had been President of the Board of Education in the second Labour Government. Her uncle, George Macauley Trevelyan, was the social historian, President of the Youth Hostels Association, and a major benefactor of the National Trust. John Dower often joined their weekend parties at Wallington , spent walking over the Northumbrian moors, looking for new hostel sites and arguing out political issues. The different strands of the national parks movement were brought together (Blenkinsop 1975). Over 40,000 copies of Dower's pamphlet, *The Case for National Parks in Great Britain*, were distributed in 1938, accompanied by a vigorous press campaign and series of public meetings. Dower prepared a draft 'Summary of Proposed Provisions for a National Parks Bill' in 1939, which envisaged the creation of a national parks commission, which would designate national parks and nature sanctuaries, and act as the planning authority within those areas. War intervened before the draft Bill could be publicised or promoted in parliament (Sheail 1995b).

It is one thing for networks to form, but another for there to be the opportunity to exploit them to effect. Such occasion might be personally tragic. As a member of the Officer Reserve, Dower joined the army as soon as war broke out, but contracted virulent tuberculosis while surveying the Dover harbour installations. He was invalided out. In April 1942, Reith's successor, Lord Portal, spoke in parliament of the need to include 'the preservation of extensive areas of great natural beauty and of the coastline' in any 'national planning of the use of land' (Cherry 1975). It provided H.G. Vincent, the Principal Assistant Secretary in the Ministry of Works and Building, with the pretext to appoint Dower, in August 1942, to carry out a factual enquiry into 'the practical needs in certain (park) areas'. Vincent and Dower knew one another through their membership of Political and Economic Planning (PRO, HLG 92, 46).

Dower recognised at once the outstanding opportunity for giving effect to the good causes he had so long championed (Holford 1948). He had in the previous few months begun to write a series of short articles for the journal *The Dalesman*, on 'Reconstruction in the Yorkshire Dales'. Where almost everyone was busy with the immediate tasks of winning the war, it was also a time to dream of 'a *forward*-looking and far bigger thing' than simply reverting to pre-war ways. Where the words 'reconstruction' and 'planning' were increasingly used, there had first of all to be a vision of what was to be achieved, and then the motivation, tools and organisation to bring it about. As Dower (1942) recalled, Patrick Geddes, the originator or inspirer of so much of what was best in modern town planning and sociology, had identified the three major elements of his social surveys as 'place, work and folk'. They also signified what was required of Dales reconstruction, where *folk* were linked through their *work* (and recreation) to the *place* where they lived. All three had to advance and accord with one another. The Dales had to be seen as a whole. Little could succeed without its meeting the needs, tastes and occupations of residents and visitors alike. No attempt to enrich the social life of the Dalesfolk – by themselves or through others – would get very far unless it took full account of their physical and economic environment.

By the time *The Dalesman* articles were published, Dower had flung himself into 'the daily work of committees'. With the strong endorsement for national parks, given by the Committee on Land Utilisation in Rural Areas (the Scott Committee), Dower was asked to prepare 'a report on the general issues backed by the specific information which he had obtained'. His 11,000-word report was first circulated for comment among Departments in November 1943. Not only was there opportunity further to develop the earlier proposals of the Standing Committee on National Parks, but the context was now much fuller. If over 80 per cent of the population of England and Wales was to live and work in towns and cities and with little or no further encroachment by way of suburbs, there must be greater opportunity to relax and enjoy the amenities of the countryside. Where town and country must remain discrete, neither should be managed without close reference to the other (PRO, HLG 92, 46 and 80).

In a paper to the Royal Institute of British Architects in March 1943, Dower spoke of how the holiday use of countryside and coast, if generously encouraged and wisely directed, might become one of the most fruitful objectives of post-war reconstruction policy. It was second to none in giving physical, mental and spiritual heath and happiness to 'the whole mass of the people'. The large and rapidly growing demand, so visible before the war, stemmed from three movements. One was the increase in leisure time. A second was the ever-widening popular appreciation of 'natural landscape beauty'. The third and most obvious was the rapid advance in 'mechanical transport' that gave easy, quick and relatively cheap access for vast numbers of people to all holiday areas even in the remotest parts of the country. All three were popular, good and irresistible movements, but a degree of control and direction – in short, planning – was needed (Dower 1943).

Dower now spoke both as a leading figure in the voluntary movement, and with the perspectives that came with the emerging powers and responsibilities of the Ministry of Town and Country Planning. He responded to an invitation from the Town Planning Institute in February 1944 to speak on 'Planning and the Landcape' – or rather, 'The Landscape and Planning', so as to emphasise the strategy required in tackling landscape problems. For him, the 'landscape' implied what 'we see about us in the countryside' that involved, through the senses, 'a continuous relation or partnership between objective and subjective, between the countryside and ourselves'. Now over a much larger canvas than had been available to him, in writing his articles for *The Dalesman*, Dower (1944) emphasised that the countryside had to be kept going, if it were to be preserved. Where the small, truly wild patches, suitable as nature reserves, would require 'a specially rigorous conservation policy', the remainder of the countryside required a reasonably prosperous farming industry. That in turn implied there should be ample scope for changes in the methods and intensity of cultivation. Although there were bound to be changes of detail in the appearance of the countryside, there was no cause for alarm. The essentials would not change. Even the hurried and drastic wartime changes in farming had generally done more good than harm to landscape values. The more gradual and considered changes of the post-war period would tip the balance even more strongly toward the credit side.

Where the cost of protecting the beauty and interest of the countryside could only be justified by there being access for public enjoyment, how might consensus be achieved where individual opinion played so large a part? What should be the basis for the legislative and administrative actions required? Dower pressed for those in authority, whether elected members or their officials, or those who managed or wrote about the land, to 'go humbly and seriously to school with Nature herself as mistress and inspirer'. Next to Nature, the poet William Wordsworth was the surest and most inspiring guide, both for his appreciation of landscape beauty and for insight into the art and practice of landscape treatment. It was Dower's 'robust faith' that a team of experienced landscape lovers would quickly emerge. From their individual and collective judgements, and reference to all the relevant facts, a scale of landscape values would be drawn up and applied in assessing the optimal location of national parks, nature reserves, a regional 'open space', or purely local designation. Through such recommendations, and the power to negotiate both informally and formally, by attaching conditions to consents, the planner would become the designer and 'expert' adviser, indicating how developments might be undertaken with much benefit, and minimal harm, to landscape beauty and interest.

It was against this background of evolving knowledge and understanding that Dower further revised his 'national parks report'. As Holford recalled, he wrote 'continuously and with increasing decision, as if he felt that the project could only be hammered out at white heat'. He was an administrative and technical committee in one, penetrating a maze of detail, 'which was all put in order and added to the argument'. In Holford's words, the further draft 'compelled the admiration of every officer that sat around the table'. Although there were some doubts and disagreements, even at that stage, the case had been made with such knowledge and conviction that it had to be given 'official recognition and public presentation' (Holford 1948). During the last days of the Wartime Coalition Government, in May 1945, W.S. Morrison, the Minister of Town and Country Planning, successfully applied to the Cabinet's Reconstruction Committee for consent to the publication of Dower's recommendations, as the work 'of a member of his Department acting as a consultant'. A Preface would emphasise how the Government was not committed 'to acceptance of the recommendations and conclusions'. The publication later that month of the 'one-man White Paper' was of pivotal importance in finally establishing the principles by which any British national parks were to be designated. Whatever their meaning in North America or Africa, Dower wrote of how they signified in Britain an extensive area of beautiful and relatively wild country in which, for the nation's benefit and by appropriate national decision and action, four objectives were met, namely that

1. the characteristic landscape was to be strictly preserved
2. access and facilities for public open-air enjoyment were amply provided
3. wildlife, and buildings and places of architectural and historic interest, were suitably protected
4. 'established farming use' was effectively maintained.

Although constrained by the Government's inability to agree on the general powers and machinery for land-use planning and development, Dower emphasised that a national parks authority should be appointed as a service or sub-department of the Ministry of Town and Country Planning. He therefore recommended the appointment of a preparatory commission, as the nucleus and precursor to a full National Parks Commission, to assist the Minister in delimiting the first park areas in consultation with the local authorities concerned, and to prepare a detailed scheme for the machinery, action and finance required at the second, executive stage. By such a two-stage procedure, the Commission would grow naturally into its task (PP 1944–45)

With hindsight, John Dower's report, *National Parks in England and Wales*, marked the culmination of inter-war attempts to combine preservation with modernity, and ensured that there was the appropriate level of 'expert' guidance in achieving that end. Although allowing such advocacy to continue, the Reconstruction Committee rejected the proposal for a preparatory Commission. There were more pressing priorities for Government. The

Chancellor of the Exchequer and Minister of Agriculture claimed it was for Ministers (as opposed to an *ad hoc* Commission) to shape and control policy. The Minister of Town and Country Planning was simply invited to appoint a National Parks Committee to explore the question further (PRO, HLG 92, 49 and CAB 87, 10). As Dower remarked, the change did not require 'any radical difference to the choice of members'. Although failing health prevented him from becoming Chairman, Dower was closely consulted as to the composition of the Committee formed under the Chairmanship of Sir Arthur Hobhouse, and exerted considerable influence over the drafting of its report. It was published in July 1947, three months before his death at the early age of 48 (PRO, HLG 93, 1; PP 1946–47a).

Dower's report had provided a 'sound foundation' for the Committee's recommendations as to the choice of park areas and how they might be administered. The Hobhouse Committee recommended the designation of 12 parks, covering 5,682 square miles, within 3 years. A further 52 areas were nominated as 'conservation areas'. Such advice seemed academic in the sense that it was hardly possible to weaken, in the park areas, the greatly strengthened planning-powers granted so recently to county councils under the Town and Country Planning Act of 1947. A compromise was therefore struck in what became, in Arthur Blenkinsop's words, 'a declaratory act'. The National Parks and Access to the Countryside Bill established a National Parks Commission with powers to designate a series of national parks, but left the planning powers essentially in the hands of local authorities. Ten national parks were designated between 1951 and 1957. Nineteen Areas of Outstanding Natural Beauty had been declared by the time the Countryside Act of 1968 subsumed the National Parks Commission within a new Countryside Commission.

Nature Reserves

It was no coincidence that the peak of game preservation in the late Victorian and Edwardian years should correspond with a rapid growth of interest in animal and plant life and rural amenities generally. Each was a function of the greater amount of personal leisure time and mobility. Not only might the denser network of railway lines, the bicycle, and the earliest motor-cycles and cars make it easier for enthusiasts to pursue their particular pastime, but for the poacher to visit the game covert and the collector of wild birds and their eggs to find and dispose of his quarry. A Society for the Protection of Birds was founded in 1889, and obtained its Royal Charter in 1904. The annual report of the Yorkshire Naturalists' Union for 1905 appealed on behalf of its Birds and Eggs Protection Committee for all ornithologists and the local authorities in Yorkshire to do everything possible to ensure that the provisions of the Wild Birds Protection Act were fulfilled, especially in respect of birds that were in imminent danger of becoming extinct as nesting species (West Yorkshire Record Office, Leeds, Yorkshire Naturalists' Union, MSS, 36–7).

It was the purpose of the Society for the Promotion of Nature Reserves (SPNR) to instil a more systematic approach to the acquisition of such sanctuaries. With the support of key figures in the British Museum (Natural History), it was founded in 1912 by N. Charles Rothschild, an active partner of Messrs N.M. Rothschild and Sons, a leading naturalist and authority on the fleas of the world. The immediate objective was

> to collect and collate information as to areas of land in the United Kingdom which retain primitive conditions and contain rare and local species liable to extinction owing to building, drainage, disafforestation, or in consequence of the cupidity of collectors.

Through the drive and resources of Rothschild, the SPNR compiled a list of 273 areas of the British Isles deemed 'worthy of permanent preservation', either as 'typical primeval country', breeding places for 'scarce creatures' and localities for rare plants, or for their rock sections and other features of geological interest (Rothschild and Marren 1997). It was not the primary purpose of the SPNR to hold such areas, but rather to use the press, personal persuasion and correspondence to emphasise their importance, whether to their respective owners or, if necessary, to such bodies as the National Trust (Sheail 1976b).

An article published in *Country Life* in 1913 cited the recent acquisition by the National Trust of Blakeney Point in Norfolk, and extension of its reserve of Wicken Fen in Cambridgeshire , as exemplars of what might be achieved. The author, William Crump, was by training a scientist, by profession a schoolmaster and then cinema owner, and by inclination a botanist and local historian. He wrote that such coastline as that at Blakeney Point furnished 'the best example of wild Nature absolutely free from human interference', where it was possible to study the characteristic vegetation and 'wild living creatures', as well as the forces that 'made and unmade the land', and thereby established new habitats. It was here that Nature presented 'that cinematographical aspect of herself essential to a full understanding of life'. The owner, Lord Calthorpe, had granted in 1910 a lease for the 'marine horticulture', as carried out by parties of students led by Frank Oliver, the Professor of Botany at University College London. In the opinion of one of his distinguished students, Edward J. Salisbury, it was this kind of survey and analysis of the physiography and vegetation of the shingle, sandhills and saltmarsh, that saved 'British ecology from becoming dominated by a more static description of vegetation units' . There was accordingly much concern as to whether the research site might be 'seized by some speculative builder', when the heirs to Lord Calthorpe offered Blakeney Point for sale. Personal donations were made by such figures as Oliver. Through the good offices of the leading authority on the British flora, G. Claridge Druce, a substantial sum was obtained from the Fishmongers' Company. As well as the purchase of the length of Blakeney Point, a further donation secured the strip of saltings, so as to encompass the entire 'natural area' of beach, dunes and marsh. It was transferred to the National Trust in the summer of 1912 (Anon 1914).

Though such inland reserves as Wicken Fen were patently less natural, in the sense of being a highly modified relic of the

A Third Force

undrained East Anglian Fen, Crump (1913) wrote of how they were no less dynamic in terms of the changes taking place in their wildlife. Where at present Wicken Fen was 'a bewildering tangle of tall grasses, rushes and herbaceous plants', the fen was drying out and becoming fen carr and eventually woodland. There were already numerous thickets of alder buckthorn and its allies. As Crump explained, such a scale and inevitability of change meant the National Trust was faced with a dilemma. If it was determined to preserve Wicken Fen as a fen, it must adopt artificial means of arresting the course of Nature. The fen would become even less primitive in its condition. If natural succession were allowed to occur, Wicken Fen would cease to be a fen. Thus, in more than one way, a nature reserve was 'no mere refuge for vanishing or persecuted species'. It was, in Crump's words,

> an outdoor workshop for the study of plants and animals in and in relation to their natural habitats; a twentieth century instrument of research as indispensable for biological progress as a laboratory or an experimental station.

Such instances of insight raise the obvious question as to why so little was achieved by way of reserve acquisition. How far did it stem from a lack of perceived need, as opposed to lack of concern or appropriate organisation? Such leading politicians as Neville Chamberlain were members of the SPNR. His personal papers contain a leaflet on the Brent Valley Bird Sanctuary, and details dating from January 1936 of bird tables (written on a leaflet advertising nesting boxes). There is correspondence from Chamberlain's Private Secretary that on 21 January 1940 the Prime Minister saw a common sandpiper at the west end of St James Park lake – a remarkable thing for that time of year (Birmingham University Library, Chamberlain MSS, 6/2/7 and 15–16).

Frank Oliver may have gone far in explaining why nature preservation excited so little interest among biologists and the public generally, when he observed, at the first meeting of the British Ecological Society in December 1913, that 'the country districts of England are not obviously and seriously threatened'. The nature-reserve movement lacked therefore 'the background for a strong popular appeal'. It was in any case remarked that interest in natural history had declined, as the leisured classes took up gardening and golf, whilst 'the masses of the people seem to be preoccupied by other matters'. And as Oliver observed, even where reserves were established, any extensive closure was 'resented by many people as a kind of game preserving'. At Blakeney Point, where the birds and their eggs could be strictly preserved between 1 March and 1 September, the autumn migrants and edible species had been shot and snared since time immemorial. Having listened to 'all shades of opinion from birdmen', the Committee of Management concluded it would be unwise to advance 'further than public opinion in the locality would be prepared to go with them'. Annual permits were introduced for shooting between September and late February. Seventy-two were taken up in the first year (Anon. 1914).

Frank Oliver became, however, increasingly concerned as to the scale of change taking place and, more specifically, the revolution in communication wrought by petrol and the motor car. As he emphasised in a paper to the British Association in September 1927, there was urgent need to protect

> representative examples of natural ground with its flora and fauna, so that these might serve as a present enjoyment and solace, and might be handed down to future generations intact, with records of their changing history. (Oliver 1928)

The pretext was the north Norfolk coast. Scolt Head Island, known locally as the 'Bird Island', had been acquired and handed over to the National Trust in 1923. Some 400 acres of partially inundated marshes at Cley, on the same coast, were acquired by public auction in 1926. This effort had been organised by Sydney H. Long, a physician at the Norwich group of hospitals, Secretary of the Norfolk and Norwich Naturalists' Society for 24 years, and the moving spirit behind its Bird Protection Committee. When the

A Third Force

National Trust refused to accept custody of this further property, it was Long who used the precedents of the National Trust (with its encouragement) to establish a non-profit-paying company, called the Norfolk Naturalists' Trust. In his paper to the British Association, Frank Oliver looked forward 'to the time when every county would have its County Trust, which would hold and administer the areas it acquires'. It was not until 1946 that a second county naturalists' trust was formed in Yorkshire.

Geoffrey Dent was a successful businessman and all-round field naturalist and sportsman. He had joined the RSPB in 1923, and had served on its Watchers' Committee and Council since 1938. Through his initiative, a small committee was formed, soon after the outbreak of war, to begin the task of preparing for post-war recovery. Under his chairmanship, a memorandum was drawn up, setting out the functions of bird sanctuaries and the need for government assistance in protecting them. Experience in America, the Dominions and 'most advanced European countries' had demonstrated that the only effective way of preserving 'native wild life for the benefit of future generations' was to supplement the preservation laws with the provision of national parks or reserves to act as breeding reservoirs for those species which might otherwise be threatened with extermination. More specifically, Dent defined the requirements of a breeding sanctuary as its having a breeding stock of the desired species, an area large enough for nesting and feeding purposes, an adequate wardening system, limitations on public access, and an assumption that agriculture was of secondary importance in peacetime. Dent assumed the sanctuaries would be selected on an ecological basis, the preservation of mammals, reptiles, insects and plants being combined with that of birds (RSPB archive, Sandy, NRIC file and Council minutes).

Dent succeeded in stimulating both the Council of the RSPB and SPNR to the extent that a joint Conference on Nature Preservation in Post-war Reconstruction was convened of representative bodies in July 1941. An immediate object was to capitalise on the publicity already being given to the proposed establishment of national parks. Ministers encouraged a deputation to form a

Nature Reserves Investigation Committee to draw up a rationale and identify a series of national nature reserves. It was assumed the designation and management of such reserves would be a responsibility of a national parks commission. John Dower made such a recommendation – his friendship with the animal ecologist, Charles Elton, ensured he was well versed as to the needs of the ecologist. It was enough to ensure that when a National Parks Committee was appointed in 1945 to assess further the feasibility of a series of national parks, a Wild Life Conservation Special Committee was formed to cover that dimension. The leading figure in British ecology, A.G. Tansley, became de-facto Chairman and Elton a member. Through their encouragement, the British Ecological Society had both participated in the wartime surveys and promoted the more positive concept of nature conservation. Tansley had at first favoured the appointment of an official body, comparable with the Fish and Wild Life Service of the United States, to promote the wildlife dimension. Through his own wartime involvement with the Agricultural Research Council, Elton had become impressed by the potential of a research council, both for co-ordinating and leading the conservation research required and in providing a statutory wildlife service that might stand above sectional interests (Sheail 1987, pp. 130–45).

It was the achievement of the British Ecological Society, and then those ecologists serving on official committees, to persuade ministers that responsibility for nature conservation should be placed not with the planning sector, but within the science sector, of government (PP 1946–47b). The decision was taken to appoint by Royal Charter a new body, the Nature Conservancy, that was, in all but name, a research council of comparable status to that of the Agricultural Research Council and Medical Research Council. The Nature Conservancy was to provide expert advice on nature conservation, designate and manage a series of national nature reserves, and to undertake such research as was relevant to those functions, over and above the more fundamental, long-term research otherwise expected of a research council (Sheail 1998, pp. 24–34).

Whilst acknowledging the pivotal role of scientists and the crucial part played by government, Geoffrey Dent emphasised the need to retain and considerably extend the popular appeal in such work. Without some good 'propaganda reserves', there would be little support for establishing any reserve-sites. Dent was perhaps the first to recognise the value of Minsmere Levels, on the Suffolk coast, as an examplar of what was required. The sluices had been opened, and the grazing marshes flooded with sea water, as a wartime defence measure and for battle training. Identified by the wartime surveys for its ornithological importance, the RSPB leased from the owner some 300 acres of brackish marsh, with a further 1,200 acres of wood, heath and seashore. The drawing up of the lease provided valuable insight in drafting the statutory powers required by the Nature Conservancy for reserve acquisition and management, under the National Parks and Access to the Countryside Act of 1949 (Sheail 1995c). The RSPB was also a pioneer in its positive management of the reserve, in terms of sustaining and creating habitat suitable for Marsh harriers, Bearded tits and Bitterns. In as much as the latter two species avoided dense, unbroken reed-beds, where there was no standing water above the reed stools, it was recognised right from the start that a programme to control the spread of reed would be needed (RSPB archives, Sandy, Minsmere file, report of 1952).

Where nature reserves crystallised and gave tangible expression to the aspirations of conservationists, they similarly reinforced the misgivings of other user-interests. The number of National Nature Reserves rose sharply following the appointment of Max Nicholson as Director-General of the Nature Conservancy in December 1952. Nicholson was a journalist, founder-member of the British Trust for Ornithology, and ornithologist on the Wild Life Special Conservation Committee. A war-time civil servant, he became the Head of Herbert Morrison's Office as Lord President of the Council. He ensured the Conservancy 'punched well above its weight'. Over 70 National Nature Reserves had been acquired during the Conservancy's first ten years. Their establishment, and the implementation of the Protection of Birds Act of 1954, often required a close working-relationship with other user-groups. A policy statement published by the Nature Conservancy and wildfowl-shooting interests, of March 1960, emphasised the need for wildfowl refuges, both for sustaining and re-stocking the marshlands generally and for supporting European conservation, in terms of migratory species. The Conservancy's monograph, *Wildfowl in Great Britain*, provided a highly relevant model of the collaboration possible between two potentially conflicting interests, and of identifying, on the basis of scientific criteria, what was required in terms of achieving the optimal protection of the wildlife communities (Atkinson-Willes 1963, p. 341).

A model of another kind was provided by the founding of a third Naturalists' Trust, that for Lincolnshire in December 1948. Through the insight, energies and persistence of its Honorary General Secretary, A.E. (Ted) Smith, the Trust simulated both the formation of further county trusts and the conversion of the SPNR into a national co-ordinating body which, in time, became the Royal Society for Nature Conservation. The number of trusts expanded from seven, with a membership of 1,750 members in 1958, to 36 with nearly 18,000 members five years later, and 39 trusts with over 40,000 members in 1970. There were by that time 400 reserves of an aggregate 35,000 acres. At the Kent Trust Conference in March 1970 the President of the SPNR emphasised how each trust continued to be completely autonomous, dependent on voluntary workers, rather than run, like so many national organisations, from a head office manned by paid officials. A levy of one shilling per member was levied on trusts to cover the costs of the SPNR. One of the most important roles of the Society had become the negotiation and disbursement of grant aid. A £30,000 grant from the Carnegie Trust enabled a number of trusts to cross the threshold from being entirely amateur bodies to ones that had begun to employ a core of paid staff and a generally more businesslike approach.

In a Presidential Address marking the twentieth anniversary of the Lincolnshire Trust, Ted Smith recalled how the wildlife of at least one-third of the Trust's 30 reserves would have been destroyed or irreparably damaged, had they not been designated. Even now, their wildlife had to be protected from the damaging effects of such activities as arterial drainage on neighbouring properties. Such management work further emphasised the need for nature conservation to be practised on all land, however modern the farming system. Citing another founder member of the Trust, Smith (1970) spoke of how

> if farmers can come to realise that they, just like their forefathers before them, carry a responsibility to future generations for the kind of countryside they will have to live in, much can be done to develop a new landscape that will be compatible with, and expressive of, modern scientific mechanised farming – yet will be pleasing to look at and still rich in wildlife.

Coastal Preservation

There was 'a national movement seawards'. This was the inescapable conclusion of a monograph published by the Council for the Preservation of Rural England (CPRE) in October 1936, on the development and preservation of the coast. The author was Wesley Dougil, a member of the Department of Civic Design at Liverpool university, who had himself carried out a survey of the Northumberland coast. The seaboard was not only recognised to be one of Britain's greatest assets, but there was now the will and means to exploit it. For a distance of 30 miles along the Sussex coast, one never lost sight of post-war houses, bungalows and shacks. It was the same from Poole, through Bournemouth, to Christchurch, and along lengths of the north Welsh coast. The movement was not only deep seated, but destined to develop immeasurably (Dougil 1936).

The point was well-taken by the Ministry of Health. Officials wrote, in internal memoranda, that if Exchequer aid were ever offered, priority should be given to preserving the coastline, perhaps as a first step in creating a Green Belt around England. An early wartime survey of the coast between the Wash and Thames estuary stressed that it was more than a question of aesthetics. Sound planning also required knowledge of coastal processes (Sheail 1976b). H.G. Vincent, the Principal Assistant Secretary in Lord Reith's Ministry, learned of how 'the geographical Dean of St Catharine's Cambridge, J. Alfred Steers, had written a book, *The Coastline of England and Wales* (Steers 1948). He was appointed, as 'an expert scientist' in February 1943, to provide a qualitative assessment of the whole coastline from the point of view of scenery and amenities and, at the same time, to record a number of physical characteristics and other features of importance to any planning considerations (PRO, HLG 92, 1). His annotated Ordnance Survey 1:25,000 maps and reports distinguished lengths of exceptional, very good, and good-quality, coastline. They provided regional planning officers with the basis for a series of national optimum-use maps. Steers presented his findings to an audience at the Royal Geographical Society in June 1944, with the Minister present (Steers 1944). At Steers's instigation, the Department of Health for Scotland obtained Treasury approval in June 1946 for a survey of the Scottish coast (Scottish Record Office (SRO) DD 12, 30–1). Undertaken each summer, the last was of Shetland in August 1953. The flavour of his individual reports is conveyed by that of Orkney. He had not seen at that time anything to compare with the grandeur of the cliffs near the Old Man and St John's Head. The many scattered sheds of the very prosperous poultry industry gave the landscape a 'shacky' appearance. The wartime camps and WD buildings were a sad disfigurement. Some had flapping sheets of corrugated iron; others remained as arc-shaped end-walls of former Nissen-type huts. Whilst Steers had again fulfilled his brief of providing a series of consistent assessments (in as much as he alone was responsible for them), the Scottish Office did not have enough planning staff to follow them up (SRO, DD 12 1067). Steers's own book, *The Coastline of Scotland*, did not appear until 1973, by which time such documentation had become an historic reference point to a further generation of coastal survey (Steers 1973).

In a paper given to the Royal Society of Arts in November 1959, the Chairman of the Central Electricity Generating Board (CEGB) and a part-time Member of the Board, Sir William Holford, the Professor of Town Planning at University College London, sought to highlight the breadth of issues raised by the term 'amenity'. The immediate pretext had been the strenuous opposition to the construction of a nuclear power station at Dungeness (Sheail 1991a, pp. 148–52). Holford warned of how 'we are approaching a situation where the greater part of our land, not already built-up, had a rarity value, and where every individual site could claim to be in a greater or lesser degree unique'. Neither the CEGB nor, indeed, any developer could be dogmatic in resisting such claims, and yet electricity was 'basic to the whole existence of this country in the twentieth century'. Obviously the Board had a right to ask for details as to what would be disturbed by the construction and operation of, say, a power station. With such information, a great deal of damage might be avoided (Holford 1959). The prospect of further nuclear power stations, and of other major developments along the coast, caused the Nature Conservancy to organise a series of exploratory meetings with interested organisations to assess both coastal resources and priorities for their protection. About 10 to 15 per cent of the coastline fell within a national park or Area of Outstanding Natural Beauty. The Nature Conservancy held some 2 per cent of the coast, and the National Trust a further 4.5 per cent, of which half was in Devon and Cornwall. Local initiatives were reported. A Cornish Coast Advisory Committee had since 1957 co-ordinated efforts within the county, alerted local opinion, and demonstrated to owners that the surest safeguard for their coastal land was inalienable ownership under the National Trust. Some 40 miles of coastline were conveyed to the Trust, mainly by gift (Nature Conservancy 1960, pp. 11–7).

Very hesitantly, the Council of the National Trust took the unprecedented step of actively seeking to acquire properties. The Department of Geography at Reading University was commissioned in 1962–63 to make an assessment, using air photography, of the entire coastal zone of England, Wales and Northern Ireland. It was found that only about 900 miles, or a little over one-quarter, remained free of development and of such outstanding beauty as to be worthy of permanent preservation by the National Trust. Plans were laid for a campaign , first known as Operation Neptune, to raise a fighting fund of £2 million, that would enable the Trust to purchase strips of coastline, as they came onto the market, for public enjoyment, recreation and scientific study (Fedden 1968).

The General Election of October 1964 returned a Labour Government. The Chancellor of the Exchequer, James Callaghan, had told an interviewer, during a pre-election broadcast, that his 'pet wish' was to do something 'to protect our coasts from further ruin'. Anthony Crosland, the new Economic Secretary in the Department of Economic Affairs, wrote personally to Callaghan, on 23 October, expressing 'the hope that you have not given up ideas of saving the British coast line'. It might 'sweeten' the Autumn Budget. He enclosed the National Trust's *Annual Report* for 1963–64, and a letter from the veteran Labour Party campaigner, Ruth Dalton, pressing for the 'nationalisation' of the coastline. Treasury officials acknowledged that a government contribution had its attractions, but also warned of how it might cause 'private springs of generosity' to dry up. A better approach might be to contribute on a pound-for-pound basis. There was risk however of the Appeal being so successful as to create a liability as great as £2 million. But there were more fundamental concerns. Much as most in the Treasury would like to see every inch of coastline preserved, Kenneth E. Couzens (an Assistant Secretary) warned that there were occasions when major installations had to be built in areas of great natural beauty. An oil refinery and terminal had been required in the Pembrokeshire National Park, and a nuclear power station at Dungeness. If the Government were to make such a cash contribution for preserving unspecified lengths of coastline, it would be even harder to resist the very strong pressure for such amenity works as that of placing underground the 400 KV line, which would otherwise have to be carried by pylons through part of the West Sussex Area of Outstanding Natural Beauty (PRO, T 224, 1117).

Callaghan persisted, informing Lord Crawford, the Chairman of the National Trust, in February 1965, that he was ready, for his part, 'to stand behind the Trust in this imaginative appeal' for a very good cause. The Duke of Edinburgh, as Patron, was to launch Enterprise Neptune on 11 May. Callaghan was keen to announce the scale of Government support in his April Budget speech. Officials saw no difficulty following such precedents as the grant to London Zoo for a new building, but warned of how the powerful House of Commons Public Accounts Committee would strongly object to any donation which, so to speak, would be 'kept in a sock'. A meeting, on 24 March, confirmed that it was the Trust's intention to invest the Appeal monies for use, as occasion offered, to purchase and repair property, and to provide public access. As Callaghan indicated, there was choice. The Government could give a large contribution (say £1 million on a pound-for-pound basis) to be spent over a number of years. That would require legislation and fairly detailed control as to how it was spent. The Trust was obviously reluctant to be bound by such regulation of its activities. Alternatively the Government could give a smaller sum to be spent over one or two years. It was Fred Willey, the Minister of Land and Natural Resources, who announced, the day before the Appeal Launch, that a contribution of £250,000 would be made as 'a substantial encouragement at the outset to those organising the appeal and that it will stimulate the generosity of other donors' (PRO, AT 25, 34; PD, Commons, 712, 19–20). Whilst the coincidence of the Appeal with a period of economic recession meant a poor response from business and industry, the Appeal had raised over £1 million by the end of 1967. Seventy-eight properties, representing 75 miles of coastline, were acquired or protected by covenant. Perhaps more important, it had helped reawaken public anxiety as to the future of such coastline (Fedden 1968).

The Appeal had two unintended repercussions, the first being the stimulus it gave to statutory planning. Richard Crossman, the Minister of Housing and Local Government, complained in his diary for April 1965 of how the Trust's intervention would put a value on land that was otherwise virtually valueless, except with planning permission. Crossman wrote of how his wife, in conversation, had suggested that he simply 'froze the coastline'. Attracted by the idea of striking 'as dramatic a blow as we struck for office building in London last autumn', Crossman had enquiries made (Crossman 1975, pp. 205, 212 and 345). Such intervention was a further stimulus to the Ministry and National Parks Commission in carrying out an intensive study of land-use planning along the whole coastline of England and Wales. To provide such detail, nine regional conferences of the relevant planning authorities were held in 1966–67. A general policy was sought of revitalising existing resorts and of creating new ones, establishing regional recreation areas and thirdly of designating special areas for industrial development. Such measures should absorb at least some of the pressure on the undeveloped coast. Thirty-four lengths of coast, or some quarter of the entire coastline, were however of such outstanding importance, yet so threatened with development, as to require stronger powers for their planning and management. On the assumption of a uniform width of 1 mile above high-water mark, they comprised 1 per cent of the land surface of England and Wales, compared with the 9 per cent occupied by national parks and a little over 7.5 per cent by Areas of Outstanding Natural Beauty. Whilst regretting the need for a further designation, there seemed no alternative to identifying such lengths of coastline as Heritage Coasts. By the end of the century, 45 Heritage Coasts, extending along 1,540 km (960 miles) of English and Welsh coastline, had been designated. They represented some 35 per cent of the total coastline.

The second unintended effect of Enterprise Neptune was the pivotal part it played in the overhaul of the National Trust itself. The costs of running the Appeal were so high, and Conrad Rawnsley, the Director, so sharply critical, that Council terminated his employment in October 1966. He and a so-called Reform Group now exploited the Trust's constitution by requiring an Extraordinary General Meeting and a poll of members to be held, as a way of pressing their case for a more open and accountable organisation (Fedden 1968, pp. 71–2). Richard Crossman, now the Lord President of the Council, pressed the Prime Minister for an independent inquiry (Crossman 1975, p. 458). His successor,

Anthony Greenwood, and Fred Willey successfully opposed such a move. Not only was the Trust an independent body, but there was nothing to suggest it had acted improperly as a charity or misused funds provided by the Government in respect of any property (PRO, AT 25, 34). The Trust had itself set up an enquiry under Sir Henry Benson, an accountant of wide experience in business and government, to examine the Trust's finances, management, organisation and responsibilities. The substantial changes recommended by his Committee in 1968 were largely adopted, thereby transforming what was described as an amateurish oligarchy into a responsible business enterprise. Considerably greater emphasis was given to raising membership and closer contact with members. Whilst much of the administrative work was decentralised to regional committees, the managerial function of headquarters was strengthened and the professional staff enlarged (Cannadine 1995).

By the turn of the century, the Neptune Coastal Campaign had raised £32 million. Some 940 km (600 miles) of coastline were protected. Re-launched in 1985 with a fresh target of 1,000 miles of coastline, it had passed the half-way mark in 1988, when a length of beach in County Durham was acquired from British Coal for £1. It had been discounted at the time of the original survey because of the waste-tipping from the nearby Easington colliery. Where the Trust's ownership continued to convey a level of protection not generally possible under statutory planning, not even the concept of inalienability could prevent such properties from being affected by oil and other forms of pollution (Dwyer and Hodge 1996).

The Challenge of Leisure

America had offered a model for national parks. The term 'nature conservation' was borrowed from America to convey a more positive form of wildlife preservation. As both concepts came to be adapted in terms of managing the British countryside and coastline, so American experience was again drawn upon – this time as guidance as to how people might be more closely involved in undertaking and supporting the conservation work required.

As Max Nicholson (the Director-General of the Nature Conservancy) wrote, following a tour of the United States in 1959, knowledge and understanding as to the management of natural substances, organisms and processes called for the highest levels of education. The conservation bodies had to be much more vigorous in promoting the purpose of their work. In its evidence to the official Committee on Broadcasting in 1961, the Nature Conservancy sought to raise the awareness of the communications industry itself as to its potential for promoting conservation. Such BBC programmes as Peter Scott's *Look* and David Attenborough's *Zoo Quest* were seen by a vast, but still passive, audience of over 10 million. It had to be stimulated into taking a more active part in the practical aspects of conservation (Sheail 1998, p. 126).

Largely at the instigation of the Nature Conservancy, the Council for Nature (to which most natural-history and nature-conservation bodies belonged) organised a National Nature Week in May 1963, to draw attention to the threats to wildlife and the part 'active conservation' could play, if supported by an informed public opinion. The Post Office marked the event by issuing two attractive postage stamps. Over 46,000 people visited the main national event, a Wild Life Exhibition sponsored by *The Observer* newspaper and opened by the Minister of Housing and Local Government, Sir Keith Joseph. A further innovation was the opening of Nature Trails. Over 1,725 schoolchildren from 81 schools walked the nature trails on Mousehold Heath, near Norwich. To the Duke of Edinburgh, paying an official visit to the Exhibition, the most remarkable aspect was the way in which the event had brought together exhibitors who might otherwise never have met. It emphasised the merits of some greater discourse between the various interests. So as to help capitalise on what had been achieved, he suggested a two-day study conference. Some years earlier, he had found this to be a useful device for securing general discussion of a particular problem, without the need to produce resolutions or recommendations. They would come later, when issues had been aired and some meeting of minds achieved. Again largely through the Nature Conservancy, the conference was

A Third Force

held in the following November of 1963. Its theme was the 'Countryside in 1970', a date chosen as being certainly in the future, but 'near enough to be realistic', yet tinged with just a little of the apprehension aroused by George Orwell's '1984'. There followed a second study conference in November 1965, and a third in 1970.

Such events were there to be exploited. The Minister of Land and Natural Resources, Fred T. Willey, achieved an acceleration of his policy for the countryside by persuading the Cabinet's Home Affairs Committee in October 1965 of the advantages of making a major statement of policy at the second 'Countryside in 1970' conference. Whilst the overriding purpose of the new Ministry, formed on the election of the Labour Government in October 1964, was to establish a Land Commission, so as to expedite the provision of land for house-building, it had also been given responsibility for national parks. For Willey and his Parliamentary Secretary, Arthur Skeffington, the obvious course was to turn the Labour Party pamphlet, *Leisure for Living*, into legislative proposals. Its chapter on 'The open air' had proposed turning the National Parks Commission into an agency for preserving and promoting the enjoyment of the beauty of the whole countryside, functioning in a way similar to that of the Arts Council and the proposed Sports Council (Sheail 2001).

The National Parks Commission pressed for a 'new-style Commission', capable of grappling with the profound changes taking place in the leisure use of the countryside. Where a beautiful countryside was both a dollar earner and source of much pleasure to domestic holiday-makers, the authorities in the Lake District and Pembrokeshire Coast national parks warned of how 'the weight of numbers of people and cars crowding into those areas threatens to kill what they come to enjoy'. The Commission pressed for fresh legislation, giving it the executive powers to plan positively for leisure both within and outside the park areas. Ministers and officials soon came to recognise how any measure confined to national parks would be outdated. An obvious course was to absorb the National Parks Commission into a 'Countryside Commission' (PRO, HLG 29, 735).

The Fourth Wave. The Challenge of Leisure was the title given to the findings of a Civic Trust survey, first published by the *Architects' Journal* in January 1965. Its author, Michael Dower (the son of John Dower), described how 'three great waves had broken across the face of Great Britain since 1800'. The first had been the sudden growth of dark industrial towns, followed by the thrusting movement along far-flung railways, and thirdly the sprawl of car-based suburbs. And in the decade 1955–65 a fourth wave had broken, in the form of an increasing demand for outdoor recreation. Also drawing on American experience, Dower warned of how this wave would bring both immense pleasure to an increasing number of leisure-seekers, and an obvious danger of damage and destruction to the very sources of that leisure. Already in Britain,

> the weekend multitudes are congesting our roads, fouling our downs and commons with litter and soiling our lay-bys; their chalets and caravans threaten all parts of our coast; their cars and motorboats echo in quiet valleys and lakes (Dower 1965).

As Michael Dower (1965) explained, leisure was a compound of six decisive factors – population, income, mobility, education, retirement and the free time of adults. Each had grown dramatically. The point was perhaps best made by a caption to a photograph of a beach packed with holiday-makers, namely that if everyone in England and Wales went to the seaside on the same day, each would get a strip of coast 3.5 inches across. Pressures were similarly building up inland. Whilst the countryside was simply not designed to withstand such weekend invasions, people properly expected there to be the physical basis for the 'freedom, informality and choice' they sought in their leisure time. That need had to be met with the least damage to 'the character of this island'.

Fred Willey began his own speech to the '1970' Conference, in November 1965, by emphasising how there was a general consensus of opinion on the need for change. So as to expedite the forward planning and research required, a new Countryside

Commission should take over the role of the National Parks Commission, and additionally have 'a new function of encouraging the provision of opportunities for the enjoyment of the countryside generally'. The centrepiece of his speech was the proposal to establish a series of country parks, so as to make it easier for people living in towns to enjoy the countryside without having to travel too far (Anon 1966). Willey deliberately used the promise of a White Paper to ratchet forward the consent of ministers to the detail of what had already been announced. The White Paper of February 1966, *Leisure in the Countryside*, set out both a range of measures requiring urgent attention and a more holistic approach to the resource planning needed for reconciling such greater access with all the other user-demands made on the countryside and coast. How could such numbers of visitors enjoy themselves, without causing harm to those who lived and worked there, and without spoiling what they had come to the countryside to seek? The essence of the Government's proposals was to give elected local bodies the powers and finance to help to ensure the resources of the countryside matched the needs of the nation. A new Countryside Commission would promote and co-ordinate action and advise the Government on the measures needed (PP 1965–66).

Although it was assumed Scotland would one day have national parks, the Scottish Office had always emphasised the crucial differences in perception and circumstances between the two countries. England was so closely populated that even the last few stretches of 'unspoiled' countryside available for public recreation were threatened by building development. Not only was the greater part of the Scottish Highlands and Islands, and the Border Country, of national-park status but, far from wanting to discourage development in those areas, there was desperate need to slow down, if not reverse, the continuing decline in population. More time was accordingly needed to consider how the economic purpose, as well as social intention, of national parks might be integrated with such specifically Scottish questions as the future of crofting, hydro-electric power development, and the management of the deer forests (Scottish Record Office (SRO), DD 12, 3011; Sheail 2000).

Although there was 'no great demand for Scottish national parks on the English model' , a brief to the Scottish Secretary in March 1964 warned of growing concern over what was happening to the countryside. There would be obvious embarrassment if England and Wales embarked on further legislation, 'when no statutory provision at all had been made for Scotland'. The dilemma previously faced by the Scottish Office was set out by Robert Grieve, the Chief Planning Officer, in a paper of January 1962, in which he spoke of how the highlands and islands had a deep place in the hearts of Scots, but there had however never been anything on which to hang 'a genuinely inspiring and positive plan'. That 'new dynamic force' had now been identified. There were unique opportunities through mass tourism to diversify and therefore revive the economy of the remoter areas. None was more expert in identifying the benefits that would accrue to the local economy from 'pump-priming' monies than the tourist industry. No other interest group could speak so authoritatively as to visitor and tourist preferences and, therefore, the balance to be struck between preservation and development (SRO, DD 12, 2656).

The same meeting of the Cabinet's Home Affairs Committee as gave Fred Willey authority to make his speech to the 'Countryside in 1970' conference, also approved the announcement of Government policy for Scotland (SRO, DD 12, 3009). Willie Ross, the Scottish Secretary of State, gave notice of a Bill to establish a Countryside Commission for Scotland. Working closely with the local authorities, it would have all the powers required 'to conserve our unique heritage of scenic beauty', and to ensure 'its recreational and tourist potential is developed in full'. A second aim would be to emphasise that the Government's proposals would be 'framed to suit Scotland's distinctive needs', and thirdly to stress how the new machinery would accord with the existing structure of local government and the voluntary bodies (PD, Commons, 720, 70–1). A leader in *The Scotsman* (18 November 1965) welcomed not only the fulfilment of a political commitment, but the rationale behind it. With the increasing pressure of people, cars and industry on the countryside, it was far better to preserve the existing popular beauty-spots than to 'tidy them up after they are despoiled'.

If the stimulus to the announcement had been the need to keep abreast of political developments South of the Border, the announcement drew heavily on a new study of the Scottish countryside. It had been made by a preparatory Study Group for the second '1970' conference, under the Chairmanship of Robert Grieve (who had left the Scottish Office for the Chair of Urban and Regional Planning at Glasgow University). The Group comprised representatives of the Association of County Councils, National Trust for Scotland, Scottish Tourist Board, land-owning and farming bodies, together with Grieve and two independent members. Its report emphasised the weakness of the Highland councils, in terms of rateable income and, therefore, the professional support they required in confronting 'an increasing tempo of change'. Scotland contained by far 'the biggest reserve of open unspoiled hill land and coastal territory in Britain'. Some of the more remote parts fell within the rare category of 'wilderness'. The same physical structure had also led to 80 per cent of Scotland's population living within the Central Belt, parts of which were the most heavily urbanised in Britain. The fact that everywhere was within 30 miles of such upland beauty meant 'a potentially explosive situation existed'. The growth of Britain's motorways was bound to increase tourist pressures on Scotland. With 'the continuing democratisation of outdoor sports', there were already more than 8,000 skiers on Scottish slopes in winter (SRO, DD 12, 2916 and 2959).

The Study Group sought a positive response to such pressures through 'the integrated multi-purpose development' of farming, forestry and recreation. Although the Government continued 'to guide, stimulate and persuade in important matters', the Group noted how there was an increasing trend towards delegating major elements of policy to *ad hoc* bodies, such as New Town Corporations. Its principal recommendation was to establish a Countryside Commission, which would act 'as a central agency to determine countryside standards and policy, to recommend grants to other authorities, and to carry out with its own executive arm those projects which cannot be handled by existing agencies'. The publication of such findings, and the support given them by Scottish Members of Parliament and public opinion generally, marked an important political watershed. The Minister of State obtained the general agreement of representative bodies to the need for a Countryside Commission in February 1966 (SRO, DD 12, 2930 and 2959, and CO 1, 5/755).

The dilemma for the Scottish Office was how to confer executive powers on the new Commission without creating even greater reluctance on the part of local authorities to take any kind of initiative. The Treasury remained sceptical of the need for any executive powers. A significant advance was nevertheless made in July 1966, when Kenneth Couzens (an Assistant Secretary in the Treasury) conceded the Highlands as 'an exceptional case'. Not only did the local councils lack the resources required for major countryside schemes, but the local population could hardly be expected to take on the burden of providing for so many tourists. Having secured the principle of executive powers, the priority for officials of the Scottish Office was to press for their extension to the whole of Scotland, albeit in reduced form. 'Prototype projects' were cited that might both demonstrate what local authorities and private enterprise could achieve and help attract officers of high calibre to the proposed Countryside Commission. Couzens conceded the case for experimental schemes, such as weekend and holiday villages, financed entirely or in part by grant aid from the Commission's own resources (SRO, DD 12, 1915 and 3010). As the Treasury correctly anticipated, 'English' ministers soon came to regard such experimental powers as an essential part of their Bill.

With the national economy showing signs of improvement, the Scottish Secretary felt sufficiently confident to submit a paper to the Home Affairs Committee, in November 1966, describing how consultations had shown 'an overwhelming body of opinion' in favour of a Scottish body, with sufficient powers to realise the potential for enlarging the tourist trade and recreational opportunities for Scots people. Such consensus had been achieved by enabling local planning authorities to provide for every aspect of recreational and amenity planning. The Secretary of State was empowered to make 75 per cent grants towards current expenditure and loan repayments for such purposes. The overriding goal of the Commission would be to establish a bond of mutual trust, whereby local planning authorities would turn immediately to the Commission whenever there was need for its specialist guidance and support (SRO, DD 12, 1136–7 and 1150; PD, Lords, 284, 1134–51).

The Scottish Bill received the Royal Assent in October 1967, and the Countryside Bill for England and Wales in July 1968. Both were praised for the ease with which they passed through their parliamentary stages, despite their touching so many interests (PD, Commons, 749, 1654–5). To a degree, the achievement was a function of the minimal powers granted. The Countryside Commissions were mainly advisory to satisfy local authorities. Finance was strictly limited at the insistence of the Treasury. There were still no national parks in Scotland. And yet, if the Bills had been perceived in such minimalist terms, they would never have obtained priority in the legislative timetable. In setting the precedent, the achievement of especially the Scottish Office had been to portray its Bill as a pro-active, positive step in the management of rural interests. It had brought that third force in the countryside (alongside farming and forestry) into a much more central position in the self-consciously political drive for modernisation. As the first report of the Countryside Commission for Scotland observed, the 'further utilisation of recreational resources and conservation of the scenic heritage' were an essential step in increasing industrial competitiveness, and of enriching 'the lives of the population'

CHAPTER 6

Environmental Conservation

Introduction

The Council of Europe formally announced in 1966 that the year 1970 would be European Conservation Year (ECY). It began with a European Conservation Conference at Strasbourg in February, with representatives from more than twenty countries. As well as five princes and ministers, there were 350 officials, business leaders and representatives of professional voluntary bodies present. The overriding purpose was to raise environmental awareness and thereby 'to encourage all Europeans to care for, work for, and enjoy a high quality environment'. It was one of the most successful 'Years' of its kind (Sheail 1998, pp. 152–5).

There was certainly reason to believe that a more strategic view of planning was emerging both within government and among the wider constituency of industry and the conservation movement. In 1969, Anthony Crosland was appointed to the new post of Secretary of State for Local Government and Regional Planning. He was to be the co-ordinating minister and sole Cabinet representative of the Ministry of Housing and Local Government, and the Ministry of Transport. As part of a wider strategy to create superministries, proposals for a Department of the Environment (DOE) were further developed by Peter Walker (Crosland's successor) in the Conservative Government elected in 1970 (Draper 1977). The DOE, together with the new Department of Trade and Industry, and a Central Policy Review Staff (a 'think tank') seemed to presage a more holistic approach to policy-making.

There were structural changes too in the environmental sciences. The science writer, Nigel Calder, drew an analogy with the

Environmental Conservation

medical sciences. Where the latter turned to any field of science which might help the human patient, so the patient for the environmental sciences was that 'wonderful, vulnerable web of living and non-living processes on and near the surface of the Earth' (Calder 1973). Increasing concern for that patient was signified by the growth of the Nature Conservancy and its absorption, under the Science and Technology Act of 1965, into a new and much larger research council, the Natural Environment Research Council. For a few years, the Science Budget grew by over 10 per cent per annum. With the creation of the DOE, there was however, a compelling logic to its absorbing both the reserves and advisory functions of the Nature Conservancy. That was effected by the abolition of the Nature Conservancy, and appointment of a Nature Conservancy Council, as a grant-aided body of the DOE, in November 1973.

There were structural changes too in the support given to both government and science in the promotion of conservation. Where the late 1960s was marked by popular protest for nuclear disarmament, the other (and related) burgeoning cause was that of environmentalism. Existing conservation-bodies grew much larger. The membership of the Royal Society for the Protection of Birds (RSPB) rose from 10,500 in 1960 to 56,000 in June 1970, with 7,500 members joining in the first 6 months of ECY. There were now 38 county naturalists' trusts in England and Wales, and a Scottish Wildlife Trust. There were new environmental groups, with much broader agendas. From a membership of less than 1,000 in 1971, Friends of the Earth (FOE) became a major force in '1970s pressure-group environmentalism'. It claimed by the 1980s to have some 200 active local groups and 27,000 supporters (Lowe and Goyder 1983). Such dramatic growth reflected not only the success of ECY in catching the public imagination but how, as material living-standards rose, there was opportunity to press for improvements beyond those of the immediate home and workplace. Where waste and pollution had always been something to grumble about, like the weather, there was now perhaps scope to do something about them. The dumping of non-returnable bottles on the doorstep of Schweppes, the soft-drinks manufacturer, in 1971, did more than anything else to establish FOE in terms of attracting media support. Although almost all its immediate objectives failed, that failure gave fledgling organisations even more of a moral edge, as they pitted their scant resources against the Goliaths of business and government. An obvious difficulty was that of holding media attention and therefore of judging how radical to become. Whilst it was FOE policy to remain within the law, the further international pressure-group, Greenpeace, had no such inhibition (Lamb 1996).

The controversy as to the optimal size of the seal colonies around the British coasts provides insight into the potential weight of such bodies in the 1970s. The Grey seal was the first mammal to be conserved under modern legislation. The Act of 1914, as amended in 1932, introduced a close season, so as to protect the seal pups unable to take to the water and therefore escape to comparative safety (Sheail 1976a, pp. 37–9; and 1998, pp. 76–82). By the late 1960s, it was the Common seal that was seriously threatened, largely as a result of the high prices offered for pup skins and persecution by fishermen. The Conservation of Seals Act of 1970 sought to strike a balance between a viable breeding population and one that would cause least damage to fisheries. Although a close season was introduced, Fisheries Ministers were given discretionary powers to extend protection to the whole year, and to issue licences to kill seals in the close season, for research purposes, conservation, or the protection of fisheries (Bonner 1989).

There had always been dispute as to the exact status of seal populations. The 1970 Act created the important precedent of requiring ministers to seek the scientific advice and, more specifically, guidance as to the management of populations from the Natural Environment Research Council (NERC). A Sea Mammals Research Unit (SMRU) was established to devise methods of estimating more accurately the size and distribution, and the fecundity and mortality, of populations and the reasons for any changes discerned. It was also to develop mathematical models which might help predict the effects of different management policies. The number of Grey seals was estimated by 1979 to be rising by 7 per cent per year. That of the Outer Hebrides had doubled since records were first kept in the early 1960s. Even on Orkney, where an annual crop of pups continued to be taken, the stock size had risen by a quarter. The Department of Agriculture and Fisheries for Scotland (DAFS) used such data as evidence of the serious threat of the Grey seal to the fishing industry. The Nature Conservancy Council (NCC) was concerned as to the impact of the higher breeding-densities on the habitats of the affected National Nature Reserves. The advice of NERC was accordingly sought in 1976 as to how the Grey seal population might be halved, namely reduced to that of the mid-1960s level of about 35,000. The SMRU believed it could be achieved over a 6-year period by an annual cull of 900 breeding-cows and their pups, and of 4,000 moulted pups. Both the need for a cull, and the strategy for attaining it, were approved by an inter-departmental Seals Advisory Committee under the Chairmanship of the Earl of Cranbrook (the President of the Mammal Society), which reported directly to the Secretary of State for Scotland. Weather and other factors prevented more than 394 cows and 286 pups being killed in the Hebrides in 1977 (Lister-Kaye 1979).

The second year's cull was abandoned after only three months, in October 1978. A press statement explained how the Secretary of State, Bruce Millan, had taken the decision in response to 'widespread public concern', so that everyone could have 'the opportunity to study the scientific evidence' on which the decision to extend the cull had been taken. His decision followed a protest petition of 42,000 signatures, including those of 1,500 Orcadians, a series of meetings with ministers and officials, and, perhaps most significantly from the viewpoint of the press and television, the sailing of the Greenpeace trawler, *Rainbow Warrior*, into the area where the cull was planned. Public opinion had already been aroused against seal hunting by the media coverage given to the brutal slaughter of north-west Atlantic Harp seals by Canadian and Norwegian sealers. A member of SMRU protested in the *New Scientist* that the Government had overridden its own scientific advisers, and had thereby abandoned any pretence of protecting fisheries from seal damage (Summers 1978). It was a further example of 'heavy sentimentalism' surrounding all things furry and helpless. The journal *Country Life* thought it high time that 'anthropomorphic emotions were forgotten, and practical conservation measures allowed to take over'.

And yet, although opponents of the seal cull heavily exploited public sentiment, something more was at stake. A report compiled under the aegis of the Council for Nature, and published in May 1979, argued that killing operations during the close season should remain permanently suspended until one of two criteria was met: the cull should be required for the protection of the seal population itself, another endangered species, or the habitat; or there must be incontrovertible evidence of the seals causing serious damage to the fish which would otherwise be caught and sold by fishermen. In as much as there was no scientific evidence of either of those two alternative goals being met, the report claimed it was misleading for the industry to present the question as a straight choice between conservation seals and the sacrifice of jobs and prosperity in the industry. Whilst the conservation bodies accepted that seals ate fish, and that the amount of fish eaten could be reasonably estimated from the energy requirements of the individual seal, there was still no evidence of what proportion of that seal food could have been commercially exploited. Most of the white fish landed in the UK were caught more than 10 miles from the coast. There was virtually no evidence of seals feeding that far out to sea.

The voluntary bodies argued that there was an important principle at stake. If DAFS were allowed to reduce the world population of the Grey seal by a quarter or more, a precedent would have been set for further arbitrary decisions, where some political gesture was required. Far from playing it down, the opposition to the seal cull highlighted the urgent need for closer scientific investigation. Instead of using scientists merely to facilitate the imposition of arbitrary decisions, greater use should be made of their work in developing the strategies required for protecting the rapidly diminishing resources of the land and sea from over-exploitation.

Agricultural Improvement

An all-party manifesto of August 1943 warned the Government that agriculturalists feared a return to the depressed farming conditions that existed after the First World War. The Cabinet agreed to an extension of price guarantees until at least 1947. In the words of the official historian, detailed discussions were held and 'a solid foundation' had been established by the end of 1944, on which 'the whole of the post-war agricultural policy was built' (Murray 1955). Under their respective Agriculture Acts, the Minister of Agriculture and the Scottish Secretary were empowered to guarantee price support for the farming industry in return for 'some guarantee of reasonable efficiency'.

As the Ministry's expert advisers explained, the strategy recognised that

> without soil and climate the only way to maintain the fertility and productivity of the land, and to ensure healthy crops and livestock, is by systems of mixed farming with a proper balance between arable and grass, crops and livestock, over as wide an area of our agricultural land as possible. (PRO, MAF 53, 162)

So as to attain that balance, an agricultural partnership was to be formed – a close and pervasive pattern of co-operation between government and the landed and farming interests. As well as through such mechanisms as an annual economic review (Winter 1996), farmers must be both encouraged and helped to emulate the best (PD, Commons, 432, 623–43). A National Agricultural Advisory Service had been established in 1944 for the purpose of 'giving free of charge technical advice and instruction, whether practical or scientific, on agricultural matters'. Perhaps most crucially in the confidence-building required of an industry fearful of a return to pre-war conditions, the Government indicated in its response to the first major post-war economic crisis that agricultural output, already one-quarter higher than before the war, was to be raised by a further one-fifth (Winegarten and Acland-Hood 1978).

Romney Marsh, the promontory behind Dungeness on the Kent–Sussex coast, was one of the areas most likely to indicate whether the goals set for agriculture could be met through partnership, as opposed to more direct State intervention. So as to prevent the world-famous flock of Romney sheep falling into enemy hands in the event of an invasion, nearly 40 per cent of the flock was evacuated in 1940. The area under tillage rose from 9 per cent in 1939 to 37 per cent by 1944. Whatever the initial doubts, it was soon clear that the owners and occupiers of the Marsh could sustain a mixed-farming economy. The annual reports of the County Agricultural Organisers testified to how the old 'prejudice against the ploughing up of old pasture has been largely broken down and the productivity of new grass appreciated' (PRO, MAF 142, 29). The fenland model became increasingly relevant, as the Agricultural Census reflected both a further decline in the sheep population and substantial rise in the area of tillage. The greatest risk was of the potato and root harvests on the newly ploughed land being badly delayed by a wet autumn. As an insurance against such weather, tile-drains were installed and ditches improved. The success achieved encouraged others to follow. The Internal Drainage Boards (largely made up of such farmers) responded with further improvements to the arterial system (Sheail and Mountford 1984).

Well-drained land warmed up more quickly in spring, could be cultivated earlier and generally grew better crops. Good drainage encouraged root development and thereby reduced damage during drought. Grants toward half the cost of approved schemes for under-drainage and ditching were first made in 1940 and were eventually put on a permanent, peacetime basis under the Agriculture (Miscellaneous Provisions) Act of 1954. About two-thirds of Romney Marsh were affected by a scheme by 1980. Because of the way the Ministry compiled its records, five periods of activity could be distinguished. The decade of greatest activity was the 1960s, when 44 per cent of the drained area was affected, compared with about 30 per cent in the 1970s and about 20 per cent in the 1950s. Over half the grants made in the 1970s occurred between 1970 and 1973, at a time when there was such interest in land as a source of investment that rents in the Romney Marsh almost doubled. Many blocks of land previously used for grazing were acquired by new owners. In as much as the Romney Marsh was now regarded as having some of the best arable land in Britain, there was little difficulty in finding such farmers with experience of bringing land into cultivation.

At a conference convened at the Royal Society of London in 1976, on the theme of 'agricultural efficiency', there was celebration of the 'very successful farming revolution' that had taken place since 1940. Farmers had achieved a more rapid transformation of agriculture than had ever been accomplished. Where home-farming had provided less than half the temperate food requirements of a smaller human and livestock population before the war, it now met over two-thirds of needs from a smaller land-area. Whilst the most visible evidence of change was the replacement of horses and, in many instances, humans, by machinery, there were equally important advances in the genetic improvement of crops and livestock, the efficacy of fertilisers and pesticides, and general efficiency of farming systems. Perhaps most significantly, farmers were now impatient for the next round of innovation, knowing that their competitive edge in the markets depended on such research and development (Cooke, Pirie and Bell 1977).

There was no lack of encouragement from the Government. In their White Paper *Food from our Own Resources*, published in April 1975, agriculture ministers warned of both shortages and higher prices on the world's food-markets. Not only did agricultural expansion provide a partial insurance, but further investment was fully justified by the industry's own record of increasing efficiency. Everything should be done to sustain the average growth rate since 1950, namely of 2.5 per cent per annum. Although such expansion might be constrained by moves to preserve the traditional appearance of the countryside, ministers believed such anxieties were misplaced. The continuing improvement of grazing and hill land should contribute to their appearance, as well as productivity. The Government was confident such higher output could be reconciled with its commitment to proper safeguards for the environment (PP 1974–75).

A far less sanguine view was taken by the Countryside Commission. A series of studies had been commissioned since 1972, under the title *New Agricultural Landscapes*. Undertaken by two consultants, Richard Westmacott and Tom Worthington, they had revealed, in the words of the Commission's Chairman, 'fresh and disturbing facts about the nature and scale of changes taking place'. Over 10,000 miles of hedgerows were being removed each year. Up to 90 per cent of field-boundary trees, and more than half the hedges, had been lost from parts of the Eastern Counties in the 25 years up to 1972. Although Dutch Elm disease had taken a heavy toll, most trees had been deliberately removed as part of the enlargement of fields required to accommodate modern cereal farming machinery. On average, only one sapling had been planted for every two to three mature trees felled (Countryside Commission 1974).

In a general review of drainage activity, Brian Trafford, the Head of the Ministry of Agriculture's Field Drainage Experimental Unit, argued that such improvements made little impact on the environment. Most were designed to improve existing farmland, rather than to reclaim new areas for farming (Trafford 1978). Conservationists argued that whilst the area of 'farmed countryside' had grown no larger, the impact of cultivation, and the more intensive forms of grassland management, was now on so great a scale as to leave few, if any, refugia for wild plant and animal life. Not only were the changes very extensive, but their impact might be as permanent as any building development. Such wider reference highlighted the weaknesses of statutory town and country planning. The powers vested in the National Parks and Access to the Countryside Act had assumed the effects of agriculture would be benign. Whilst the Nature Conservancy was required to notify the planning authorities of areas scheduled as Sites of Special Scientific Interest, those authorities had no powers to prevent changes taking place in the agricultural use and management of the land (Sheail 1998, pp. 195–224).

Although the scale of Exmoor's problems was small in national terms, the national park came to exemplify the ambiguities and confusion that caused the writers Ann and Malcolm MacEwen to ask whether such designation was more a matter of cosmetics than of conservation (MacEwen and MacEwen 1982). The Exmoor National Park Committee, with members nominated by the county councils and Minister, felt something of 'a pig in the middle' between agricultural and conservation interests. At its instigation, a map showing the 'Critical Amenity Area' was drawn up in 1967, and 'a gentleman's agreement' reached, whereby farmers would give six months' notice of any intention to plough up the moorland. The intention was to use such time to negotiate management agreements, with compensation paid for any losses arising from the preservation of the moorland. In practice, the Committee found itself with little choice but to concede further ploughing. It had neither the statutory means to prevent such ploughing nor the resources to pay the very large sums that would be demanded in compensation. To do so would merely encourage further proposals for destroying the moorland. Not only were farmers free to plough whenever they chose, but up to half their costs would be met by grant aid from the Ministry of Agriculture, which claimed it was obliged to make such payments, even in the Critical Amenity Area.

Such evidence of a conflict between the policies of the DOE and Agriculture Departments caused the respective ministers to take the exceptional step of inviting Lord Porchester (a landowner and farmer, Chairman of the Hampshire County Council, and former member of the Nature Conservancy and Sports Council) to carry out an informal inquiry, by way of visits and private research. He found the character of Exmoor to be threatened by both too little, as well as too much, farming. The fact that the heather moors called for careful regulation of stocking densities, and cutting back of gorse and bracken, emphasised the importance of retaining the goodwill of the farming community. There was however a world of difference between providing grant aid for such purposes of sustaining both the farming community and character of the landscape, and of making it automatically available for ploughing any, and every, part of the national park. Although farmers might argue 'the more food we grow, the less food we (as a nation) import', that derived from the Critical Amenity Area was minuscule in terms of national output, whereas Exmoor was 'exceptional in the variety of scenery to be found within its compact area' (Department of the Environment 1977).

With so comparatively little moorland at risk, Lord Porchester rejected both the use of compulsory purchase powers and the extension of statutory planning to cover moorland reclamation. They would unnecessarily risk the goodwill of farming interests. Of the 41,000 acres of moorland within the Critical Amenity Area, Lord Porchester found some 12,000 acres were already owned by local authorities and the National Trust. A further 8,000 acres were registered as common land. Of the remainder, only 12,500 acres were physically improvable and, even here, two of the larger landowners had indicated their wish to retain the moorland. It would be sufficient, Lord Porchester believed, for the National Park Committee to be given 'back-up powers', namely the authority to issue a moorland conservation order, which would 'prevent such operations and practices as are likely to alter the vegetation or the general character of moorland to any material degree'. In the event of an order being invoked, the farmer would receive a once-and-for-all payment in compensation for 'the depreciation in the value of his land brought about by the imposition of the restrictions'.

The further Countryside Bill of January 1979 set the important precedent of being sponsored by both the Secretary of State for the Environment and the Minister of Agriculture. Although assuming the national park and local planning authorities would make the fullest use of voluntary procedures, they were empowered, as a final resort, to issue moorland conservation orders. There were enabling powers for the orders to be made outside Exmoor. The National Farmers' Union was particularly critical of the substitution of once-for-all compensation for annual payments. The Devon and Cornwall branch threatened to withdraw its 'voluntary cooperation and goodwill towards the National Parks Authority'. In parliament, the Conservative Opposition also challenged the basic conclusions of the Porchester report. An amendment to the Bill was tabled, urging the House of Commons to refuse a Second Reading to a Bill 'which focuses attention on a limited area, where provisions are adequate to deal with existing problems'. The Opposition Spokesman on the Environment warned that the 'whole gamut of bureaucratic legalistic intervention' would be unleashed 'on a handful of farmers in the corner of Exmoor'. Although the amendment was defeated, the Bill's fate was sealed by the Dissolution of Parliament and refusal of the Conservative Opposition to allow it to pass 'on the nod' (PD, Commons, 961, 1283–92).

The new Conservative Government issued in October 1979 a Consultation Paper, reaffirming the need to protect the characteristic moorland of Exmoor as a matter of national concern. It promised a new Countryside Bill, whereby any owner or occupier contemplating any kind of operation likely to affect the character or appearance of moorland, would be obliged to give the park authority 12 months' notice. In as much as such persons were likely to forgo agricultural improvement in return for reasonable compensation, the case for back-up powers was rejected. In taking such a view, the Government was encouraged by local farmers who had, since the Porchester report, shown much greater interest in concluding such management agreements. The conservation bodies attributed such eagerness more to a desire to fend off the threat of controls than to any sudden conversion to the protection of amenity and wildlife. The Consultation Paper conceded that, should its faith in the farming community not be realised, the Government was prepared to reconsider the position. Such a threat, occupying only one sentence in a Paper otherwise full of confidence, was poor comfort to the conservation bodies. How many more landscapes and wildlife communities had to be sacrificed before a national park was given some primacy over agriculture? At what point would the growing number of conservationists prevail over the small minority who actually owned and farmed the land? Rather than a piecemeal approach, as embodied in the concept of moorland conservation orders, the answer was to come through an all-encompassing formula for the countryside, as embodied by the Wildlife and Countryside Act of 1981 (Cox, Lowe and Winter 1986).

Arresting 'the Engine of Destruction'

It was both the extent and the rapidity of 'modernisation' that caused farming to replace urban development as the greatest threat to the appearance, wildlife and recreational value of the countryside. Although it contributed only about 2.5 per cent of the UK gross domestic product in 1976 (roughly the equivalent of that of the electrical engineering industry), farming was the foremost rural industry, in terms of both the proportion of land occupied and the unfettered manner in which it pursued its goals.

Within a month of taking office, the Conservative Government announced its intention of introducing what became the Wildlife and Countryside Bill. The Bill represented a major step forward, in the sense of emphasising how it sought to avoid favouring any group at the expense of another. But where it had been perceived by ministers as 'a nice, quiet little Bill', its passage proved long and difficult. There were over 200 hours of debate. More than a thousand amendments were tabled, and many significant changes made. The underlying theme of the debate, as it affected nature conservation and the amenity of the countryside, was the balance between the needs of agriculture and those of the natural environment. During the Committee Stage, Lord Sandford (the Parliamentary Under-Secretary for the Environment) recalled how Lord Porchester had been confronted by two irreconcilable positions. Officers of the Agricultural Development Advisory Service (ADAS) believed it was their duty to support every application for a viable agricultural scheme. The National Park Committee believed there should be some form of statutory control over the more damaging activities of farmers. In these circumstances, Lord Porchester had no alternative but to recommend moorland conservation orders (PD, Lords, 417, 464–66, and 424, 509–11).

As Lord Sandford pointed out, an alternative approach had

become possible. The mechanisms for grant aid to such areas as Exmoor had been subsumed by the European Directive on Less Favoured Areas, following the UK's adoption of that Directive in 1975. The Countryside Commission wrote to Roy Jenkins, the President of the European Commission. In his reply of December 1977, Jenkins indicated that it had never been the intention of that Directive to require projects to be carried out where they would have an undesirable effect on the countryside. To that extent, the Minister had discretion as to where grant aid might be given. In accepting that interpretation, Lord Sandford said that whilst ministers might continue to speak of farmers operating in 'a wholly voluntary system', they were so dependent on grant aid in such areas as Exmoor that the Ministry could in practice force them to follow any guidelines laid down. In short, there was now a mechanism that removed any need for the negative statutory-device as a moorland conservation order (PD, Lords, 417, 464–66). If the Minister of Agriculture decided, after consultation with the Secretary of State for the Environment, that an application should be refused for grant aid towards a farm-improvement scheme, the fresh powers introduced by the new Bill would require the National Park Committee or the Nature Conservancy Council (in the case of Sites of Special Scientific Interest) to offer a management agreement within guidelines laid down by Ministers (PD, 1980–81, Commons Standing Committee D, Wildlife and Countryside Bill, 509–27, and Lords 424, 513–17). A Lords Amendment, whereby the cost of such compensation would be met by the agriculture budget, as opposed to the conservation bodies, was defeated by the narrow margin of 59 to 57 votes. The Nature Conservancy Council (NCC) welcomed such an obligation, in the sense of removing the uncertainty that had previously bedevilled negotiations with farmers. It placed a firm commitment on the Government to provide the necessary funding (PD, Lords, 424, 498–518). The Bill received the Royal Assent in October 1981.

The extraordinary impact of Marion Shoard's book, *The Theft of the Countryside*, reflected both her skills as a polemicist and a sense that the dominance of farming in rural affairs was beginning to slip. The book described how the unique character of the English countryside was being destroyed by 'a far-reaching agricultural revolution'. It called for the extension of statutory planning to cover the agricultural use and management of land. A farmer seeking to destroy a wood would have to seek planning permission in the same way as a householder wanting to extend a house. Rather than farmers deciding the destiny of the countryside, there should be regional countryside planning authorities, representative of the whole community (Shoard 1980). Not only was there abundant visual evidence of large-scale changes occurring on agricultural land, as a result of modern farming operations, but the Nature Conservancy Council had, at long last, begun to assemble quantitative data as to the scale of impact on wildlife. A summary outline, under the title *Nature Conservation in Britain*, illustrated the minimal contribution to wildlife habitats made by afforestation, the creation of reservoirs, and adaptation of abandoned mineral workings and amenity tree-planting, compared with the widespread and sometimes catastrophic losses of existing habitat. Agricultural intensification had damaged or destroyed the wildlife interest of 97 per cent of Lowland neutral grasslands since the war (Nature Conservancy Council 1984). Research commissioned from the NERC Institute of Terrestrial Ecology (the successor body to the research branch of the Nature Conservancy) found evidence of species decline in every 'wetland' area. In the Idle/Misson Levels, on the Lincolnshire/Nottinghamshire/Yorkshire border, where most of the pastureland had been ploughed up following a major arterial scheme, only 8 species had shown signs of increasing their range and level of abundance, compared with 122 species that had become less common since the 1880s. Even in the Somerset Levels and Moors, where habitat changes had been less extensive, 101 species had undergone a decline – a marked decline in 43 cases (Wells and Sheail 1988).

As on Exmoor, local conflict forced the pace of policy-making. Angry farmers were televised burning effigies of leading figures in the NCC and RSPB, following the decision of the NCC to schedule the West Sedgemoor area of the Somerset Levels as a Site of Special Scientific Interest (SSSI), under the Wildlife and Countryside Act. Tom King, the Secretary of State for the Environment, was the Member of Parliament for the nearby constituency of Bridgwater. At a highly charged meeting on West Sedgemoor in March 1983 he emphasised how 'we are right in the front line of battle to preserve the voluntary approach to conservation'. As well as giving assurance of compensation for any loss of capital value arising from the scheduling of the land, King announced that one of the Ministry of Agriculture's specialist staff would be seconded to the NCC to help negotiate the necessary management agreements. It enabled all parties to claim some measure of success. Farmers had obtained concessions and assurances that went beyond the terms of the Act. The NCC had nevertheless scheduled 10 SSSIs by 1990 which, along with the Shapwick Heath National Nature Reserve, covered 6,900 hectares (over 17,000 acres) of the Somerset Levels and Moors.

With the workability of voluntary management agreements under such fierce challenge, the Halvergate Marshes of the Norfolk Broads became the most contested area in the early 1980s. A leader in *The Times* of 17 March 1984 described them as 'the Flanders of the great war between farming interests and the objectives of nature conservation', namely the Countryside Commission and the Broads Authority, a body appointed in 1978 'to conserve and enhance the natural beauty and amenity' of Broadland. Considerable publicity was given to the fact that more than a thousand acres (400 hectares) had already been ploughed in the two years since the 1981 Act. As Lords Buxton and Onslow warned, in a letter to *The Times* of 18 February 1984, any prospect of saving some of the remaining 5,000 acres (2,000 hectares) would depend on the taxpayer meeting an estimated annual cost of £1 million in compensation. Not only was it a huge sum, but few of the hundred farmers stood to benefit. Over half of them occupied livestock-holdings of less than 25 acres (10 hectares) each. Their incomes would decline as the productivity of the pastures deteriorated following the drainage improvements demanded by the few large farmers bent on large-scale cultivation. The higher drainage rates would make it even more difficult for stock-holders to remain in farming (Sheail 1998, pp. 232–4).

The Lower Bure Internal Drainage Board (IDB) brought matters to a head by proposing a three-part drainage scheme, costing £2.33 million. Although the Ministry refused grant aid for increasing the capacity of the existing pumps, there remained the question of compensating those farmers who threatened to plough up the pastures that remained. One-third of the budget of the Broads Authority was already absorbed by such payments. Ministers agreed in March 1984 to look for alternative financing, on the condition that farmers agreed to suspend operations. There was sufficient assurance for the Minister of State for the Environment, William Waldegrave, to inform parliament on 4 April that 'Halvergate is safe for a year'. The Department was in consultation with the Ministry of Agriculture 'to see whether we can ensure its long-term security, which is of great importance' (PD, Commons, 57, 954).

It was now individual sites that drove public policy-making. A farmer dissatisfied with the promised level of compensation engaged a contractor to clear his ditches, prior to ploughing the grassland. *The Observer* newspaper published a full story on the morning that work was due to start. Local members of Friends of the Earth (FOE) sat peacefully on the contractor's equipment. The farmer resumed negotiation. In the same month, June 1984, negotiations broke down with another farmer, about to plough up marshes in the Yare valley. He had shown no interest in a management agreement. At the instigation of the CPRE, but formally through the Broads Authority, the Department of the Environment was pressed to issue an Article 4 Direction, namely the withdrawal of the rights of a landowner to execute development, otherwise permitted under a General Development Order arising from the relevant Town and Country Planning Act. The effect was to bring the intended drainage works under statutory planning control. It was a device previously used by local planning authorities to protect buildings of architectural or historic interest. Despite the alleged opposition of the Minister of Agriculture, the

Prime Minister, Margaret Thatcher, was reported to have insisted that such an exceptional step be taken. The Department of the Environment confirmed the Direction on 25 June, emphasising that it was designed to lead to a management agreement, rather than any imposition of planning controls on agriculture to achieve a conservation objective.

It was an uncertain victory. There was vindication of the CPRE's persistence in exploiting the potential of an Article 4 Direction. Volunteers and sympathisers of FOE might have antagonised local farmers but their intervention caught the imagination of both the local and national media. Writing of the environmental pressure-group, the leader writer in the *Eastern Daily Press* observed:

> not for them the compromise of Westminister . . . they have objectives which they pursue in the most direct and peaceful manner. A nation, sickened by political cant and public violence, warms to them and their methods.

It was however far from clear what had been achieved. Whilst an Article 4 Direction might be used against engineering works, it could not be applied to such acts as ploughing, re-seeding and fertiliser use. The Broads Authority rejected as impractical its extension to the whole of the Broads area. Not only was the Secretary of State unlikely to agree but, where given, the statutory procedures of an appeal and public inquiry came into play. There was simply no precedent as to how such questions as compensation for loss of development rights would be resolved (O'Riordan 1985).

The Countryside Commission had, in the meantime, offered the farming industry an alternative to the wider use of statutory planning. On the condition that the Ministry withheld grant aid to landowners for the conversion of grasslands to arable, the Commission offered to mount an experimental scheme, whereby the equivalent of a livestock support payment would be given over a 3-year period to any landowner in the Broads, whether or not arable conversion was being considered. Out of the offer, there emerged the Broads Grazing Marshes Conservation Scheme in May 1985, based on the alternative and more positive approach long canvassed by the Countryside Commission. Instead of compensation paid for profits forgone (as now enshrined in the 1981 Act), farmers would receive subsidies for voluntarily continuing with traditional stock-grazing methods. The Treasury consented to the Ministry and Countryside Commission offering an annual payment of £50 per acre over a 3-year period, in return for agreeing not to plough or otherwise destroy the marshes and following specified grazing-practices. Payments totalling nearly £420,000 were made in the first year to 102 applicants. Just over 90 per cent of the grasslands of the experimental area were protected by the Scheme or some other conservation designation. There had been no further ploughing.

The House of Commons' Environment Committee could not have wished for more striking demonstration as to the mechanisms available for site protection. Its report of January 1985 focused on the operation and effectiveness of the wildlife and landscape provisions of the Wildlife and Countryside Act. Among witnesses, only FOE pressed for the extension of town and country planning to cover major farming operations. Whilst the CPRE was sceptical as to whether a voluntary approach would suffice, there was almost universal acknowledgement among witnesses of 'a climate of change in the farming world'. The Environment Committee was greatly impressed by the remark of the Chairman of the Countryside Commission, Sir Derek Barber, that 'once you get farmers hooked on conservation there is a tendency for them to be hooked for life'. According to the Agricultural Development Advisory Service (ADAS), many were already pursuing practical measures, quite often at no cost to the public purse (PP 1984–85).

The Committee's proceedings were perhaps most significant for the evidence given by William Waldegrave, the Parliamentary Under-Secretary of State for the Environment. He claimed it would be both cumbersome and wasteful of resources to resort to statutory planning of the kind used for 'urban detailed planning'. The solution was 'to go a little further back into the grant-giving structure itself'. In Waldegrave's much-quoted words, the important thing for most of the countryside was to get the basic balance of agricultural and other land-use incentives right, so that the engine of destruction was removed.

As more explicitly expressed by the Environment Committee, it was illogical that the Ministry of Agriculture should offer financial inducements for something which another part of Government (the DOE and related bodies) had then to prevent happening. 'The whole jigsaw' would fall into place if such grant aid was redirected towards conservation objectives. Management agreements would become promotional, rather than simply preventative, mechanisms. Rather than being compensated for doing nothing, farmers would be further encouraged to embark on positive conservation.

Towards 'Creative Conservation'

In his foreword to the *Annual Reports* of the Countryside Commission, the Chairman, Sir Derek Barber, characterised the 1980s as the decade when it all happened. Changing agricultural policies created a vacuum in rural land-use, which began 'a warm embrace with rural conservation'. Where the Countryside Commission had endeavoured throughout the 1970s to raise awareness as to what was happening to the countryside, it was now essential 'to hammer out policy recommendations at a time when the old farming order was changing and public aspirations for countryside conservation and enjoyment were being more strongly felt and firmly stated'. There was 'a veritable cascade' of booklets published on agriculture, recreation and access, national parks, common land and forestry (Countryside Commission 1988 and 1991).

Whilst the agendas might be considerably more ambitious, there was also continuity in the sense that the Countryside Commission was special among government agencies. As Michael Dower, the newly appointed Director General, wrote, in the Commission's twenty-fifth *Annual Report*, it sought to promote 'a sustainable, multi-purpose countryside' – one that was 'beautiful, environmentally healthy, diverse, accessible and thriving'. The Countryside

Commission covered 'the broad sweep of human activity', and yet the realisation of that mission was entirely in the hands of others. It owned no land, and still had only some 230 staff. Its grant-in-aid of £19 million was largely disbursed as grants to other bodies. Most crucially it had powers to instigate surveys and experiments. The Demonstration Farms Project had enabled over 9,000 farmers and land managers to see at first hand how good conservation practice could be adopted by working farms, without detracting from the commercial viability. Through such practical example, and its conscious promotion of partnership with the farming and other rural industries, the Commission's outlook both anticipated and accorded well with the political philosophy of the time (Countryside Commission 1992).

But before moving into the 1990s, some further historical context is required. A response of the National Farmers' Union and Country Landowners' Association to the mounting criticism of the 1970s had been to publish a guide in November 1977, entitled *Caring for the Countryside*, which gave practical advice as to how members might combine food production with conservation (National Farmers' Union 1977). It drew on an initiative that had begun earlier, when a small group of farmers and conservationists had taken part in an exercise in July 1969 to discover what was practical by way of conservation, given different farming scenarios. The farm chosen for study was owned by the *Farmers Weekly*, near Tring in Hertfordshire. Participants were accommodated at the nearby Silsoe College. So as to retain the rapport established at what became known as 'the Silsoe exercise', a Farming and Wildlife Group (FWAG) was formed, and a part-time adviser appointed to organise further Silsoe-type exercises. Local FWAGs were formed so that by the mid-1980s there were 62 county FWAGs with over 30 full-time advisers (Moore 1987).

There was response too from the Minister of Agriculture, who asked his own Advisory Council for Agriculture and Horticulture, in May 1977, to review ways in which economic production might be reconciled with other national objectives, in 'the light of public interest in recreation and in conservation and amenity'. Its report of May 1978 warned of how 'only imaginative action, and adequate resources of manpower and money' could avert further conflict. Through its close working-relationship with farmers, and access to relevant expertise in the conservation bodies, the Agricultural Development Advisory Service (ADAS) was uniquely placed to demonstrate how appropriate management on the ground might simultaneously protect conservation interests and increase farm income (Advisory Council 1978).

Such insight and experience proved invaluable to ministers in seeking accommodation with conservationists during the debates on the Wildlife and Countryside Act of 1981. They had successfully fended off demands for an extension of statutory planning by offering such mechanisms as those available through the agricultural infrastructure in the form of grant aid and expert guidance from ADAS. It proved a double-edged sword, in the sense that it provided obvious pretext for conservationists to make further demands, whenever the scale and character of agricultural support was under consideration. Such a situation arose during debates on the Agriculture Bill of 1986, and the introduction of a charging policy for the advice given by ADAS staff to farmers. Conservationists protested that such a move would destroy the liaison that was beginning to develop with its officers. Ministers conceded that no charge should be made in respect of advice given on the conservation of natural beauty and wildlife, or 'any other agricultural activity or other enterprise or benefit to the rural economy' (PD, Commons, 87, 614–23).

Such admission by the Agriculture Ministers of their responsibility for protecting the wider environment prepared the way for further concession. In debate, John Gummer, the Minister of State for Agriculture, conceded 'the changed circumstances of the politics of plenty' called for a wider policy for the countryside (PD, Commons, 87, 695–7). Indeed, as food surpluses mounted under the European Common Agricultural Policy (CAP), economists joined conservationists in challenging the primacy given to food production through public subsidies (Hawarth and Rodgers 1992; Whitby 1996). An earlier enquiry by the House of Lords

Committee on the European Community had accused the Ministry of being altogether too negative in its approach to the drafting of a revised Regulation to reform farm structures. The draft was still 'too closely production-orientated' (PP 1983–84). In replying to the Committee's criticisms, Lord Belstead (the Minister of State for Agriculture) insisted that the Government could not act in isolation from the rest of Europe. He nevertheless undertook to press for powers that would 'enable us in environmentally sensitive areas to encourage farming practices which are consonant with conservation' (PD, Lords, 455, 88–93).

It fell to the Minister, Michael Jopling, and officials to explain to their counterparts in Brussels the concept of making payments to farmers to farm below the maximum. Whilst the experiment under way in the Halvergate Marshes had persuaded the Ministry as to the practicality of achieving that end, such explanation was typically met with incomprehension and apathy in Brussels (Smith 1989). Member-states and the Commission asserted it would be legally impossible to accommodate conservation requirements within the amended regulations covering agricultural structures. Perseverance nevertheless paid off. Much of the UK draft text became the basis of Article 19 of EC Regulation 979/85, which permitted member-states to make payments to farmers for the provision of 'public goods'. A further Regulation allowed an element of EC funding.

The way was clear for the Agriculture Act of 1986 to confer powers on the Agriculture Ministers to channel agricultural moneys for the first time to conservation. Following consultation with the Countryside Commission and NCC, as required by the Act, Ministers were empowered to identify and administer a scheme for the Environmentally Sensitive Areas (ESAs), modelled on the pilot scheme in the Broads. Where designations had previously drawn a distinction between amenity, recreational, wildlife and historic value of features, the ESAs treated them as a unified whole, under the all-encompassing concept of 'national environmental significance'. Entirely voluntary in concept, ESA payments were offered to farmers 'who followed farming practices which respect the environmental needs' of those areas where 'uncontrolled agricultural change would put at risk our rural heritage' (PD, 1985–86, Commons, Standing Committee B, Agriculture Bill, 6–7).

The impasse had been broken in terms of creating a sense of partnership between agriculture and that 'third force' in the countryside, namely the protection of amenity and wildlife, and promotion of outdoor recreation. In a very short space of time, farming interests became among the most innovative in perceiving a wider role for themselves in the countryside (Sheail 1995d). In a speech to the Country Landowners' Association in July 1994, its President anticipated the collapse of the £29 billion a year CAP following the entry of East European countries into the Union, as well as the implementation of the GATT settlement of 1993. He called for a cheaper, 'greener' farm policy. Prices should be allowed to fall to lower world-market levels, while farmers should receive subsidies for such public benefits as wildlife conservation and public-access agreements (*Daily Telegraph*, 30 July 1994).

It could not be assumed that conservation benefits would flow automatically from any reduction in intensive farming. There had to be both encouragement and guidance. Thus, the Countryside Commission introduced, on an experimental basis, a Countryside Premium Scheme, whereby those farmers in receipt of payments under the Ministry's 'Set-aside' basic scheme could receive additional grants for undertaking conservation works and providing public access. The Commission was successful in obtaining funds, totalling £25 million over 3 years, for a Countryside Stewardship Scheme. Launched jointly by the Secretary of State for the Environment and Minister of Agriculture in June 1991, the scheme was initially targeted at farmers either conserving or restoring one of five types of English landscape. There were a third more applications than moneys available. Additional funds enabled 900 contracts to be let in the first year, covering nearly 300,000 hectares. The Commission was particularly encouraged by some 22 per cent of the agreed area including provision for public access (Countryside Commission 1993).

There was movement too in the provision of new woodland and

forests for recreational purposes. The Countryside Commission had endeavoured since the early 1980s to publish a policy statement on forestry in the countryside. It had been thwarted by acrimony arising from the substantial increase in the commercial planting of conifers by the private sector. By the mid-1980s, the prospect of food surpluses raised the possibility of woods and forests becoming an alternative use of land, where the visual, wildlife and recreational benefits of tree planting might be set alongside commercial timber-production. The policy statement, *Forestry in the Countryside*, was published in December 1987. As a means of illustrating how a renewed national commitment to multi-purpose forestry might be achieved, the last two pages of the booklet briefly outlined two proposals. They rapidly became the best remembered part of the whole policy statement. The first was a proposal that 'urban fringe forests should be established close to, and around, some of the major conurbations', taking Cannock Chase and Epping Forest as models. The second proposal recalled how the New Forest, with its blend of wooded areas, open heathland and villages, gave pleasure to millions of visitors each year. A new forest located in the East Midlands could provide both a major recreational and tourism resource, and a means of enhancing the landscape and wildlife interest. It would make a significant contribution to the national timber supply (Countryside Commission 1987).

The concept of a new Forest had been under active consideration since December 1986 when, as a characteristic first step in the Countryside Commission's development of an experimental programme, the head of its Conservation Branch drafted a series of questions. Could such a Forest evolve under private ownership? Would a new body be required to provide overall direction and to raise funds? How might the Forest capture and hold public interest? At a brainstorming meeting of the Commission's officers in late January 1987 there was consensus that a feasibility study should be made of establishing a public open-space of similar size to the New Forest (of some 40,000–50,000 hectares), largely under trees, near a major centre of population. Although massive in terms of the English countryside, the venture would fail unless highly ambitious. Scale was needed to accommodate the mix of topography and woodland types that would capture public and corporate imagination from the outset. Although planting and management regimes would be tailored to allow large-scale open access, it was essential that agriculture should continue, and that commercial timber-production should develop, as a source of funding in the longer term (Sheail 1997c).

With hindsight, a second stage was reached in confidence-building within the Commission, with the decision to make informal soundings of persons with 'considerable understanding of forestry'. Roderic M. Hewitt, the recently retired Conservator for the Forestry Commission in the East of England, was commissioned to make a 6-week assessment of its feasibility. His report of October 1987 suggested there might be social and financial benefits from using the Forest concept as a means of rehabilitating derelict land. News of Hewitt's enquiries prompted requests for interviews from radio and television. The Director of Planning for Nottinghamshire County Council pressed for a meeting to discuss a joint experiment in 'landscape restructuring', centred on Sherwood Forest. A letter from the Director of Planning for the Leicestershire County Council in September 1987 described the Council's own Countryside Action Programme and, in particular, the concept of a Leicestershire Forest. Finance and staff had already been committed to an integrated package of environmental measures, required to 'refashion' north-west Leicestershire. As well as improving the management of Bradgate Park and other areas of Charnwood Forest, that were under considerable pressure, the Programme offered 'a dramatic opportunity to achieve regeneration' in the close-by abandoned Leicestershire coalfield.

A third stage in confidence-building had been reached. At their meeting of December 1987, the Countryside Commissioners formally approved the reference to a new East Midlands Forest in the policy statement *Forestry in the Countryside* (published that month), and the commissioning of a more formal feasibility study. A consortium of landscape consultants, economists and planners was appointed in October 1988. Its report hailed the Forest as a creative opportunity to establish a new landscape which future generations will come to love and revere, as they do other great national landscapes, such as the Lake District and the New Forest.

At a time when new landscapes were being created, whether by design or chance, or a combination of both, in many parts of the country, the new Forest would act as a model in showing how they might be both economically sound and multi-functional. The concept of landscape design, taken so much for granted in urban parks and New Towns, could now be used to rebuild a rich rural landscape in the Midlands. Not only might it help reverse the 'disastrous loss' in wildlife and finely textured landscapes, but the Forest would provide outstanding opportunities to apply the considerable research and practical experience gained in habitat creation.

The publication of the policy statement by the Countryside Commission, and appointment of consultants, had acted as a further fillip to local-authority interest. Preliminary discussions were held between the County Councils of Leicestershire, Derbyshire and Staffordshire, with a view to inviting the consultants to consider a Forest that might extend from the Charnwood Forest in north-west Leicestershire to the Needwood Forest in south Staffordshire, and include part of south Derbyshire.

A fourth stage had been reached. Sufficiently assured by the rationale set out in the consultants' report, and the obvious local-authority interest, that the Forest had the potential to become a 'flagship' policy for the Commission, the emphasis shifted towards that of instilling sufficient confidence in ministers that decisions could be taken as to its location, funding and administrative framework. As well as the publication of a consultative document and meetings with interest groups, a survey was commissioned from National Opinion Poll (NOP) before Christmas 1989 of 250 households in each of the 5 candidate areas shortlisted by the consultants, namely Arden and the Severn Valley in the West Midlands, Rockingham and Sherwood Forests in the East Midlands, and the Charnwood/Needwood Forest that encompassed parts of both. Ninety-four per cent of those questioned applauded the Forest concept. The submission of the Nottinghamshire County Council, *Sherwood Reborn – a New Midlands Forest*, comprised a 13-page booklet, setting out what it described as a 'compelling' case, based on 'its historical association, existing features, future potential, and the enthusiasm of the local population'. About half the population of England lived within two-and-a-half hours' driving-time of Sherwood. Its development would undoubtedly help reduce visitor pressure on the Peak District National Park. Charnwood/ Needwood emerged as the clear front-runner. It contained the highest proportion of industrially derelict land. There was greater enthusiasm for the developmental, as opposed to the protectionist, elements in the Forest concept. In terms of assertiveness, none surpassed the assertiveness of Leicestershire. In a telephone poll conducted by the *Leicester Mercury* over a 48-hour period, only 115 of the 10,513 respondents were hostile (Sheail 1997d).

The Countryside Commission had to display great sensitivity in publishing its recommendations to Government. It had to retain the enthusiasm and goodwill among the four candidate-areas that had 'lost'. The Commission also had to avoid giving the appearance of trying to bully ministers into funding the whole Forest project. Not only would such an impression be counterproductive, but the Commission itself wanted to maximise private-sector support. It was more a question of balance, and here, worryingly, the Government did not seem to realise that 'quite substantial public funds' would be needed if farmers and landowners were to be encouraged to plant trees, at a time when the timber market and the existing forms of grant aid for forestry made it, quite simply, 'a very poor investment'. The Commission believed there had to be 'a careful blend of mechanisms', the main one being an additional tier of incentives to encourage existing and future landowners to plant voluntarily new woodlands of a high environmental standard, with provision in some cases for additional public access. Such Exchequer support should be complemented by private-sector finance. Given the kudos attached to the Forest, an exceptional level of interest might be expected from philanthropic, corporate and marketing sponsorship. At a time when industry was consciously seeking a green image, significant funds might be expected from such utilities as the energy industry.

At their meeting of 4 October 1990, Commissioners formally agreed their preference for Charnwood/Needwood. At a press briefing to announce the decision, the Commission emphasised how its main consideration had been that of environmental improvement. The other concerns had been the need for countryside recreation, the potential for regional development, and the scope for farm diversification. Close account had been taken of the level of public support and the availability of land for planting. There was considerable publicity in the press, and on radio and television, the next day. The *Leicester Mercury* was published under a single banner-headline, 'Victory', together with a special supplement of five pages. Evidence of the success of the Countryside Commission and relevant local authorities, in terms of securing a political response to such raised public interest, came four days later, when the Secretary of State for the Environment, Chris Patten, used the platform of the Conservative Party conference to announce 'the first national forest', with the hope that another would soon follow. In his words,

> the Countryside Commission wants to plant a brand-new forest in the Midlands. It will be the first new forest planted in this country for over 200 years. It will bring together local authorities, farmers, businesses, voluntary groups and schools to take part in the venture. But it needs Government help. I can tell you today that we intend to provide that help. Work on that 150 square mile forest will therefore start next year.

On 4 November, Sir George Young, the Minister for Housing and Planning, joined the Commission's Chairman, Sir Derek Barber, local dignitaries and children in the ceremonial planting of the first spinney.

A fifth stage could now be discerned, namely that of retaining the enthusiasm of all interests, following the Government's acceptance in principle of the concept. The Commission's grant-in-aid was increased, so as to enable a business plan, or forest strategy, to be prepared. At 'a robust and lively meeting' in February 1991, the new Secretary of State, Michael Heseltine, expressed doubt as to whether farmers would put their land under trees. Not only had little interest been shown in existing forms of grant aid, but too much reliance should not be placed on further Exchequer grants filling the funding gap. Whilst agreeing that its Development Team, appointed in April 1991, should take the closest cognisance of private-sector support, the Commission emphasised how the implementation of the Forest concept depended on each element playing a mutually supportive role. That implied an assumption of much higher Exchequer planting incentives. Any indication that the Government was distancing itself from the earlier enthusiasm shown by the Secretary of State would have the most damaging effect on chances of securing the private and voluntary support.

Throughout this critical fifth stage of iteration, the maintenance of consensus was critically important. The Leicestershire County Council had immediately set aside £35,000 for practical work, including the purchase of land and planting of its existing properties. As well as promising expert assistance, the Director-General of the Forestry Commission spoke at the Annual Dinner of the Wood Processors' Association in December 1990 of how the proposed Midlands Forest had caught the public imagination. It was evidence of how the timber industry had to recognise the desire of the British public for hardwoods and, therefore, multi-purpose forestry. The draft strategy, published by the Development Team in the autumn of 1993, drew a large and almost wholly favourable response. Among the 1,200 individual responses, some 99 per cent endorsed the concept of the Forest. Even the misgivings of the various user-interest groups could be used to effect. The Country Landowners' Association warned, in a press release of April 1991, that nothing would be achieved by way of planting unless members were given the right encouragement in terms of grant aid. The Commission's hand was further strengthened by the firmness with which the Development Team rejected pressure from the Ramblers' Association that its draft strategy should be amended to accommodate large-scale land purchases and the imposition of permanent and definitive rights of access, wherever grant aid was given for planting.

It was not until July 1994 that the Secretary of State, John Gummer, announced his acceptance of the strategy plan. The opening words of his written reply to a Parliamentary Question caught the essence of what had ensured consensus throughout the eight years of discussion. The National Forest was

> an ambitious and imaginative environmental project to create a new forest in the heart of the country, in an area where much of the land has been despoiled by mineral working. (PD, Commons, 246, 501–2)

It was an excellent example of sustainable development, where environmental improvement brought economic regeneration. The recent consultation exercise had confirmed overwhelming local support. As with the Forest of Dean or the New Forest, this new Forest would provide a national asset to be enjoyed by future generations. A new 'lead' body would be created, as a company limited by guarantee. As the shareholders, the Secretary of State and Minister of Agriculture would appoint the chairman and directors. Through targeted project-funds and existing forms of grant aid, the intention was to establish new woodlands by voluntary means over about a third of the Forest area. Besides planting, the new company would encourage the development of leisure and recreation, rural enterprise, habitat protection, restoration of mineral workings, and community involvement (Wade, Sheail and Child 1998).

CHAPTER 7

Transport and The Environment

Introduction

In its report, *Transport and the Environment*, the Royal Commission on Environmental Pollution further highlighted the deep and widespread concern as to the continued increase in traffic. Road construction and the pollution caused by vehicles had become highly controversial issues (PP 1993-4). Some hundred years earlier, a balance had also been sought in the developing technologies and institutional arrangements required for capitalising on the undoubted benefits of modern communications, whilst minimising the unintended consequences for both the individual and society at large (Bagwell 1988).

A priority for the new pattern of local government in the late nineteenth century had been to confront the appalling state of the roads. Each of the county councils and county borough councils, established in 1888, was to be responsible for 'the main roads' of their administrative area, namely those that had ceased to be turnpikes after 1870 and those designated for their importance in linking urban centres, or as thoroughfares to and from railway stations. The borough councils, and urban and rural district councils created under a further Local Government Act of 1894, were responsible for the lesser roads. One of the more innovative counties was Nottinghamshire. The Chairman of the County Council, Lord Belper, convened a meeting of district councils in May 1895, so as to enable the County Surveyor, Edgar Purnell Hooley, to share the experience already acquired in repairing and maintaining the county's 350 miles of 'main road'. Hooley (1894) described them as 'a patchwork quilt . . . of multitudinous patterns in appearance'. Their neglect was on such a scale that it was not until 1898 that their condition had been sufficiently overhauled as to require only regular maintenance and therefore 'normal' expenditure. A new waterbound coating, covering and binding was required every five to nine years.

As the author of a textbook, *Modern Road Construction*, remarked, the road engineer was severely tested not only by the extraordinary variety of conditions encountered in Britain, but also by the new forms of transport. They called for an entirely new approach to road construction (Wood 1912). There were as many as 520 traction engines, or 'road destroyers' as Hooley called them, in Nottinghamshire by 1908. Where local carts, with 3-inch tyres, might weigh 1 ton, such engines might pull 20-ton loads on tyres of only three-quarters of an inch in width. Owners were asked not to use them in wet weather, when the roads were 'licking up'. Hooley identified 1896 as the year when 'a new form of road damager', the motor car, first appeared in the county. There were 296 cars and 347 motor cycles registered with his Office by April 1905. The chief concern of many witnesses to the Royal Commission on Motor Cars was the great nuisance caused by the larger clouds of dust, sometimes rising up to 40 feet in the air. Lord Montague of Beaulieu claimed dust was 'the cause of nine-tenths of the unpopularity of motor cars'. An estate agent described how the herbage along lengths of the London to Bath Road was absolutely useless, whether for feeding cattle or haymaking. It was impossible to sell or let some houses because of the dust nuisance. The Royal Commission concluded that the possibility of 'dustless' cars was a chimera. The solution was with dustless roads (PP 1906).

Hooley was one of the more successful innovators. As he wrote, everything depended on there being some medium, such as the road scrapings and finer material, that would knit the whole together. When torn or 'sucked' out by 'the scrubbing action of motor tyres', the entire road surface became a series of holes, some as deep as 4 inches. By allowing the wetness to penetrate the very foundations, the complete road might rapidly disintegrate after the first winter frost. Trials with simple tar-washing, and tar mixed with granite, slag and limestone by the roadside, proved disappointing. As Hooley went on to discover, if the slag were taken directly from the furnace, heating was not only absolute but

> by the judicious mixing of a toughening adjunct, a hard water-tight joint can be obtained, and a water-proofed road presented.

Hooley obtained a patent in April 1902 for the mixture, called tarmac to distinguish it from ordinary macadam (Earle 1974). The road from Radcliffe to the county border was the first rural highway to be constructed from machine-fixed tarmacadam. The *Newark Advertiser* of July 1904 reported how, after a year, its condition was 'as good today as when laid'. The County Surveyor for Buckinghamshire was one of the earliest to recognise the merits of the new material, surfacing a short length of the London to Bath road in March 1904. Although the grant aid provided by the Road Board, following the Development and Road Improvement Act of 1909, was small, the fact that it covered the difference in cost between the two types of treatment greatly accelerated adoption of the new surface. Almost half the main roads of Nottinghamshire had been resurfaced by the end of the Great War (Haller 1921).

As so often happens, the means by which one environmental problem was resolved might so easily instigate another. As the Road Board emphasised in its first report for 1910–11, its priority was 'the alleviation of the intolerable and injurious nuisance arising from mud and dust', and to find ways of reducing maintenance costs (PP 1911). There was, however, much consternation when, in 1910, a Kent farmer won a court action for compensation for the loss of a cow, which had allegedly died from drinking streamwater contaminated by tar washed from a nearby road. The first scientific appraisal of the newly tarred roads was made by W.J.A. Butterfield, a leading authority on the chemistry of tars and related compounds. In a paper to the Institution of Municipal and County Engineers in February 1912, he reported how experiments with gudgeon and dace had indicated fish deaths were unlikely if the coal tar was 'freed' from ammoniacal liquor and 'light' oils, the distilled tar contained less than 3 per cent by volume of crude tar acids, and the area of the tarred surface was no greater than one-twentieth of the total area of ground draining into the watercourse. A small sub-committee was appointed by the Roads Board to consider the matter further, with Butterfield as chemical adviser (Butterfield 1912; Sheail 1991b).

Alarmed by plans to spend £40 million on road surfacing with tar, the Freshwater Fishery Committee of the Board of Agriculture and Fisheries wrote in January 1919 drawing the Road Board's attention to the circumstantial evidence that road-tarring had a deleterious effect on neighbouring trout and other freshwater fisheries. Treasury approval was obtained for both Boards to share the costs of experiments. There remained concern however as to the legitimacy of using the Road Fund for 'interesting experiments on the influence of toxic solutions of known concentrations on stream life such as snails, shrimps, weeds, &c'. A Joint Sub Committee organised a series of laboratory trials, mainly on perch and trout, to help identify simple and speedy methods of characterising the toxicity of washings. Through the good offices of the County Surveyor for the Hampshire County Council (a member of the Joint Committee), an experimental station was established on a site between the Alresford to Winchester road and a chalk stream of the upper Itchen. It was transferred from the Ministry of Transport (as the Road Board had become) to the Fisheries Department of the Ministry of Agriculture and Fisheries in March 1922 (PRO, MT 39, 21 and MAF 41, 308). The washings from the waterbound granite surface of the old road had no significant effect on the trout kept in the specially excavated ponds. The fish, together with shrimps and sticklebacks, died within 15 minutes of the first rain-washings from a length of newly tarred road in August 1921. Whilst no further harm was reported, the restocked fish were killed in the following winter by the higher concentrations of tar derived from the break-up of the worn road surface (Ministry of Transport *et al.* 1922).

The prospect of the county councils taking over roughly two-thirds of the roads managed by the district councils in the early 1930s, and the likelihood that an even greater proportion of them being tarred, meant there was added urgency to finding a formulation of tar that could be used safely near watercourses. The only alternative was an asphaltic bitumen, derived from natural bitumen, which had to be imported. Two adjacent stretches of the Alresford–Winchester road were resurfaced in August 1931, one with a new dressing, Brotox, provided by the British Road Tar Association, and the other with bitumen, the cost being met by the Association. The fifteen trout of both ponds were still in excellent condition when the experiment was brought to an end in March 1933. The Fisheries Department pressed for a circular being sent to highway authorities, indicating that Brotox was excluded from the general ban on tar products. The Association made increasingly urgent telephone-calls. Although sympathetic, officials of the Ministry of Transport were concerned lest any new circular would amount to a free advertisement. Other associations, such as cement manufacturers, would demand official recognition for their equally unobjectionable products. Officials insisted the Association's own publicity would suffice (PRO, MAF 41, 308 and MT 39, 33).

The Alresford Experimental Station was the first inland fisheries research station in the UK. As with many later threats to the environment, it was never possible for the scientist to say exactly at what point fisheries might be endangered. Fish stocks could never be monitored so closely, or the effects of road-dressings distinguished exactly from those of other, possibly unsuspected, pollutants. The various parties were, however, in no doubt that such collaborative research had averted a serious clash between those promoting much-needed road improvements and the increasingly popular recreation of fishing. Whilst it was a further salutary lesson for the Ministry of Transport in the difficulties of securing standards of management through circulars and the manipulation of grant aid, officials also recognised that through a constructive response to allegations of pollution, and their use of expert committees and advisers, the road-improvement programme had proceeded with a minimum of disruption and adverse publicity.

'Mixed Blessing'

The first book to survey the general impact of the motor vehicle was published by Colin D. Buchanan in 1958. With the title *Mixed Blessing*, the book traced the way the motor vehicle had come to penetrate and dominate social and economic life. The author's purpose was to dispel any idea of there being an easy solution to the problems created by the ever-increasing volume of motor traffic (Buchanan 1958).

Though the motor vehicle had considerably widened personal horizons, there had also been less attractive social and longer-term consequences. Urban expansion had previously been checked by the distance people had to walk or cycle to work. But with the introduction of the motor-omnibus and increasing access to a motor cycle or motor car from the 1920s, those living in the Victorian or Edwardian terraces of the town centre could begin to realise their dream of a home in the countryside – or at least more rural surroundings. In meeting that demand, there were economies to be made by building alongside the roads leading into towns. The house purchaser was attracted by both the convenience of the position and the savings made by the builder in terms of the ready provision of a road and access to utilities. On the deficit side, such ribbon development both separated the road from the countryside and blurred what many regarded as the essential discreteness of town from country. In a debate in the House of Lords, Lord Crawford, as President of the CPRE, stated:

> I do not want to reduce the number of cottages or bungalows up and down the country by one per cent. All I ask is that they shall be properly planned. (Sheail 1979b)

Whilst no one doubted the need to balance the interests of the individual with those of the community, the difficulty was in finding a formula that was politically acceptable and capable of being implemented immediately and effectively. The fact that local planning authorities were liable to claims for compensation from property-owners adversely affected by a scheme meant such schemes were weakest where they were most needed. Land values were likely to be highest on the main roads leading into towns. Nor was there a certain method of preserving the line of future roads. Where built, traffic movement was often seriously impeded by vehicles parked outside the houses springing up through ribbon development, or was interrupted by vehicles entering or leaving the many side streets constructed in a similarly uncontrolled manner. In as much as it was too late to widen the road, there was often no alternative but to build a by-pass (PRO, PREM 1, 167 and HLG 52, 572–3).

The unanimity among professional and voluntary bodies for some kind of regulation was unexpectedly strengthened from a highly emotive quarter. The purpose of the Road Traffic Act of 1934 was to arrest the rising number of road accidents by introducing speed limits in built-up areas, pedestrian crossings, and tests for new drivers (Plowden 1971). Since three-quarters of road accidents occurred along built-up lengths of road, the Oxford Preservation Trust argued that one of the most effective ways of reducing the slaughter was to end ribbon development. A report containing these views was forwarded to the Ministers of Health and Transport by another government minister, Viscount Halifax, with the comment, 'Try to do something about it!' (PRO, MT, 39, 613 and HLG 52, 573). Although the Ministry of Transport remained sceptical, the Trust had succeeded in stigmatising ribbon development as a cause of death and injury, especially among children. In the words of *The Times*, ribbon development presented a death-trap – where country lanes became 'an approach to the hospital and the cemetery' (PRO, PREM 1, 67 and MT 39, 613; Cambridge University Library, Kennet MSS 47, 1).

The King's Speech to parliament in November 1934 anticipated a Bill 'if time permits'. The Prime Minister, J. Ramsay MacDonald, virtually promised a Bill. An inter-departmental conference of officials of the Ministry of Health and Ministry of Transport found that it was beyond the realms of practical politics to grant absolute immunity from the risk of ribbon development. Not only would it be impossible to 'confiscate' every piece of land abutting a road, but there would be claims for compensation of 'an almost unlimited magnitude'. The risk could however be substantially reduced by a two-part Bill. The first part would generalise powers already taken by the Middlesex and Surrey County Councils, whereby a local planning authority could prohibit the provision of any access or erection of a building in front of an Amenity Building Line of 200 feet of a 'main thoroughfare'. A second part would seek to check the grosser forms of ribbon development by enabling the highway authorities to prohibit building within 80 feet of a road, without liability to claims for compensation. In as much as this would make it a Transport Bill, there was considerable embarrassment among officials when the Minister, Leslie Hore-Belisha, rejected the 'confiscatory' element, claiming it would turn an otherwise popular measure into one hotly contested by a section of the Government's supporters, in the last stages of office before a general election (PRO, HLG 52, 573 and MT 39, 205 and 612).

It required the intervention of Ramsay MacDonald to secure the Cabinet's agreement that an *ad hoc* Committee should be appointed under the Chairmanship of Sir Philip Cunliffe-Lister, the Colonial Secretary, to reconcile views. As Chancellor of the Exchequer, Neville Chamberlain, claimed the only way of reducing ribbon development was to impose a Road Improvement Line without liability for compensation. Viscount Hailsham, the Secretary of State for War, objected that, even if that were true, it was 'wholly unjustifiable to confiscate private property'. Cunliffe-Lister found it illogical that a highway authority should have to purchase the land on which to build the road, but escaped the costs of sterilising land up to 80 feet from the road. As Chairman, he insisted the overriding consideration should be to avoid any landowner incurring personal loss from the Bill. With that fundamental point agreed by all members of the Committee, attention turned to minimising the highway authorities' liability for such claims for compensation.

Arbitrators would be instructed to take full account of the benefits of the new road when assessing levels of compensation (PRO, CAB 23, 81, and CAB 27, 581). The Restriction of Ribbon Development Act received the Royal Assent in August 1935. Whilst the Town and Country Planning Act of 1947 removed the liability of compensation payments, the separation of the responsibilities of the highway authorities from town and country planning remained.

Nothing seemed to curb what Colin Buchanan called 'the public's lust' for greater personal mobility. Motor traffic doubled in the decade following the Second World War. There were so many private vehicles that even London continued to function without serious interruption during the railway strike of 1955. As Buchanan (1958) warned, it was not so much a public-transport stoppage, but a paralysis in the supply of petrol and diesel oil that was most to be feared. The country had become dependent on the motor-vehicle family, which grew with such astonishing fecundity as to turn many cities and towns into 'a motor slum'. The conventional arrangements of buildings and streets were becoming obsolete. The vehicles had become so penetrative, their destinations so numerous, that streets were turned into 'rivers of jostling, lethal vehicles'. Buchanan believed the only hope of extracting most of the benefits, with as few drawbacks as possible, was to canalise pedestrian and vehicle circulation. His fear was that, rather than grasping such a radical, albeit expensive, solution, compromise would be found in the piecemeal widening of streets, with even larger roundabouts. As Buchanan (1958) emphasised, the priority was not so much to keep traffic moving but to preserve civilised urban life.

A major landmark in the development of such thinking was the appointment of Colin Buchanan as Urban Planning Adviser to the Minister of Transport in June 1961, 'to study the long term development of roads and traffic in urban areas and their influence on the urban environment'. The report of his Working Group was published in July 1963. In commending the report, an accompanying report by a Steering Group, under the Chairmanship of Sir Geoffrey Crowther, characterised the dilemma as one where we are nourishing at immense cost a monster of great potential destructiveness. And yet we love him dearly.

Although from a social perspective the motor car menaced civilisation, it was also 'one of our most treasured possessions or dearest ambitions, an immense convenience, an expander of the dimensions of life, an instrument of emancipation, a symbol of the modern age' (Ministry of Transport 1963).

The Buchanan report (as it was known) broke new ground in the sense of being the first comprehensive and quantitative study of *Traffic in Towns*, that explicitly related the planning and location of buildings, on the one hand, with the planning and management of traffic on the other. With due acknowledgement to the necessarily crude nature of the methods and assumptions used, it attempted to put precise figures upon traffic flows and the capacity of the various methods for accommodating them. It was an exploratory study in the sense of illustrating the potential impact of new thinking on, say, the structure and life of actual towns and cities, namely Newbury, Leeds, Norwich and part of London (Cullingworth 1988).

As the Steering Group warned, in its commentary on the report, Britain was only now reaching the point where most households expected to own a private motor vehicle. As well as work, sleep and leisure, a fourth dimension had already been added to life in towns, namely the time spent sitting in vehicles that were either stationary or moving far too slowly. From the experience of North America (which was a generation ahead), there was no comfort to be drawn from assuming congestion itself would set a limit to car ownership. It was likely to rise four fold in 50 years, with an annual increase of 6 per cent over the next two decades.

There were three possible ways of alleviating the situation. American experience pointed to a large-scale, urban road-building programme. Not only were British city centres tightly packed with buildings but with history. As increasingly found in America, the opening of a new motorway seemed only to call into existence new traffic sufficient to create new congestion. An obvious, second approach was to persuade more commuters to use public transport. Whilst that must be pursued, it was unlikely to have much impact, except perhaps in catering for the 'semi-commuter', who might drive to a suburban station or bus-stop with the certainty of being able to park the car cheaply or for free. And thirdly, there had to be some deliberate limitation. It was simply impossible for many city centres to accommodate all the cars wanting to move within them. From such an analysis, the Steering Group believed there had to be an integrated response, applied by a single authority, and on a sufficiently large scale, if there was to be 'any chance of living at peace with the motor car'.

The major contribution of the Buchanan report was to outline the philosophy, or set of principles, required to attain a new kind of city comprising of primary road networks and environmental areas. Within such a patchwork

> there must be areas of good environment – urban rooms – where people can live, work, shop, look about and move around on foot in reasonable freedom from the hazards of motor traffic, and there must be a complementary network of roads – urban corridors – for effecting the primary distribution of traffic to the environmental areas. (Ministry of Transport 1963)

Where such corridors and areas might be laid out side by side in the smaller towns and cities, the main 'primary distributors' might have to be built below the present surface in the larger cities, with the secondary distributors and parking at ground level, and new environmental areas some feet above. Although the impelling force would be to cope with the volume of motor traffic, there would be an extra dividend of replacing 'slums and unworthy housing'.

The difficulties of linking towns and cities proved no less daunting. As Colin Buchanan wrote, in his book *Mixed Blessing*, the saving in costs from speeding up the movement of industrial and commercial traffic would greatly improve Britain's competitive position in world markets. As Buchanan (1958, pp. 208–11) perceived it, the difficulty was one of striking a balance of investment between the new motorways and other parts of the road system, and with the 'genuine modernisation' of a nineteenth-century railway network. The argument had however considerably widened by the time Peter Walker became Britain's first Secretary of State for the Environment in the early 1970s. He later recalled being often tempted to withdraw every proposal and threaten the closure of every motorway. It seemed the only way of making the public recognise that, far from banning them for the impact they made on the countryside, more motorways had to be built, both for the convenience of travelling long distances quickly and also for the peace they brought to the by-passed towns and villages. As in towns, the future lay with canalising movement (Walker 1977).

The motorway programme of the 1950s had envisaged a thousand miles of new road by the early 1970s. A Special Road Act of 1949 provided for 'the construction of roads reserved for special classes of traffic'. The Preston by-pass was opened to motorway standards in December 1958, and an initial 55 miles of the M1 in November 1959. About 843 miles of motorway had been opened by 1971. Not only were there shortages of moneys, but the procedures laid down by the further Highways Act of 1959 proved drawn out and intricate. The concept of a motorway from London to the South-West was first mooted by the County Surveyors' Society in 1938. It was opened in 1971. The 23 years taken to plan and build the 59-mile length of the M40, from Oxford to Birmingham, included two public consultations, the first in 1973 being the first time there had ever been such consultation with the public as to a proposed road scheme. Although it met the immediate object of reducing traffic on the M1 by 10-15 per cent, and the M34/A41 by up to 70 per cent, there was considerable criticism, not least from the Confederation of British Industry (1992), as to how it was perceived simply as a corridor of movement. The failure to involve the local planning authorities, businesses and other interests more closely during the initial planning phases not only caused much of the acrimony behind the 5 public inquiries and 4 appeals required by the planning process, but opportunities were lost for better integration at both the regional and more local scale.

Whilst there was frustration on the part of business, the impact of such new routeways on amenity gave rise to some of the most bitter conflict – and none more so than the decision taken in February 1990 to build a motorway in a deep cutting through Twyford Down, to the east of Winchester. It isolated the most easterly part of the St Catharine's Hill Site of Special Scientific Interest and part of the East Hampshire Area of Outstanding Natural Beauty. Martin Biddle (the distinguished archaeologist and President of the Twyford Down Association) attacked it as 'possibly the greatest single act of visible destruction ever worked on the scenery of southern England'. As the last undeveloped length of chalk downland abutting Winchester, the ridge provided 'a magnificent backcloth to England's ancient capital'. It had supported human habitation and civilisation since earliest times. 'Here, perhaps alone in modern urban England,' Biddle wrote:

> it was possible in the course of an hour or so to walk from the twentieth century to the prehistoric past, or even to glance from one to another in the course of a moment at work or in school. (cited in Bryant 1996)

Although the contentious 3-mile M3 extension was eventually built, the Twyford Down protest and, more particularly, the media coverage given to it, were an immense fillip to other anti-roads campaigns. In 1993, an alliance of up to 3,000 people from local, radical and mainstream environmental groups forced the Government to back down on a proposal to take the East London river crossing through Oxleas Wood in south-east London. In autumn 1994, police had forcibly to remove protesters, who had barricaded themselves into houses in the path of the East London extension of the M11. Brian Mawhinney, the Minister of Transport at the time of the protests against the Newbury by-pass, complained that whilst he had taken unprecedented steps to ensure environmental considerations were a legitimate aspect of transport policy, and that 'ordinary' people should be given a more direct and active role in seeking the outcome they wanted, there were also groups of people who dug tunnels, built tree-houses and indeed did everything possible to thwart a democratically determined decision that had the force of law. Millions of pounds had to be spent on law enforcement that would otherwise have been spent, say, on health or education. Even more disturbing was the support and sustenance offered by those in the local community, who saw themselves as strong upholders of law and order (Mawhinney 1999).

Where nothing could be done to hide the huge white gash made by the M3 Extension through the downland to the east of Winchester, some 'creative conservation' was possible. Opponents had dismissed as 'restoration rhetoric' the undertaking by the Department of Transport to infill the deep cutting of the now-redundant A33 with infill from the motorway, and to establish a downland sward (Eden *et al.* 1999). A contract was awarded to the Institute of Terrestrial Ecology (ITE) (a component body of the Natural Environment Research Council) to survey the wildlife resource. Although the line of the motorway had been fixed, there was considerable scope for modifying the actual earthworks so as to maximise opportunities for creating wildlife habitat. Most crucially, whilst the rhetoric of opponents had given the impression that the new cutting would destroy ancient chalk grassland, the entire route crossed arable land where the wildlife interest had largely been obliterated. By reclaiming both the A33 cutting and some of the previously cultivated land, now incorporated in the associated earthworks, a net increase in calcareous grassland was achieved. Far from the Chalkhill blue butterfly becoming extinct, as many opponents of the scheme had predicted, the population of this and other invertebrate species expanded (Institute of Terrestrial Ecology 1997).

For the more extreme opponents, it was an all-or-nothing situation. Where the Chief Scientific Adviser to the Government, Robert May, saw Twyford Down as a model of the kind of close collaboration between ecologists, planners and engineers that should occur everywhere, the Campaigns Director of Friends of the Earth claimed such accommodation as afforded by scientists had simply made it easier for motorways to inflict greater damage, in terms of 'global warming, acid rain and a wide range of other environmental problems' (*The Observer*, 20 October 1998). The view of the ITE scientists was that of an officer of the Hampshire Wildlife Trust, namely that the best for wildlife had been achieved, given the decision to build the motorway.

London's Third Airport

The most novel form of communication in the twentieth century was that of flight. By the 1920s, the location and design of aerodromes and the buildings required to accommodate the planes and fare-paying passengers had begun to tax the minds of architects and planners, as well as the industry itself. A competition aroused so much interest that John Dower persuaded the Council of the Royal Institute of British Architects in May 1929 to examine further the architectural design of aerodromes. Its first report, written by Dower, emphasised the importance of considering such ventures in their 'broader town planning aspect'. There was bound to be fierce competition for prime development land within 30 minutes' travelling time of the city- and town-centre. The vicinity of the airfield had to be kept free of tall buildings and such structures as the pylons of the National Grid, then under construction (Anon 1931; Dower 1932).

An object of the Doncaster Corporation Act of 1931 was to enable the Corporation to acquire land as an aerodrome, and to make the appropriate by-laws, using the precedent of the Derby Corporation Act of 1929 and Bournemouth Corporation Act of 1930. Doncaster was located on a straight line between London and Newcastle, and between Hull–Liverpool and Dublin. As the Estate Surveyor reasoned, the better weather conditions east of the Pennines meant the East Coast route from London to Scotland was bound to be the more popular. The projected site was 2 miles from the centre, close to the Great North Road and racecourse. As well as being a 'satisfactory landing ground for the heaviest aircraft', there was plenty of flat and gently undulating land should a forced landing be required (Doncaster Record Office, AB9/TC3/527).

Rather like John Dower, Colin Buchanan's interests were wide-ranging. He was intimately involved in the debates as to location of London's Third Airport. As he recalled in his volume *No Way to the Airport*, it was

> a long and extraordinary story of committees and commissions, recommendations made and rejected and made again, rows and ructions and furious reactions, resistance movements and demonstrations. (Buchanan 1981)

With Heathrow and Gatwick heavily used, an inter-departmental committee under the Chairmanship of the Under-Secretary to the Minister of Aviation warned, in June 1963, that 'a third airport will be required for London by the early 1970s'. Stansted (which had been taken over from the United Air Force in 1951) 'was the only one with clear prospects of making a good airport for London'. The demand of the North West Essex and East Herts Preservation Association for a public inquiry was powerfully reinforced by the report of a Committee on the Problem of Noise, published a month later, which emphasised the acute noise problems caused by aircraft taking off and landing at Heathrow. Far from easing, the problem of noise had considerably worsened, following the introduction of the heavy long-range jets in 1958 (PP 1962–63).

The Minister of Aviation in the new Labour Government ordered a public enquiry, which closed in February 1966. The Inspector found 'it would be a calamity for the neighbourhood if a major international airport were placed at Stansted'. It was so objectionable on planning, access, noise, environmental and agricultural grounds that such a development could only be justified by national necessity. No such case had been made. The Inspector continued, 'In my opinion a review of the whole problem should be undertaken by a Committee equally interested in traffic in the air, traffic on the ground, regional planning and national planning.' Such a recommendation caused the Minister to delay announcement of the finding for a year, until May 1967, during which time a further inter-departmental committee both studied and confirmed the choice of Stansted. The necessary planning permission would be granted by a Special Development Order under the Town and Country Planning Act of 1962. However, the Order required parliamentary sanction. Not only was there considerable outcry from both local and national bodies, but an Opposition motion in June called for an independent committee of inquiry into national airport policy. Although rejected on party lines, all but two of the speakers in the debate attacked the choice of Stansted. Among the Government supporters abstaining, Renee Short complained of how the officials on the inter-departmental committee had been 'judge and jury of their own case' (PD, Commons, 749, 769–894).

A new minister, Anthony Crosland, the President of the Board of Trade, announced in February 1968 that having further reviewed the question he had decided to suspend moves to obtain a Special Order. In as much as all the critics of the Stansted decision had conceded the need for a third London airport in the South-East, he had decided to take advantage of the powers granted under the newly enacted Town and Country Planning Act to appoint a special Planning Inquiry Commission (PD, Commons, 759, 667–74). As agreed with the Opposition, such a Commission would be appointed

> to inquire into the timing of the need for a 4-runway airport to cater for the growth of traffic at existing airports serving the London area, to consider the various alternative sites, and to recommend which site should be selected.

Its Chairman was Mr Justice Roskill, a judge in the High Court. The members included Colin Buchanan. A long list of 78 possible sites was reduced to one of three sites, namely Cublington in Buckinghamshire, Nuthampstead in Hertfordshire, and Thurleigh in Bedfordshire. At Buchanan's suggestion a fourth site, Foulness, was added, both because of obvious public interest and as a further basis for comparison. Stansted had come ninth. A series of local hearings was followed by a public inquiry, lasting 74 days. Although the aviation authorities appeared ready to accept the Commission's nomination of Cublington, there was strong opposition from all the county councils and resistance associations to the inland sites. There was a measure of support from the Essex County Council, Southend Borough Council and certain entrepreneurs for Foulness. The Commission submitted its report in December 1970. It recommended Cublington, with Buchanan dissenting in favour of Foulness (Bromhead 1973).

As Colin Buchanan later recalled, events moved with merciful swiftness. Of the 40 speeches made in both Houses of Parliament, in February and March 1971, only one favoured Cublington as the new airport. Whilst all hell had broken out at Cublington itself, ministers made clear there could be no further enquiry. Buchanan had provided them with the 'one straw to clutch at'. John Davies, the Secretary of State for Trade and Industry, grasped it in his statement of April 1971, that the Government had decided that an airport and associated port facilities must be made operational at Maplin Sands, off Foulness, by 1981. Where some commentators believed the rejection of some two-and-a-half years of enquiry was simply a matter of politics, Buchanan (1981) identified three 'fairly solid reasons'. Dominated by economists, both the Commission and research team had fed on one another's vanity in basing their findings entirely on the technique of cost–benefit analysis, which the public found impossible to understand. Secondly, they had underrated the importance the public would attach to the protection of the countryside. To Buchanan, it was inconceivable that a huge industrial complex 'could be laid athwart the Vale of Aylesbury', and thirdly, therefore, the majority of the Commission had ignored the local uproar at the various sites.

The Secretary of State appointed in August 1971 a progress review body and a technical planning team. A Consultation Document was issued in April 1972 on runway location and alignment and, in August, a Maplin Development Authority was established to be responsible for land reclamation (PD, Commons, 842, 1744–52). The objections to Foulness remained. Not only was it 50 miles from London, but the airport would inflict colossal damage on one of the few undeveloped parts of South-East England. The RSPB had vigorously protested at the choice of Maplin. One-fifth of the world's population of the dark-bellied Brent goose wintered at Foulness. The Nature Conservancy had expressed its considerable concern at an inter-departmental level. Having undertaken a survey of the affected area in 1971, it was well-prepared to carry out a series of impact studies, commissioned by the DOE in August 1972.

A Maplin Development Bill was given a Second Reading in February 1973. Among the expert witnesses during the Select Committee stage was Derek Ranwell, the head of the Conservancy's Coastal Ecology Research Station. He described how the Foulness/Maplin area, of some 22,500 acres, was of national and international importance for its wildlife and physiographical interest. As well as a winter population of over 6,000 dark-bellied Brent geese, 20,000 wading birds and 4,000 wildfowl, there was one of the largest British breeding colonies of the rare and decreasing Little tern. The most continuous area of sand and silt flats in Britain, the lime-rich sands and silts carried a rich resource of molluscs, marine worms and crustaceans. There was the largest population in Britain of *Zostera noltii*, a protein-rich food that was especially important for the Brent geese, as they arrived exhausted from their autumn migration from the Arctic. There were similarly the most extensive tracts of the rare and diminishing salt-marsh grass, the small cord-grass, *Spartina maritime*, possibly in Europe. The Bill was amended at Committee Stage, so as to require the Maplin Development Authority to consult the Conservancy before beginning any work of reclamation. In as much as the Authority was to pay the Conservancy such sums as approved by the Secretary of State (and with the consent of the Treasury) as were needed for conserving any fauna or flora adversely affected, funds were to be available for such purposes as the purchase or leasing of 'substitute' sites for the types of wildlife presently found on the Sands (Natural Environment Research Council archives, Swindon, CRS 05/G1/02/2).

It was Anthony Crosland (now the Secretary of State for the Environment in a new Labour Government) to announce, with Peter Shore (the Secretary of State for Trade), the suspension of all work on the airport, pending a reappraisal of the project (PD,

Commons, 870, *107*, and 1334–40). In a further statement in July 1974, Peter Shore confirmed the abandonment of the project which, by that date, was forecast to cost £650 million – nearly twice as much as the next most expensive alternative considered by the reappraisal. Forecasts of air-passenger demand had fallen significantly following the dramatic increase in fuel prices. Not only was there a growing use of wide-bodied aircraft, but the next generation was expected to be considerably quieter. No further main runways, nor increase in passenger accommodation, would be required at any airport before 1990 (PD, Commons, 877, 675–92). There followed further consultation documents and a White Paper on airports policy in February 1978, indicating that a new airport for the South-East would be needed by 1990. Departmental Committees were appointed in August to review the long-term options. There was an immense outcry when it was revealed that four of the six sites under investigation had already been considered by the Roskill Commission. So as to forestall further outcry, the Government announced, within a few days of publication in December 1979, that the British Airports Authority had been invited to proceed with a planning application for Stansted as London's third airport, subject to a public inquiry (PD, Commons, 976, *35*).

By the end of the century, Heathrow was the world's busiest airport for international travellers. Gatwick had the world's busiest single runway, and Stansted was the fastest-growing major airport in Europe. Traffic had risen by over one-third in 1999, and had doubled in the previous four years. Foulness had, in the meantime, received the full weight of British and European protection, namely as a Site of Special Scientific Interest, a designated site under the Ramsar Convention, and a Special Protection Area. It formed part of the larger Essex Estuaries candidate Special Area of Conservation.

Commercial Pipelines

Rather than further explore these highly publicised controversies, the remainder of this chapter will focus on another revolutionary development that, paradoxically was so invisible and silent as to be almost overlooked by those who thrive on dissent (Davies 1962). If the water industry was a pioneer in transporting huge amounts of water from upland reservoirs to towns and cities in the nineteenth century, the oil industry, some hundred years later, constructed the first explicitly commercial, long-distance pipelines. The movement of materials by underground pipeline made not only economic sense, but seemed entirely in accord with the 'green image', which the oil industry had consciously cultivated since the inter-war years, when petrol-filling stations and their associated advertisements first attracted unfavourable publicity (Brown 1993).

By the time the UK Department of Trade and Industry published a set of *Guidelines* for the environmental assessment of cross-country pipelines in 1992, the industry was already well established and regulated. The immediate pretext for the guidance was the implementation in the UK of provisions of a Directive of the European Economic Community. As the Department of Trade and Industry (1992) emphasised, no one method of environmental regulation and assessment was applicable to all situations. Detail had to be tailored to meet the needs of each particular project.

As the particularly rich archives of the earlier Ministry of Power and Esso UK make clear, it was the extraordinary variety of purposes and circumstances of the pipeline industry that most taxed the minds of the industry, officials, ministers and parliament. Earlier Private Bills, and most notably the Esso Petroleum Act of 1961, had led directly to the Pipe-lines Act of 1962, which continued to define the basic parameters of the pipeline industry. As a case study of the expertise and experience gained by the industry, and the wider debate within Government departments, historical context is provided as to how the UK became a pioneer in the development of good practice and was, thereby, well placed to promote further measures, within a European context, for the safe and productive management of industrial resources.

With the decision taken in 1945 to refine as much petroleum as possible within the United Kingdom, there was a tenfold increase in refinery capacity between 1947 and 1960. The small works established at Shellhaven on the Thames estuary in 1916, Llandarcy in South Wales and Fawley on the Solent in 1921, and Grangemouth on the Forth and Stanlow on the Mersey in 1924, were enlarged to become essentially new refineries. Fawley became the largest in the Commonwealth (PRO, POWE 61, 164).

A defence network of pipelines, some 1,200 miles long, had been built during the war for the large-scale movement of products between the Bristol Channel and Thames estuary, and northwards to the Mersey, which was linked to the Humber. There were extensions to East Anglia, and southwards to Southampton Water. Parts of the system were used by the four main commercial distributors, Shell Mex/British Petroleum (BP), Esso, Regent and Mobil, on a fee-paying basis. Not only did this provide an annual income of £60,000 by 1960, but it helped to keep the system in a state of readiness for an emergency, without the full cost falling on the taxpayer (PRO, POWE 61, 86 and 165).

The first cross-country pipeline built solely for commercial use was opened in 1951, linking Finnart on the west coast of Scotland with the BP refinery at Grangemouth. As larger tankers came into service, pipelines were needed to carry the crude oil from the deep-sea anchorages to refineries. A 9-mile pipeline was opened between the newly opened Tranmere terminal and the Shell refinery, at Stanlow, in 1960. The most ambitious was a 62-mile pipeline, authorised under the BP Trading Act of 1957 and opened in 1961, which carried crude oil from the Angle Bay Ocean Terminal in Pembrokeshire to the BP refinery at Llandarcy. Esso announced in September 1959 that it was to proceed with a project to construct a 10-inch diameter pipeline over a distance of 72 miles from Fawley, under Southampton Water, and through East Hampshire and Surrey, to a terminal at West Bedfont, close to London Airport and 12 miles from the centre of London. The pipeline would carry as many as 14 products, the most important being aviation fuel for London Airport, where the development of large jet airliners, such as the Boeing 707, had caused demand to rise from 3 million gallons (mg) in 1958 to a projected demand of over 45 mg in 1961. Whilst it was hoped there would be no undue difficulty in purchasing wayleaves, preparations were made for a Private Bill, so as to ensure the pipeline was ready by January 1963 (PRO, POWE 61, 165).

The aid of the Minister of Power was sought, particularly in soliciting the co-operation of other ministers. Although the formal response was guarded, there was never any doubt among officials that the Minister would support the venture. Not only was it the first important commercial pipeline of its kind in the UK, but there were considerable advantages in duplicating lengths of the defence system, in the event of their being destroyed in war. Letters were prepared for 'conditioning other Departments as to both the commercial and defence potential of the Esso proposals'. They described how the defence system was currently used to carry the fuel needed for jet aircraft from Fawley to Aldermaston, from where it was taken by road to London Airport. Eight 4,000-gallon tankers each made 2 or 3 journeys a day, 7 days a week. All other fuels for the London area had to be sent by sea tanker from Fawley to the Esso terminal at Purfleet, and then up the Thames by barge to Fulham. Whilst garages in east London would continue to be served from Purfleet, those up to 40 miles of Fulham would now be served by the pipeline. A further pipeline of up to 2 miles in length would be built from West Bedfont to supply London Airport. The number of road-tanker deliveries from Fulham was expected to fall from 200 to 20 a day (PRO, MT 96, 116 and POWE 61, 165).

Esso was also developing plans for a second pipeline, which would carry ethylene gas from Fawley to the ICI petro-chemical plant, being built north of Avonmouth. Half the output of glycol and other derivatives of ethylene oxide would be used in the manufacture of Terylene, and the rest for explosives, detergents and other products for home and export markets. A pipeline was the only continuous and reliable method of conveying ethylene from Fawley to the plant at a cost that would enable ICI to be competitive in world markets. A fleet of specially built refrigerated lorries would be both uneconomic and add to the congestion of already overcrowded roads. Esso estimated the cost of building the pipelines to London and Severnside to be £2.5 million and £800,000 respectively.

Negotiations with individual owners and occupiers got off to a bad start when a land agent visited the Hampshire home of Lord Chesham, the Parliamentary Secretary to the Ministry of Transport. Lord Chesham was astonished to be told that his Minister had welcomed the project as a means of easing road congestion around London Airport. The Minister, Ernest Marples, strenuously denied giving such encouragement (PRO, MT 96, 116). It was however a meeting of the Alton branch of the National Farmers' Union in April 1960 that provided the immediate pretext for ministers to intervene. Representatives were outraged that a private company should be permitted to secure a permanent right of way that would sterilise a width of up to 400 yards of farmland for all time. Even if permitted in the national interest, the compensation offered for such disruption was entirely inadequate. As a Government Whip reported, opinion among landowners, farmers and Members of Parliament was undoubtedly inflamed by the fact that Esso was a subsidiary of Standard Oil of New Jersey, and the consequent belief that all the financial benefits from the pipeline development would accrue to American shareholders. The Government Chief Whip, Martin Redmayne, recommended that before the Bill to promote the two pipelines made any further progress it should be considered by the Cabinet's Home Affairs Committee (PRO, POWE 61, 165).

A meeting at the Ministry of Power in May 1960 became the first of many to cover two broad areas of concern, namely the impact of the project on individual owners, lessees and occupiers, and its importance in the wider national context. Esso accused farmers of acting as 'outright land speculators rather than agriculturists in negotiating claims for compensation'. The Bill followed closely the precedents set by the four earlier (and largely unchallenged) pipeline Acts. Compulsory powers would lapse after three years. Permanent access was essential in order to inspect and maintain the lines in the interests of safety and efficient operation. In practice, only a band of 40 feet would be required so as to provide access for pipe-laying machinery. The actual trench might be only 2 feet across for laying the pipe. Behind the scenes, officials drafted a paper for the Minister of Power, Richard Wood, to submit to the Home Affairs Committee. It described how the Esso Bill was entirely in accord with the Government's general economic policy based on competition. The refineries and their expanding network of pipelines , far from simply benefiting foreign investors, were 'a considerable magnet' for American and foreign investment. Home refining contributed £150 million a year to the balance of payments. Any move towards a Government-owned system was likely to encourage demands that petroleum distribution as a whole should be nationalised.

Critics of the Esso proposals made great play of the United States' inter-state pipeline system, which had operated on a common-carrier basis since the Hepburn Act of 1906. The Ministry of Power believed it to be quite inappropriate to the UK, where distances were much shorter and alternative means of transport more readily available. In practice, Shell Mex/BP (with its strong British element) and Esso were the only companies with a sufficiently large density and volume of traffic to warrant pipelines. Together, they had over 80 per cent of the trade. They would resent the imposition of common-carrier obligations for the unfair advantage it gave competitors in finding markets for their surplus oil. The Ministry similarly had no desire to help the Russians, Italians (who used Russian oil) and other newcomers to win part of the market share without having to make any investment in refining and pipeline facilities. If there was to be competition, it had to be fair. Everyone should pay for what they used.

The Home Affairs Committee, at its meeting of May 1960, agreed that the Esso Bill should be allowed to take its course. Parliamentary procedures offered the best opportunity for exposing and discussing objections. There was concern however as to whether, as the number of pipelines increased, their control should be left entirely to private legislation. The Minister of Power was invited to prepare a further memorandum on the need for Government regulation and the form it might take (PRO, CAB 134, 1980 and 1982, and POWE 61, 165).

A vigorous campaign was launched against the Bill by the

Country Landowners' Association (CLA), National Farmers' Union (NFU) and the Federation of Property Owners. Each emphasised the unprecedented scale of the project. Over a thousand owners would be affected. Five Conservative Members of Parliament, whose constituencies would be affected, tabled a Motion that recognised the advantages of moving petroleum products by pipeline, but asked the House to decline a Second Reading until the Government had completed

> a full examination of the problem arising in connection with the laying, maintenance and operation of such pipelines and the protection of the interests affected.

From the wording of the Motion, a leader in *The Times* of 27 May 1960 commented on how one might be forgiven for thinking 'some vast and permanent blight' was about to descend 'on the fair face of England'. Compared with motorways or overhead power lines, the effect of a pipeline, once installed, would be negligible. Where it was usual and entirely legitimate to demand compensation on the most advantageous terms, a policy of general obstruction to an enterprise of such obvious advantage was both shortsighted and vain.

The petroleum industry tried hard to break down the public image of gigantic pipelines undermining the countryside. Representatives assured a joint meeting of the Conservative Transport and Power Committees in May 1960 that the pipelines required to carry refined products in the UK would have a much smaller diameter than those in the Middle East. The risk of accidents and of 'having one's best acreage ankle-deep in high octane petrol' (to cite an article in *The Observer* of 8 August 1960), were grossly exaggerated. As a Government Whip reported, the conciliatory answers on procedures and compensation sounded almost too good to be true. There was a feeling among the 25 Members present that Private Bill procedures should be replaced by public legislation, that would ensure pipeline development was properly planned and co-ordinated (PRO, POWE 61, 165–6).

In the late evening of 28 June, the Second Reading debate on the Esso Bill was opened by the Labour Member, William Warbey, who described how pipeline development promised to become second only to the National Grid as the country's largest transport system. Unless urgent steps were taken, its haphazard construction would soon resemble that of early railway development. The Labour Member for Fulham, Michael Stewart, spoke of how compulsory powers of purchase were essential if Esso was to avoid paying an 'extremely heavy tribute' to landowners. Conservative Members pressed for alternative ways of scrutinising such major projects. The Bill was given a Second Reading following an assurance from the Minister that the project was of urgent national importance, and that the Government had already begun to examine the general problem of pipeline development. By an arrangement already struck, where the opposing Motion was withdrawn, it was ordered that the exceptional step should be taken of committing the Bill to a special Select Committee, thereby ensuring adequate safeguards were provided for owners, lessees and occupiers of land (PD, Commons, 625, 1273–1316).

The Select Committee took evidence in July 1960, under the Chairmanship of the Conservative MP, John Arbuthnot. The CLA and NFU indicated that they had advised their members to negotiate on the basis of the model deeds, which had been agreed for granting wayleaves. The local authorities had also withdrawn their petitions. As the Clerk to the Hampshire County Council told the Committee, the pipeline would not only reduce road-tanker traffic in the county, but encourage development of the petro-chemical industry in other parts of the country, away from the immediate vicinity of the refineries. Although approving the Bill, Arbuthnot warned the Minister that evening that the Committee would strongly recommend that there should be no further Private Bills dealing with pipelines. With the further modifications required by the Committee, a 17-page Private Bill of 31 sections grew to one of 43 pages of 55 sections. It received the Royal Assent in March 1961 (House of Lords Record Office, printed evidence on Private Bills, 1960, Esso Petroleum Company Bill; PD, Commons, 639, 737–41; PRO, HLG 54, 588, and POWE 61, 165–6).

The Pipe-Lines Act

Given the Minister's assurances to parliament during the passage of the Esso Bill, rapid progress had to be made in the wider enquiry as to the development of commercial pipelines. Although a Working Party was set up under the Ministry of Power, it was the Board of Trade that came to play the larger role, insisting that it was no longer enough for parliament to hold the reins between the developer and landed-interests. Something more was needed to ensure such development was both efficient and economical. Whereas a 'national grid' might one day be envisaged for the transport of oil, there was unlikely to be much 'trunking' in the chemical industry, where each pipeline tended to be 'tailor-made' for the particular raw material. On the safety aspect too, there was a wide divergence of experience. Whereas oil-pipeline techniques were pretty advanced, the chemical industry was still very much at the experimental stage (PRO, BT 213, 146 and BT 258, 1151).

The Working Group's report was submitted to the Home Affairs Committee in February 1961. In rejecting any notion of the Government becoming a monopoly developer and operator, the Group believed sufficient co-ordination would be achieved by establishing some kind of central registration, with powers for the Minister to intervene where wayleaves could not be privately agreed. There was however such a 'considerable divergence of opinion' on the Home Affairs Committee that the question had to be referred to an *ad hoc* meeting of ministers, under the chairmanship of the Paymaster-General, Lord Mills. That meeting acknowledged the great potential for pipeline development but agreed that industry was more likely to accept supervision if it were introduced at the outset. At first comparatively relaxed, control might be increased as the number of pipelines grew. As Lord Mills reported, 'we are fully satisfied that Government legislation' was needed. No one wanted to see the 'plate of spaghetti' that had emerged from the earlier development of the canals and railways. Such orderly and economic development could only be achieved through control of all future projects. To that end, a minister should be notified of every proposal for a pipeline that extended beyond the developer's own property. Where compulsory rights were sought, the consent of the minister would be required, following, if necessary, a local inquiry (PRO, CAB 130, 176, CAB 134, 1984–5 and 2170, POWE 61, 9–10, and 86, and BT 258, 1151).

Richard Wood was authorised by the Home Affairs Committee to say, in reply to a Parliamentary Question, that the Government had decided it was necessary to legislate, so as to secure in the national interest the orderly development of privately-owned industrial pipelines. The legislation would

> provide that, where there are objections by public bodies or private individuals to a project, these objections may be heard at a Public Inquiry and that, in appropriate cases, the Minister's decision will be subject to the approval of Parliament.

The question of ministerial responsibility had been studiously avoided. Ernest Marples, the Minister of Transport, wanted ultimate responsibility for regulating pipeline development, but argued he was already so heavily committed to promoting a Bill to reorganise the British Transport Commission, and a Road Safety Bill, that Richard Wood should continue to promote the present Bill. To officials of the Ministry of Power, this sounded very much like trying to get the best of both worlds. Given however his earlier undertakings to parliament, Wood had no alternative but to concede (PRO, POWE 61, 9 and 86–7, and PREM 11, 3388).

As Lord Mills recounted, in moving the Second Reading in the House of Lords in March 1962, the origins of the Pipe-lines Bill were to be found in the Esso Bill two years earlier. It had three principal objectives, namely to confer control on cross-country pipelines in the national interest; to enable developers to obtain compulsory powers without having to promote a Private Bill; and to ensure that pipelines were safely laid, operated and maintained (PD, Lords, 238, 1120–21). In Committee, the Opposition spokesman, the Earl of Lucan, complained at the absence of any concept of the pipeline network as a public service. Although the minister might be able to withhold authorisation, and thereby prevent duplication of lines, there was no scope for stimulating development where it would be most beneficial for the public interest. Development would only occur where individual operators believed they could make a profit (PRO, POWE 61, 217; PD, Lords, 239, 353–4, 651–774, 784–831 and 977–9).

As the Parliamentary Secretary of the Ministry of Power, John Peyton, remarked, during the Third Reading of the Bill in the House of Commons, the word 'planning' had become a missile that meant different things as the occasion demanded. It had acquired a sort of magical content of its own. In the context of the Bill, it did not mean setting up detailed planning machinery right from the outset. Rather, the initiative had deliberately been given to those skilful, successful and enterprising commercial pioneers, with the most intimate knowledge of what the market for pipeline development required. However, once that initiative had been taken, and an application had been made to build a pipeline, the public interest was protected by 'every conceivable power and discretion that could be necessary'. The Minister would have complete discretion as to whether an application might be granted, or refused (PD, Lords, 239, 177–9, and Commons, 663, 1477–81, 659, 456–71, and 663, 1477–81; PRO, POWE 61, 187).

Considerable discretion had to be accorded the Minister in deciding matters of pipeline safety. Not only would the drafting of detailed regulations, applicable to the safety of all types of pipeline, have considerably delayed the Bill, but there were fears that parliament might want to extend them to the defence pipeline-network, with obvious financial implications for the Exchequer. The obvious course was to make provision as each pipeline Order and consent came to be considered. At its meeting of July 1961, the Home Affairs Committee approved the Minister having powers to impose conditions on the construction, operation and maintenance of all types of line. Provision was made for the appointment of inspectors (probably 2 or 3) to devise and ensure their enforcement. So as to give the inspectors time to consider what might be required, the developers had to give 3 months' notice of a proposed scheme, even where it might otherwise be exempt from scrutiny (PRO, BT 213, 146 and POWE 61, 172 and 198).

The Bill eventually received the Royal Assent in August 1962, the same day as the Transport and Road Traffic Bills. A major consideration had been its robustness in responding to the changing economy and technology that would surely occur in pipeline transportation. The changing perception of the fuel and power industries was reflected in the structural changes of Government . The Ministry of Power became part of the Ministry of Technology in October 1969. Some two years later, that Ministry was merged with the Board of Trade to form the Department of Trade and Industry. However, with the Middle East oil crisis, and the prospects of Britain rapidly developing its own oil and gas resources in the North Sea, responsibility for fuel and power was again hived off in January 1974, this time to a new Department of Energy. Where commercial pipelines on land continued to be regulated by the Pipe-lines Act of 1962, Part III of the Petroleum and Submarine Pipelines Act of 1975 covered offshore lines. The Pipelines Inspectorate had oversight of the construction, operation and safety aspects under both Acts. The archives of Esso UK, preserved at Fawley, provided insight into the opportunities taken by one of the more major refiners and distributors over that period.

For Esso, the first major test of the 1961 Act's robustness was the application for an entirely new pipeline. Called the Mainline, it would link the company's other refinery in south-west Wales to the Midlands. Three oil companies had opened refineries beside the magnificent deep-water harbour of Milford Haven in Pembrokeshire, namely Esso (the first in the field), Gulf and Texaco. In November 1970, they formed a consortium with a shareholding of 75 per cent Esso, 20 per cent Texaco and 5 per cent Gulf, for the purpose of constructing the pipeline to the Midlands, and thence northward to Manchester and eastward beyond Birmingham. A Public Inquiry was held under the Act of 1962, first for three days at Haverfordwest and then for a further two days at Dudley in Worcestershire during the summer of 1971. Emphasis was laid on the fact that the Inspector was an officer of the Department of the Environment. The Minister gave his consent to the construction of the line in July 1972. It was commissioned in March 1973.

By that date, there appeared to be an unstoppable momentum. If Esso was to retain its market position in east London, an alternative had to be found to conveying supplies by sea from Fawley to Purfleet. The obvious course was to build a pipeline from Alton, on the Fawley to West London line, to Purfleet, on the north bank of the Thames. Operating costs would be reduced by 40 per cent. No longer would there be any need to worry about fog, snow, or inclement weather at sea. The pipeline would be invisible, operating silently and unnoticed beneath the ground, every hour and day of the year, almost entirely free from any risk of disruption. The construction of such a pipeline would mean that over half the company's 'white' oil products were distributed directly by pipeline to marketing terminals.

Detailed planning was disrupted by the uncertainties of the Arab-Israeli War and the international energy crisis. It was resumed in the late 1970s, by which time it had become even more essential, if Esso was to maintain its volume share of 25 per cent in the general airlines market that a pipeline should be built to supply fuel oil to Gatwick airport. Together, Heathrow, Gatwick and Stansted accounted for more than four-fifths of total airline demand. The concentration in the South-East seemed likely to continue. A formal application for a Construction Authorization was made in August 1979. Meetings with officials of the Department of Energy emphasised the need for early approval. Some 10 trains a week carried jet fuel from Fawley to a jointly-operated facility near Gatwick. The company's existing agreement to use the facility ran out in December 1980 and, without a pipeline, supplies during the peak summer months would soon be in jeopardy. Officials made clear that the Pipelines Inspector would have to be satisfied not only as to 'the purpose of the line and its compatibility with the non-proliferation intent' of the Act, but also by its technical integrity and the company's operational competence. He would have to satisfy himself on operating procedures and safeguards, and the emergency-response capability. Time soon slipped by. It was not until December, having consulted with Government departments, that the Department of Energy gave consent for the application to proceed. Only then could advertisements be placed in specified national and local newspapers, and a copy sent to each local authority and owner and occupier affected. Each had a statutory period of 28 days to lodge an objection.

It was difficult to see what more Esso could have done to expedite progress. Out of a total of 250 owners and occupiers, along a route of some 72 miles (116 kilometres), only 25 had objected. Members of the Project Management Team had responded to invitations to attend meetings of parish councils, each of which had then withdrawn its objection. Some statutory undertakers had lodged a formal objection simply as a device to ensure that negotiations already under way were brought to a successful conclusion. The Planning Inspector from the Department of the Environment wrote that the remarkably small number of objectors at the Public Inquiry held at Maidstone in October 1980, reflected the considerable care the company had taken in choosing the route. In March 1981, the Secretary of State announced that he had accepted the Inspector's report. Some 18 months after the company had submitted its relatively straightforward, non-controversial application, the formal Construction Authorization was received on 4 April 1981.

By the early 1980s, it was the turn of Mainline to respond to changing market conditions. On the one hand, there was a surplus of refining capacity. Following the closure of the Esso refinery at Milford Haven in April 1983, the fuel carried by Mainline across Wales to the Midlands and North-West had to be supplied by sea from Fawley, round Lands End. On the other hand, the key area for UK sales had become a 'corridor' some 50 miles wide, stretching from Manchester and the North-West to London and the South-East, through the Midlands. In June 1983, Esso applied for a Construction Authorization for what became known as the Midline, a 14-inch pipeline from the recently enlarged refinery at Fawley, that would convey 'white' oils over a distance of 132 miles

(208 kilometres) directly to the Mainline point station at Seisdon in the Midlands. The route along the edge of the New Forest would use the corridor already occupied by the Fawley to Severnside pipeline, cross the eastern edge of Salisbury Plain, skirt Swindon, and cross the Cotswolds and the river Avon at Evesham.

Much to the company's relief, all the formal objections to the pipeline came from individuals – there was no sign of an 'activist' group emerging. Criticised by Esso headquarters for the slow progress made in reaching agreements, both the project manager and land agents stressed the importance of each negotiation being handled sensitively. People would react strongly and negatively to being bulldozed. Esso had to show an understanding of owners' problems. Some additional cost and inconvenience must be accepted. And yet, however many layers of kidgloves were worn, some critics would always accuse Esso of 'threatening behaviour'. Nor was it always possible to meet objections that were of a general kind. A resident of Grafton Flyford, in Worcestershire, complained that the pipeline would bring no benefit to the locality. Nor was the adoption of an alternative route always warranted. One property-owner, who collected derelict cars and forklift trucks, took the strongest objection to the devaluation of his land and disruption of rural life. The only alternative to a wayleave through his land was down a narrow residential lane, already full of main services. The Public Inquiry of July 1984 lasted only three hours. It took a further 20 months for the formal Construction Authorization to be obtained.

The company's statutory responsibility for restoring agricultural land was embodied in the Deeds of Grant signed during the negotiation of easements. Most Deeds followed the general guidelines drawn up by the Country Landowner's Association (CLA) and National Farmers' Union (NFU). It was perhaps inevitable that the construction of the South-East Pipeline, which passed through such heavily-used countryside, should give rise to complaints of dust and noise, and local disruption. There was however considerable criticism of the contractors' use of heavy machinery in wet weather, when no farmer would have dreamt of putting a tractor on the land. A letter sent by the Ministry of Agriculture to the Pipelines Inspector in mid-December 1981, warned of how such damage would have to be taken into account when considering future applications for pipelines. In his response of early January 1982, the project manager set out in detail the steps taken, both directly and through the CLA and NFU, to mitigate disruption and assure the farming community. Some 50 kilometres of the line had already been restored and handed back, without complaint.

Every effort was made within Esso to apply the lessons learnt from the South-East Pipeline to the planning and construction of Midline. There was not only closer supervision of contractors, but each was required to start work by April, so as to finish before mid-October. The CLA sought a revision to the standard Deed of Grant, so as to give the landowner the right to call a halt to construction work in adverse weather conditions. Esso refused, claiming that no developer could possibly give individual owners a right to dictate when and how construction work might proceed. Rather, the company offered to meet the reasonable expenses of an expert adviser employed by the farmer, and to employ itself a land-drainage consultant to advise on the engineering aspects and reinstatement of the route. The CLA signified in December 1983 its consent to a revised Deed of Grant drawn up by Esso, and already agreed by the NFU.

Both sides looked for evidence of good faith in the other. Esso was irritated by some of the press releases and articles issued by the CLA and NFU and yet, overall, such publicity benefited both parties. The CLA and NFU were able to assert themselves as an active and indispensable interface between their members and Esso. The guidance and information put across by the two organisations won far greater respect and understanding than if Esso had said the same thing more directly through its own press releases. In having to defend their own negotiating position, the CLA/NFU highlighted not only the concessions they had wrung from Esso, but were required to explain as lucidly and cogently as possible the reasons why the company could not concede on other points. Thus, the CLA Land Use and Valuation Adviser explained how he had not only secured the best possible terms for members, but that such pipelines were by far the most efficient, unobtrusive and safest means of bulk transport.

In an appreciation written in February 1987, the project manager attributed the remarkably trouble-free construction of the Midline to careful preparation in the early stages, good liaison and public-relations work, and the engagement of a 'land owner undertakings monitoring team' through the construction period, that had remained independent of the construction organisation. Except for the gaps in the hedges, it was already difficult to see where all the activity had taken place only two years earlier.

Environmental Assessment

It was not easy for those developing the commercial pipeline system to gauge the level of support for environmental protection. An Esso review of corporate responsibility in December 1980 found, on the one hand, a growing reluctance on the part of Government to impose further controls and, therefore, costs on industry. The deteriorating economic climate had, however, done nothing to curb media and public concern. The sense of outrage at oil spills was as strong as ever. European Community legislation was also becoming more important. The corporate review concluded that the most effective way of protecting the company's interests was to participate as fully as possible in the environmental debates that were increasingly setting the policy agenda.

It was however one thing to make such general statements, and another to ensure they were followed in practice. During preparations for the Public Inquiry into the South-East Pipeline, the view was expressed that the company need only refer to its good safety record and codes of practice. Anything more might result in costly precedents or demands for a re-evaluation of existing pipelines. Those officers directly responsible for UK pipeline operations reacted angrily. Not only did the company's public standing require it to co-operate fully with the reasonable requests of Government but there was simply no alternative. Under the Pipelines Act of 1962, as modified by Regulations in 1974, the Pipelines Inspectorate had become an agent of the Health and Safety Executive, in securing the safe construction, operation and use of those pipelines covered by the Act. There was invariably substantial agreement as to general philosophy and specific measures, before any formal application to the Inspectorate was made.

In their evidence to Public Inquiries, the company's witnesses emphasised how pipelines had a much better safety record than other forms of transport. Although they might carry extremely dangerous substances, their high standard of construction, maintenance and operation meant the risk of leakage was very low. Within the files of the individual pipelines, copies were preserved of the annual returns required by the Pipelines Inspectorate, giving details of throughput, modifications, cathodic survey results, pressure test results, patrolling, and other relevant information. Lists were updated and revised as to who should be notified in the event of an emergency. In the course of negotiations with the Thames Water Authority, in regard to the South-East Pipeline near the Darenth Pumping Station, a safety evaluation estimated the risk of slight contamination was 1 in 27,000 years, and of severe contamination as 1 in 100,000 years. The supervisory system would detect any significant leak and, the instant it happened, shut the pipeline down.

Whilst accepting the enormous odds against a leak, and the assurances of a rapid response to any emergency, water undertakers emphasised that even the most minimal danger to their boreholes could not be tolerated. That concern was increased by the knowledge that the greatest danger to a pipeline arose from the actions of third parties. Esso had always been acutely aware of this. On Salisbury Plain, a cover of reinforced concrete had been provided where tanks might cross the pipeline . An Esso engineer was in attendance when a farmer near Salisbury carried out drainage and ditching work in April 1968, so as to ensure there was no risk to the pipeline and its protective wrapping. It became the practice for the entire route of each pipeline to be flown over by helicopter once a fortnight. A ground inspection was made once a year.

There was nothing inherently novel in the making of environmental impact assessments. There had been no end to the number and variety of 'environmental considerations' voiced, nor to the planning authorities, national pressure groups and individual members of the public who believed they had the right to be consulted. As the Esso Environmental Co-ordinator remarked in July 1981, it had always been the practice closely to scrutinise major capital projects, as the first preparatory move to consulting the appropriate regulatory agencies and interested external groups. The whole review process was so all-embracing, and so much taken for granted, that it was difficult to see what industry had to learn from the so-called 'new' concept of Environmental Impact Assessment (EIA).

A suspicion that statutory EIAs were being sought as a further mechanism for impeding industrial development was reinforced by reports of their use for that purpose by environmental pressure groups in the United States. Early drafts of a European Environmental Directive were closely modelled on that 'specific rigid numeric assessment system'. The public response of UK industry had been twofold. Most of business and industry, including the Confederation of British Industry, was forthright in its opposition. The response of the Gas Corporation, Central Electricity Generating Board, and such companies as ICI and BP, had been more subtle. They had emphasised in their publicity how they already practised a form of EIA. By doing so, the Gas Corporation claimed to have reduced the average time taken to gain planning approval for the construction of its natural-gas system to 22 weeks. Esso decided to follow that more constructive response, but with a much lower public profile.

Esso accordingly supported the UK Petroleum Industry Association in urging the Department of the Environment to drop its outright opposition, and to participate in the drafting of an EEC Directive. Whatever the pace and course of inter-governmental negotiations, the company was convinced an Environmental Impact Statement would eventually be required for all future pipeline schemes. If used intelligently, it would provide 'valuable reassurance' when objections of a general nature were made. It was an obvious reference-point in responding to specific concerns voiced about a scheme. As a major part of the company's evidence to a Public Inquiry, it would set out as clearly as possible the need for the pipeline, the alternatives considered, and the key elements favouring the route chosen.

The Environmental Assessments prepared for both the South-East Pipeline and Midline began by citing the Company's obligations under the Pipe-lines Act of 1962 and, more particularly, those parts that required the preservation of amenity, wildlife and the historic environment, protection of water resources from pollution, and the restoration of farmland to a condition equal at least to that before the work commenced. Over and above these statutory requirements, the Assessments emphasised how Esso (as one of the largest and longest-established oil companies in the UK) took seriously its responsibilities for public safety and environmental concerns. It was the company's policy to combine high standards of safety with operating efficiency, and to give every consideration to eliminating or minimising risk of damage to the environment. There followed sections devoted to ecological and archaeological considerations, the transmission of diseases to livestock, and the intended methods of operating and monitoring the pipeline.

A priority for any Assessment was to describe how the pipeline was to be built. Although the 'spread' method of construction had been used since the earliest days in the United States, it was not adopted in Britain until the mid-1950s. The term 'spread' derived from the way the entire construction might extend over several miles of the route, with each task being operated by separate and specialist crews. A width of 60 feet was usually sufficient. High-speed, rotary-bucket excavators would remove the top soil and subsoil, depositing them separately on one side of the trench. The steel pipe, of up to 40 feet in length, would be welded together at a rate of up to 2 miles a day. Once the pipes were lowered into place, the trench was backfilled so as to ensure the subsoil was consolidated and the top soil left loose and friable to its original depth.

It was explained to both Public Inquiries that a cross-country route would cause the least general disruption to the public, and was the quickest and cheapest to build. Two major obstructions on the South-East Pipeline could not be avoided, namely the Thames crossing and the built-up area of Dartford. It was the first time the technique called 'horizontal directional drilling' had been used on a large scale in Europe. A half-mile pilot hole was bored from the north bank of the Thames, under the river on a curved trajectory, to the surface on the south bank. There were 170 crossings on the Midline, which included 3 motorways, 42 major roads, 94 minor roads, 11 railway lines and 4 canals. As well as the Avon, 15 more minor rivers and streams were crossed. The more major crossings were thrust-bored and an open-cut method was used for the remainder. Particular care was taken at river crossings, to avoid pollution and any interference to fisheries, wildlife and recreational use.

In its formal response to the Midline proposal, the Countryside Commission had drawn attention to the need for professional guidance and 'proper sensitivity' for the landscape, especially in the two Areas of Outstanding Natural Beauty, the North Wessex Downs and Cotswolds. A meeting of March 1983 provided an opportunity for representatives of the company to outline the numerous steps being taken to 'fine tune' the route. So as to avoid crossing the open downland, the pipeline would follow an existing track across Broughton Down. It would be re-routed to avoid the large and important Site of Special Scientific Interest of North Meadow, Cricklade. In order to avoid felling mature trees, the route through Poulton Park in Hampshire had been modified so as to follow the existing pylon-route, where the trees had already been felled.

Whilst the Nature Conservancy Council (NCC) would have much preferred Thursley Common to have been avoided altogether, it became clear in the course of negotiation that it would agree to the South-East Pipeline crossing the National Nature Reserve, subject to a series of deviations. As well as agreeing to these, the company offered to reduce working widths and to keep construction work to the minimum during the nesting season. It would erect more long-term fencing to assist the recovery of mature heather, help establish a site suitable for a sand-lizard population, and fund a studentship for three years to monitor the recovery of those parts of the common most directly affected by the pipeline.

Close account had also to be taken of archaeological sites. The Archaeological Officer for the Hampshire County Council co-ordinated the task of marking on a set of Ordnance Survey 1:10,000 maps every site known to exist along the Midline. Esso had already gained considerable experience of working with archaeologists from the South-East Pipeline. A donation of £5,000 had been made to the Kent Archaeological Rescue Unit, of which £500 was used to cover the costs of publishing a book describing ten years of rescue archaeology in the county. The page describing the Rescue Unit's work on the Esso pipeline recounted how bulldozers had been followed, as they stripped off the topsoil, and the excavation of the trench closely watched. It was 'a splendid opportunity to study a very wide area of countryside, mostly little known, with the contractor doing the excavation'. Whilst no known major sites had been destroyed, 6 new sites had been revealed. The new Iron Age sites were particularly important, showing a density much greater than had previously been suspected for that part of West Kent.

CHAPTER 8

Environmental Hazards

Introduction

If there is anywhere on earth where a community might feel 'safe' from natural hazards, it must be the British Isles, where the elements (on land at least) are relatively benign. More often than not, an environmental hazard has arisen only through some human activity. A devastating example was the Aberfan coal-tip disaster of October 1966. Whilst the processes that caused the down-slope movement of the coal wastes onto the Welsh valley village were natural, the loss of the 144 lives stemmed from the creation of the tip in the first place and the inadequate management of its drainage. Such a combination of natural and human forces, and their impacts, have provided writers with plenty of scope for mounting a 'vigorous indictment of ruthless, profit-seeking industry', the indifference of central and local government, and of public apathy (Barr 1969).

One of the few large-scale natural hazards commonly to afflict the UK has been flooding. Its impact has often been magnified by the concentration of housing and industry in the riparian zone. Such an event may be illustrated by the flood that struck Norwich in November 1912. Where the rain gauges had recorded 6 inches of rainfall over the previous fortnight, it was assumed the improved engineering and drainage works, undertaken since the previous major flood of 1878, could cope with the swollen rivers. Six inches of rain then fell within 12 hours – an intensity never previously recorded in the British Isles. The accompanying storm blew down trees by the hundreds. Almost every low-lying part of Norfolk was under water. The trams in Norwich were stopped by the depth of water in the main streets. All but two of the dynamos in the electric-lighting station were flooded. The church at Trowse was inundated to a depth of 3 feet, and many of the gravestones washed out of position. The President of the Local Government Board, John Burns, 'paid a flying visit to the city, his object being to make a personal inspection of the flooded area'. The Secretary of the Alliance Cage Bird Association reported ruinous losses among 'many working-men canary fanciers', who supplemented their earnings in the boot-and-shoe trade by breeding such birds in specially constructed sheds in their back gardens. Scores of cages could be seen floating in the streets of the Heigham district, the centre of the industry and where the floods were most severe. Many strains of canaries were wiped out altogether (Goose 1912).

The most extensive and locally devastating natural disaster was the East Coast Flood Disaster on the night of 31 January 1953, caused by a combination of a very high storm surge and a fairly high tide, together with severe wave action in the North Sea. The coasts of the Netherlands and Belgium were inundated even more catastrophically. As the surge swept southward along a thousand miles of coastline, it grew to some 9 feet or more, causing the level of over 8 feet at Southend in Essex to be the largest known. The sea defences were breached in 1,200 places (Grieve 1959). Not only was much expected of government but, as the Prime Minister, Winston Churchill assured the House of Commons on 2 February, every effort was to be made to ensure 'all the resources of the State' were employed. A Cabinet Committee of eleven ministers had already met to decide priorities and co-ordinate the response. Its Chairman, the Home Secretary, Sir David Maxwell Fyfe, spoke the next day of how the greatest use was being made of the armed forces in both evacuating communities and repairing the breaches of the sea and river defences (PD, Commons, 510, 1480–4 and 1665–71).

The first full Cabinet discussion was held on 17 February, its purpose being to prepare for a debate in the House of Commons. As Maxwell Fyfe reported, two days later, 307 had died. Over 25,000 houses had been flooded. Three oil refineries had been inundated and a considerable part of the stock of 66,000 tons of raw sugar at Purfleet destroyed. Up to 175,000 acres of agricultural land had been flooded, of which one-third had been seriously affected by salt water. Upward of a thousand cattle, 8,000 sheep, 1,500 pigs and 20,000 poultry were lost (PD, Commons, 511, 1456–1580). As the emphasis shifted from the immediate relief and repair work to longer rehabilitation, Harold Macmillan, the Minister of Housing and Local Government, warned the Cabinet on 14 March that little progress would be made in the rebuilding of the sea defences and infrastructure of the affected communities until the Government announced the scale of its financial assistance. There had not been 'a disaster of this magnitude for centuries past'. The Chancellor of the Exchequer, 'Rab' Butler, accepted that 'the Government must adopt a generous standard in providing financial help for the work of rehabilitation'. Some £30 to 40 million had already been spent on short-term works. Farmers had been promised help in rehabilitating land affected by the salt water, and for reinstating crops, orchards, hedgerows and fencing. As part of the Government's reassurance as to the protection of coastal communities, Maxwell Fyfe announced the appointment of a Departmental Committee under Viscount Waverley. Its interim report of July 1953 recommended an improved flood-warnings system, claiming that had it been in operation earlier there would have been minimal, if any, loss of life (PRO, CAB 128, 26/1 and 129, 60; PD, Commons, 513, 32–47 and 496–601).

The Committee's more substantive report of May 1954 emphasised how it would be prohibitively expensive to provide complete protection against every conceivable combination of tide and surge. If a surge of the greatest dimensions had struck at a time of high water of the maximum spring tides, the flood waters would have been several feet higher. The Liverpool Observatory and Tidal Institute calculated, on the basis of measurements taken at Sheerness and Southend since 1820, that the risk of the water levels rising to that of January 1953 were no greater than once in 200 years. Given the protection afforded to human life by the improved warning system, the Committee recommended that the standard set for each length of coastline should be determined on the basis of the extent and value of the properties to be safeguarded. Rather than the responsibility and, therefore, cost of making such provision falling entirely on central government, they should continue to be borne by the individual, local and national interests (PP 1953–54a).

In the sense of being quite without precedent, the most shocking, man-induced disaster in peacetime was, perhaps, the grounding of the Liberian-registered oil tanker *Torrey Canyon*, between the Isles of Scilly and Land's End on 18 March 1967. As the official report observed, its scale in terms of oil pollution, was 'as unprecedented as it was sudden' (Cabinet Office 1967). Politically, the priority for the Government was to defend itself from charges of being slow to react. It was not until the tanker's back had broken, and all hope of salvage finally abandoned, that approval had been given for bombing missions designed to burn as much oil as possible before it left the tanker. At the personal instigation of the Prime Minister, Harold Wilson, a White Paper was hurriedly drafted and published on 4 April, describing how naval vessels, together with chartered boats, had begun spraying the oil slicks with detergent within hours of the wreck. The oil had first come ashore on the 25 March, the same day as the Minister of Housing and Local Government left for Cornwall to assure local authorities that they would receive grant aid of up to 75 per cent of the cost for cleaning-up operations (PP 1966–67). In a Commons statement that same day, Wilson further emphasised that everything was being done, for example, to protect the Cornish tourist industry, which had an estimated value of over £100 million per annum (PD, Commons, 744, 38–54)

As the Government's Chief Scientific Adviser, Sir Solly Zuckerman, wrote, later that year, 'practically every issue on which decisions for action had to be taken during the period of crisis was at least partly of a scientific or technical nature'. The condition of the tanker had so deteriorated by the late evening on 21 March that Wilson had first telephoned him. Under Zuckerman's Chairmanship, an inter-disciplinary committee of scientists was assembled the next morning. There was considerable criticism of the damage caused to marine life by the excessive use of detergents on the beaches. A priority therefore was to develop emulsifiers which combined the maximum effectiveness with minimum toxicity and persistence (Cabinet Office 1967). For the Nature Conservancy, which had played so large a part in both monitoring and endeavouring to alleviate the worst of the damage, the most pressing need was to ensure that in any future emergency such 'expert' advice was followed by those physically responsible for carrying out the cleansing operations. During the *Torrey Canyon* operation much of the detergent had simply been used because it was to hand. It was the most obvious way of being seen to do something to stem the disaster (Sheail 1998, pp. 177–80).

The twentieth century is conventionally divided by its two world wars, and perhaps by a third staging point at the end of the Cold War, in 1989. But an environmental perspective, and a good deal of hindsight, might also bring to the fore the years leading up to 1970. As well as pictures of the oil-stricken Cornish beaches and wildlife, television and the press gave considerable prominence to the thalidomide scandal, where appalling injuries were inflicted on unborn babies through their mothers taking the anti-depressant drug, thalidomide. It was a time of marked disenchantment with science and technology, as developed through 'big business' and government. Rachel Carson's polemic, *Silent Spring*, had been published earlier in 1962. That angry, challenging book described how the indiscriminate use of insecticides, used both to protect agricultural crops and combat disease, threatened the delicate balance of nature. The irresponsible use of such compounds had already wiped out countless forms of animal life (Carson 1963). It was a time of mounting public pressure for a nuclear-test-ban treaty. As Thomas Dunlap commented, the image of contaminated rain, and of strontium 90 passing through grass into the milk of cows and nursing mothers, and into the next generation of children, did more than anything else 'to make Americans suspicious of the utopian dreams of technology' (Dunlap 1981).

It was not just the military authorities that were stigmatised for their commitment to nuclear power. The electricity-generating industry had perceived nuclear power as the fuel of the future. Whereas there was a dependence on others for coal and oil, the industry might become entirely self-sufficient in nuclear power. There was, however, unprecedented opposition to its adoption. Although the Government's decision to locate the first nuclear power stations well away from closely inhabited areas was intended to reassure the public, it also encouraged speculation as to their potential dangers. It was not until February 1968 that any relaxation in location policy was announced. As Minister of Power, Richard Marsh, emphasised, in a statement to Parliament of February 1968, the UK now had 132 reactor-years of commercial experience, during which time there had been no accidental release of radioactivity producing significant effects beyond the site boundary (PD, Commons, 758, 235–8).

The Central Electricity Generating Board (CEGB) had to pay increasing attention to those who opposed, on a point of principle, any form of nuclear power. The CEGB *Annual Report* for 1976–7 commented on how Britain was not alone in being

> on the horns of a dilemma, and yet from where we stand – at the cradle of commercial nuclear power – three acknowledged factors should make the issues clearer to see.

First, the nuclear power industry was unique in its awareness of the impact its activities might have on health, safety and the environment. No other industry, nor indeed country, was so closely regulated. Secondly, the licensed operators of commercial power stations in Britain had proved their ability to develop such an energy source so responsibly, reliably and economically. The third reason, and one most often overlooked, was that those persons most closely involved – the workforce and their unions, and the populations living nearest to the stations – had accepted nuclear power in their stride. The levels of radiation derived from the nuclear power industry were extremely small in comparison with the natural background levels and, say, those of diagnostic and therapeutic use in medicine (Central Electricity Generating Board (CEGB) 1977).

The focus of public concern appeared to shift during the late 1970s, away from the safe operation of the power stations to that of reprocessing the irradiated nuclear fuel and the storage of active wastes. Increasing attention was directed towards the activities of British Nuclear Fuels Ltd at Sellafield in Cumbria, and the UK Atomic Energy Authority. A Nuclear Industry Radio-Active Waste Executive (NIREX) was established in November 1985. Parliamentary approval was given in May 1985 for four sites to be investigated as to their suitability as near-surface radioactive waste repositories. There was such fierce opposition from the respective local communities and the anti-nuclear lobby (Openshaw *et al.* 1989) that Nicholas Ridley, the Secretary of State for the Environment, accepted the advice of NIREX, shortly before the General Election of 1987, that such appraisal should be terminated, and resources concentrated on evaluating options for a deep repository. As the CEGB *Annual Report* recounted, such studies had confirmed both the technical feasibility and safety of low-level waste disposal in a near-surface repository. There was however very little saving in costs against the excavation of deeper repositories, that might also accommodate intermediate-level wastes (CEGB 1987).

Public perception of nuclear-power development counted for more and more. The Secretary of State for Energy, Anthony Wedgwood Benn, announced in January 1978 that the Government had authorised the CEGB and South of Scotland Electricity Board to proceed with the ordering of one Advanced Gas-cooled Reactor station each, and to carry out preliminary station design-work for a Pressurised Water Reactor (PWR), the main reactor system used abroad – the aim being to establish a flexible strategy to meet developing circumstances (PD, Commons, 942, 1391–408). There was, consequently, considerable concern when, in March 1979, an accident occurred at the PWR Three Mile Island Unit, at Harrisburg, in the United States. The reactor core and fuel pins sustained substantial damage, very large quantities of radioactive waste were spilt inside the main reactor building, and a radioactive plume escaped into the locality. A CEGB study team, which left straight away to inspect the damaged plant, found nothing to suggest any fundamental weaknesses in the PWR design. The incident had arisen from a series of small deficiencies in design and operating procedures.

Far from casting doubt on its own operations, the CEGB argued that the Harrisburg incident had demonstrated the effectiveness of safety systems in nuclear power stations, when correctly used. As the Prime Minister, James Callaghan, assured parliament, in early April 1979, no such accident could occur in Britain. Studies of the Pressurised Water Reactors in Britain continued (PD, Commons, 965, 1161). In December of that year, David Howell, the Secretary of State for Energy in the new Conservative Government, confirmed that he had accepted the advice of the generating industry, namely that, even by the most cautious of estimates, there was need to commission one new plant each year over the decade beginning in 1982 (PD, Commons, 976, 287–304).

The prospects for a rapid acceleration of the nuclear power programme remained confusing. There was encouragement from the commitment of the Prime Minister, Margaret Thatcher, to the development of cheaper electricity from nuclear power, and her public support for the PWR programme, given during a visit to the Heysham nuclear power station in the autumn of 1985. The CEGB had made a formal application in January 1982 for statutory consent and a nuclear licence for a PWR station at Sizewell 'B' on the Suffolk coast. A programme of local press briefings and public exhibitions had been put in hand immediately. A Special Inquiry held under the Town and Country Planning Act of 1971 proved, however, to be the longest and most exhaustive planning inquiry ever conducted. Under the Chairmanship of Sir Frank Layfield QC, it opened in January 1983, and took evidence from 195 witnesses on 344 occasions. There were 340 volumes of daily transcripts. It took from March 1985, when the Inquiry closed, until December 1986 to write the bulk of the report (O'Riordan *et al.* 1988).

The purpose of the meeting of the Generating Board, in May

1986, had been to decide the corporate response to the problems of the nuclear industry, including specific actions that might be taken to improve its public image. Instead, the meeting opened with a statement from the Chairman of the Board, Lord Marshall, referring to 'the disastrous accident' which had occurred some 10 days earlier at the Chernobyl nuclear power station in the Ukraine. The explosion, and its effects on Britain and other countries, had dramatically altered the context of discussion. The Board's Executive called for an urgent reassessment of levels of investment in research and development into non-nuclear generation options, in the light of the disaster and its impact on political and public perceptions of the acceptability of nuclear power.

But ministers continued to support the nuclear option and, therefore, the application of the CEGB for Sizewell 'B' and proposals for further stations. At a special conference convened by the International Atomic Energy Agency in Vienna, in late August, the Russian delegation acknowledged there had been no 'safety culture' of the kind which governed Western practice. As Lord Marshall, who had led the UK delegation, confirmed to the Board at its meeting in October 1986, it would have been impossible for such gross mismanagement, through the deliberate and repeated violation of operating rules, to have occurred in any CEGB station. Six years and one month after the Board submitted its application, and after listening to debates on the Layfield Report in both Houses of Parliament, the Secretary of State for Energy, Peter Walker, gave consent in March 1987 for the construction of Sizewell 'B' (PD, Commons, 112, 475–90). The Board particularly welcomed the Minister's reasoned conclusions that the nuclear accident at Chernobyl was not material to his decision to give consent for Sizewell 'B' (CEGB 1987). Construction works began in July 1988.

Meanwhile, the complex repercussions of such accidents became clearer. Where models had predicted reasonably well the behaviour of fallout in the intensively farmed parts of Britain, they had failed to anticipate the behaviour of a major contaminant, radiocaesium, in unimproved upland ecosystems. Fallout in the UK had been greatest where the passage of the Chernobyl cloud coincided with heavy rainfall in north Wales, Cumbria, and parts of Scotland and Northern Ireland. A combination of soils with a high organic matter content, the presence of such plant species as heather that had a high uptake-rate, and the preference of individual sheep within the flocks for such plants, meant the concentrations of radiocaesium activity in some livestock and game animals remained so high as to prevent their meat being sold or otherwise entering the food-chain (Institute of Terrestrial Ecology 1998).

Dereliction

The nineteenth century afforded much evidence of grim environments being tolerated, where such industrial activity brought profits and employment. In his twentieth-century environmental history of America, Hal Rothman wrote of bargains being struck, whereby employees and their families accepted the price that had to be paid in terms of the risks arising from such dangerous workplaces to their health and the general well-being of the town and countryside around. Both in Britain and America, such bargains became strained and torn apart as industries declined and closed through the exhaustion of their natural resources or markets for their products. Far from remaining muted, those former employees could now emerge as the most authoritative critics of the abuses so long suffered (Rothman 2000, pp. 131–2).

The late nineteenth century saw the exhaustion of the South Staffordshire coalfield and the first tentative steps taken to 'beautify the Black Country'. A Midland Reafforesting Association was founded at a public meeting in Birmingham, in February 1903, by which time 14,000 acres were adjudged to be ready for immediate reclamation. Some 30,000 acres might ultimately be afforested. The Travellers' Rest Mound, at Wednesbury was planted in collaboration with the Patent Shaft and Axle Company. The most important and enduring project was the planting of 60,000 trees of various species on some 34 pit mounds, sand pits and slagheaps within the grounds of the Moorcroft Isolation Hospital at Moxley. The

Association claimed its achievement was not so much the area planted but the experienced gained. A total of 83 acres had been planted on 36 sites by the time it became moribund in the 1920s. The most depressing feature was the extent of vandalism, especially by children. The saplings planted at Pelsall in 1909 were 'beaten up thoroughly' in 1911 (Wise 1962).

It was more than a question of rehabilitating the landscapes devasted and abandoned by industry. There was need also to prevent present-day and future industries from having a similar effect. As the intended location of a flourishing iron-and-steel industry, the predominantly rural county of Northamptonshire was confronted by such a challenge in the late 1930s. As the County Land Agent remarked, the use of land was not a commercial activity that could be 'scrapped', or got rid of simply 'by a transaction of hard cash'. However ill-used, it remained as someone's responsibility (PRO, MAF 68, 645). Yet, as the 15-year history in tackling the dereliction caused by ironstone-working in the East Midlands demonstrated, there was no miraculous cure. However comparatively simple the solutions might appear, an engineering inspector warned that 'the more one delved into the problem the much more difficult it became' (PRO, HLG 89, 108).

The Scottish steel-making firm, Stewarts & Lloyds, had obtained a government loan to set up a modern steel-works based on local ores around Corby, in Northamptonshire (Scopes 1968). By the mid-1930s, over 1,600 acres of countryside had been transformed by iron-ore extraction into hill-and-dale, with ridges 20 feet high and up to 60 feet from crest to crest. It was anticipated some 25 square miles would be affected over the next 25 years. As the Mid-Northamptonshire Planning Committee protested in 1938, whilst the best engineering skills were being devoted towards the winning of the minerals in the most economical manner, no serious regard was being paid to the effect on the countryside. It was estimated to cost about £320 per acre to reinstate farmland worth less than £15 per acre (PRO, HLG 52,1; Northamptonshire Record Office, X1589, TP 29P; Sheail 1983; Moore-Colyer 1996).

Although there had been no outcry from amenity bodies, such as the Council for the Preservation of Rural England (CPRE), officials of the relevant government departments expected this to change dramatically once those without local or vested interests in the industry discovered the enormity of the changes being wrought on the rural landscape. A Committee under Lord Kennet, which reported to the Minister of Health in March 1939, strongly urged the case for restoration, emphasising that whilst the main responsibility should rest with landowners, a central authority was also needed to implement a long-term, restorative and preventative programme of action. Although war prevented any further initiative, the Minister of Town and Country Planning appointed in May 1943 Major A.H.S. Waters (a Past-President of the Institution of Civil Engineers) as Chairman of a fresh committee of enquiry. His 'extremely useful' report of May 1945 described how quarrying technology had taken an unexpected turn. The earlier Kennet report had expected larger and increasingly powerful mechanical shovels to exploit areas of thicker overburden. The long-scraping, upwards movement of the shovel meant it was impossible to separate the topsoil from underlying strata. There was no way of avoiding the creation of hill-and-dale of ever-increasing dimensions. Since devastation was inevitable, the Kennet Committee saw the challenge as 'one of undoing something already done'. The further enquiry by Waters found the situation transformed, in as much as dragline excavators had been introduced which, although capable of as much devastation, were also able to cut the waste horizontally and spread it over a greater area. It was therefore possible to separate out the overburden, including say layers as thin as 6 inches of topsoil. For the first time, it became possible to excavate and restore a site simultaneously (PRO, HLG 89, 109 and 112; PP 1945–46).

The principle of a levy had been conceded by all parties towards the costs of restoration. Waters recommended that the companies and local authorities as well as the landowners (or royalty owners) should contribute to the levy. Each should be represented on the statutory body that decided, before quarrying began, both the standards and costs of restoration. Through their participation, both the landowners and companies would have every incentive to achieve restoration as effectively and efficiently as possible. Central government also had a leading role to play. Not only would the failure to achieve a constructive solution undermine the concept of statutory planning, but it would further highlight the impotence of local government in the face of a large industrial undertaking. But for the Ministry to intervene, there had to be a long-term policy. The first and most obvious step was taken under the Town and Country Planning Act of 1947, whereby it became possible for local planning authorities to regulate the incidence of quarrying, and to insist on restorative work, without incurring heavy claims for compensation. Officials were, however, concerned as to the precedents set for the other extractive industries and, most obviously sand-and-gravel working.

The dilemma remained. As the Minister, Lewis Silkin, asserted, in reply to an Adjournment Debate in 1949,

> one has to face the fact that, unpleasant as the land in the area may be, what is going on in Northamptonshire and in the surrounding counties is an essential process in the economic life of the country. One cannot do without this iron ore. (PD, Commons, 470, 1835–44)

His successor as Minister, Hugh Dalton, was much less inhibited. He wrote, in a Cabinet paper, of being shocked by what he saw during a tour of 'two or three days' spent visiting areas which resembled 'deserts of the Moon'. They were, he later told Parliament, 'horrible to behold', and had 'a most depressing effect upon the morale of all those living near them'. The land had been robbed of its wealth, agricultural fertility and natural beauty. It was, Dalton wrote, 'capitalism with its b . . . claws out'. Company directors had 'made a profit out of this land and bunked off' (PRO, CAB 132, 14 and 15; PD, Commons, 477, 230–33, 486 and 644–757).

Under the compromise worked out, Dalton announced two measures in July 1950. Under the Town and Country Planning (Ironstone Areas Special Development) Order, all operators were henceforth obliged, as part of their planning consents, to restore the

Environmental Hazards 231

overburden within two years of excavation 'as completely and as speedily as possible to agriculture'. Only where this was impossible was the land to be afforested. Secondly, Dalton announced a Mineral Workings Bill, empowering the Minister, on the advice of an advisory committee, to administer and finance restoration. The cost of restoring pits where the overburden exceeded 35 feet in depth was to be met by operators, landowners and the Exchequer. The level of grant aid for each pit would be assessed *before* any excavation took place. Although there were no divisions on the Bill, which received the Royal Assent in August 1951, critics accused the Government of dealing out 'rough justice', in failing to take due cognisance of local operating difficulties or the individual circumstances of the operator or owner. Government spokesmen agreed, but pleaded that the arbitrary, yet simple, arrangements made for 'easy book-keeping' and followed the 'old sick-club principle'. A year later, the Cheshire Brine Pumping (Compensation for Subsidence) Act introduced a basically similar procedure in the form of a levy on producers of white salt.

In the event, the ironstone restoration programme became a model of its kind. The operators exploited and restored over 3,600 acres (1,440 hectares), of which 2,926 acres (1,170 ha) were levelled and top-soiled. Of the 1,400 acres (560 ha) of derelict land in 1951, some 1,200 acres (480 ha) had been restored by 1963 (Cowan 1961). Drawing on the practical experience gained, an inquiry into planning controls over all types of mineral workings (the Stevens Inquiry) of the mid-1970s recommended the general adoption of such a procedure, whereby operators were required to restore land to high standards with appropriate after-treatment (Department of the Environment 1976). Such a generalisation of practice was embodied in the Town and Country Planning (Minerals) Act of 1981.

There had been little opencast coal mining before 1942. Whilst representing less than 5 per cent of the output from deep mines, one ton of open-cast coal could be quarried with only one-quarter of the labour force needed for deep-mined coal. The work was done by civil-engineering staff, as opposed to skilled miners.

Renewed annually, the wartime emergency powers enabled the Ministry of Fuel and Power (MFP) to prospect for coal, requisition sites and extract the deposits, subject only to the statutory provision of compensation and the requirement that other government departments should be consulted. The Defence Regulations overrode the rights of both land owners and occupiers, and planning authorities, to lodge objections. By the end of the Second World War, it was the largest civil engineering operation in the world under a single direction (Court 1951; Sheail 1991c and 1992).

Whilst the winning of opencast coal had been perceived as a wartime expedient, the continued shortages of deep-mined coal meant it had to continue. It took an average of only 15 weeks from the application to work the coal to the granting of the Minister's consent. The same coal engineer engaged to excavate the coal undertook the work required to restore the land to agriculture. It was usual to acquire a site twice the area to be excavated. Although the area taken out of farming remained fairly constant at 25,000 acres (10,120 hectares), the total area remaining under requisition rose as the period of agricultural after-care was extended. Of the 43,000 acres (17,400 ha) under requisition in May 1952, 19,000 acres (7,700 ha) were being farmed under supervision (PRO, POWE 4,40 and MAF 141, 3 and 376).

Although studies of the impact of opencast working focus on the battles with amenity and agricultural interests, some of the most formidable opposition came from the water-supply industry. The dilemma was highlighted by the application to prospect in the water-catchment of the Borough of Llanelly in South Wales in 1956. Although opencast coal was important for such a heavily industrialised region, an adequate supply of water was also essential in attracting new industry and modernising the existing tin-plate works. The attitude of the Ministry of Health had noticeably hardened following the pollution of a reservoir supplying a third of the needs of the Ashton-in-Makerfield Water Board in Lancashire, as a result of opencast working adjacent to the gathering grounds (PRO, BD 11, 2971; HLG 50, 2383).

The handling of such conflict between the basic utilities provided important context for assessing how amenity and agriculture might fare. As an official of the Ministry of Town and Country Planning remarked in June 1950, it would be quite wrong to regard consent for opencast working as a victory for the Ministry of Fuel and Power, and its denial as a success for the department. That would be to perceive planning as a purely negative activity. Millions of tons of coal would be lost each year if opencast working was confined to where nobody wanted to live, farm or walk on Sundays. A balance had to be struck between the nation's need for coal, and the demand for amenity, housing, farming and forestry. Each piece of land had to be put to the best possible use (PRO, HLG 89, 254).

In as much as a monetary value could be placed on agricultural land, farming was even worse placed than amenity in resisting the demands for opencast working. As the Minister of Fuel and Power, Philip Noel-Baker, pointed out (in an Opposition Debate of July 1950), coal was 30 times more valuable than the food produced from the same area of land that would, in any case, be restored once the coal had been extracted (PD, Commons, 477, 2269–78). The steps already being taken to restore sites to agriculture were incorporated into a code of practice in 1951. Whilst no one challenged the need for an overall improvement in standards, there was considerable debate as to who should bear the responsibility and, therefore, the cost. A Deputy Secretary of the Ministry of Agriculture insisted in December 1950 that it must be fundamentally right that the coal industry, having overturned the soil, should carry that responsibility. There would otherwise be no incentive to minimise the amount of damage caused. The Ministry of Fuel and Power was nevertheless justified in arguing that farming should bear some of the cost, especially at a time of more exacting standards of restoration and after-treatment. There was otherwise risk of its demands becoming unreasonable (PRO, MAF 141, 3, 6 and 10).

Decisions taken at Cabinet level forced the pace of resolution. The severe public censure of government, following the Crichel Down enquiry, as to its methods of retaining farmland originally requisitioned for military purposes, meant ministers were especially anxious to abolish all wartime Defence Regulations. A Bill of 40 clauses and 6 schedules was drawn up in 1957, so as finally to put the opencast coal industry on a peacetime footing. The National Coal Board was required to apply to the Minister of Power before any site was worked – that consent would carry 'deemed planning permission'. It would be a condition that the land was restored to a standard 'reasonably fit for agricultural use' (PRO, CAB 134, 1501 and 1970, and POWE 37, 439).

In moving the Second Reading of the Opencast Coal Bill, the Paymaster-General, Reginald Maudling, appealed, in January 1958, for a sense of perspective. Not only was the impact on agriculture and amenity only temporarily devastating but, in extracting some 160 million tons of opencast coal since 1942, less than one-quarter of 1 per cent of all agricultural land had been affected. The purpose of the Bill was not to extend working, but further to minimise its impact. During the drafting stages, officials had resisted moves to incorporate a formal 'Code of Restoration' into the Bill, arguing that this would make it even harder to take account of local conditions, or more recent advances in restoration and aftercare. The Agriculture Departments and Forestry Commission (in the case of woodland) would act in a consultative capacity throughout the Board's occupancy of the land, and serve as agents of the Board in carrying out the after-treatment required (PD, Commons, 580, 1056-71; PRO, POWE 37, 464).

There continued to be misgivings on the part of Members of Parliament representing affected constituencies. As the Conservative Member for Hexham warned, it was not enough to compensate the individual landowners and agricultural interests. For many who lived or visited the area, the term 'restoration' meant the reinstatement of amenity. Something more than concrete posts and wire was needed, where trees and hedgerows had been removed. The Labour Member for Ince in Lancashire cited the case of Winstanley Hall where, despite almost 200 acres of woodland having been destroyed over some 14 years, replanting had only just begun. 'You do not restore a forest by return of post.' In his reply, the Parliamentary Secretary to the Ministry of Power emphasised the Government's intention that the standards of amenity restoration should be progressively improved. They should receive as much attention as the 'more commercial matters of the productivity of the soil' (PP, 1957–58). The Act received the Royal Assent in August 1958.

In the event, the year 1958 also marked a peak in output of 13.8 million tons. Rising coal stocks caused the Minister to restrict opencast working to very large sites in Wales, Northumberland and Scotland. Where this limited the number of areas affected, the greater size of the individual sites, and depths to which coal could be excavated, meant an even greater local impact. As was argued by the Stevens' Committee on Planning Control over Mineral Working in its report of 1976, such instances of local devastation and increasing public expectation as to conditions, standards and attitudes towards restoration and after-care demanded a major recasting of the legislative framework (Department of the Environment 1976). Not only did many of the Committee's recommendations, as incorporated in the Town and Country Planning (Minerals) Act of 1981, embody the experience of the Ironstone Restoration Fund but, as the National Coal Board pointed out, both the Government and industry could be confident, in the light of the expertise and experience gained since the Opencast Coal Act of 1958, that such conditions would be met (Tomlinson 1982; Horne and Frost 1991).

Before 'Silent Spring'

One of the books to have made the greatest impact on twentieth century thinking on the environment was Rachel Carson's *Silent Spring*. Written for an American audience, the British edition was published in February 1963 (Carson 1963). The Duke of Edinburgh distributed some advance copies. In acknowledging his copy, the Minister of Agriculture, Christopher Soames, welcomed the book for the way it stimulated thought and discussion. UK policy was one of ascertaining the facts on each pesticide used in farming, deciding on its effective and proper use, and then making sure full instructions were provided. As the Ministry's Chief Scientific Adviser wrote, there was nothing in the experience of the UK 'to justify Miss Carson's gloomy assertions' (PRO, MAF 284, 352).

Such replies prompt the question as to how far Britain, prior to *Silent Spring*, had achieved the higher productivity that came through the use of agricultural chemicals without risk to human health and the wider environment. More generally, such inquiry might throw light on 'why environmental protection is so slow?' Was the problem one of a lack of communication between the scientist and society, the deliberate neglect of scientific information, or the robustness required of the evidence before corrective action can be taken (Doos 1994)? Most histories of pesticide use have portrayed the agricultural industry as grudgingly yielding ground to the proof of conservationists as to the damage being caused (Sheail 1985). The release, under the 30-years' rule, of the relevant files of the Ministry of Agriculture afford opportunity to trace more closely the responses of ministers, officials and their expert advisers as to how they sought to reconcile the respective sectional interests with what they perceived to be the wider public interest.

Chemical pesticides had become an essential tool for improving both yields and quality. Yet by doing their job they involved considerable risk. Eight agricultural workers were poisoned by the weed-killer sprays they were using. Organo-phosphorus insecticides caused serious illness. Following the recommendations of a Working Group, under Sir Solly Zuckerman, an Agriculture (Poisonous Substances) Act of 1952 gave Agriculture Ministers (the Minister of Agriculture and Secretary of State for Scotland) powers to make regulations requiring operatives applying dangerous chemicals to wear protective clothing (PRO, MAF 284, 377). It was much harder to decide how pesticides should be regulated in order to minimise contamination of human foodstuffs and to lessen their impact on domestic, game and wild animals. Little was known about the presence, movement and significance of residues. Two further Zuckerman Working Parties accordingly recommended that the Ministry of Agriculture and the Association of British Manufacturers of Agricultural Chemicals (ABMAC) should establish a non-statutory Notification Scheme, whereby manufacturers would notify the Minister before marketing a new chemical for use in agriculture or food storage, or recommending a new use for an existing one. They were required to provide extensive data on the chemical, its behaviour and any possible risk. An Advisory Committee on Poisonous Substances, and a Scientific Sub Committee, were appointed to assist in both the administration of the 1952 Act and the voluntary Notification Scheme. Where satisfied adequate safeguards had been taken, the Advisory Committee recommended that dossiers as to the safe use of the chemicals should be published and widely circulated.

One of the most major advances in the use of agricultural chemicals was the introduction of dual-purpose seed dressings, against fungus and insect pests. Aldrin and dieldrin were first used on a commercial scale in the mid-1950s, shortly before the Notification Scheme was established. It was the coincidence of their introduction with the first reports of unusually large numbers of seed-eating birds dying that caused those chemicals to become 'such dirty words in the ears of bird lovers'. It was a letter from Major John Morrison, as Chairman of the British Field Sports Society, that first raised the issue with the Minister. Morrison was also Chairman of the parliamentary Conservative Party's Committee of Backbenchers. He cited a paper published by the *Veterinary Record* in March 1957, describing how wood pigeons and pheasants had died from ingesting dieldrin-dressed grain in trials conducted at the Royal Veterinary Laboratory (Carnaghan and Blaxland 1957). As Morrison related, Shell, the manufacturer of both aldrin and dieldrin, claimed the reports of the mysterious deaths on farmland had been exaggerated. The loss of a few birds was, in any case, a small price to pay for the agricultural benefits. The Advisory Committee came to a similar conclusion. A 'Bird and Seed Dressings Panel' was highly sceptical, in a report of March 1959, about there being any major hazard to bird populations from eating the seed. From the growers' viewpoint, the effect was likely to be more beneficial than harmful. The Nature Conservancy's representative protested that, before coming to any conclusion, a survey should be made of the 'true losses' in birdlife. Others on the Advisory Committee argued that if the Conservancy felt so strongly, it should itself finance and organise such a survey. It so happened that the Conservancy had obtained consent for establishing a new Experimental Station at Monks Wood in Huntingdonshire. Plans were being laid for its having a Toxic Chemicals and Wild Life Section (PRO, MAF 284, 62–3).

There was no hiding the concern felt. A leader in the *Kent and Sussex Courier* of 6 May 1960 acknowledged that farm output had risen, but warned of how there was public anxiety over both the cruelty involved and the way birds and bees were 'an integral part of the marvellous pattern of nature'. Their indiscriminate destruction would be to 'our ultimate peril'. The Ministry's Infestation Control Laboratory was increasingly concerned about the implications of such pesticides whose residues persisted so long in animal tissue and the general environment. Whilst it might require an adult to eat 14 pigeons a day to suffer any ill-effect, it was clearly undesirable that birds containing such levels of pesticide residue should come onto the market in any number. The risk of that happening became all the greater as the number of incidents sharply increased in the spring of 1960. Not only was the ground very hard and therefore more seed was left exposed, but there had been a switch from merely dusting the seed with dieldrin to more efficient liquid dressings. The Laboratory of the Government Chemist was persuaded to develop a technique first used in determining residue levels in sheep carcases following dipping, so as to measure them in bird corpses collected from the field. The Minister, John Hare, emphasised how everything should be done to establish the truth of whether aldrin and dieldrin were responsible for killing wild birds, and whether game birds were also affected. The Ministry had to be well prepared for discussions with manufacturers before the next sowing-season.

In developing a 'defensible' programme, Ministry officials sought to strike a balance between doing nothing and seeking a complete withdrawal of the dressings. Any refusal on the part of industry would force the Minister 'back on legislation'. The obvious course was to mount with industry a vigorous publicity campaign to persuade farmers to use the dressings in a safe and responsible way. Since even this might have 'a boomerang effect', in terms of triggering off 'anti-seed pressures', officials emphasised the scientific component of 'the holding programme'. Without such survey and experimental data, the Minister would be unable to defend himself from charges of doing too little or, from industry, of over-reaction. Not only did the number of casualties increase, but most corpses collected in the course of investigating incidents were found to contain residues of dieldrin. Industry had also become more accommodating – the recent criticisms voiced in parliament had made Shell's flesh creep. The company announced in the spring of 1961 the introduction of a new formulation, Kotox, as a seed dressing. Its substitution for use against such pests as wireworm meant that aldrin and dieldrin dressings would only be needed for controlling the wheat bulb fly in the autumn, when there was, in any case, an abundance of alternative food for wildlife. Although welcoming the obvious shift in the company's stance, officials were concerned that Shell might take all the credit for the proposals already being developed by the Ministry (PRO, MAF 284, 246).

By the time of a meeting in June 1961 to review the experience of the previous sowing-season, the Ministry had obtained the agreement of those organisations representing the manufacturers, merchants and farmers to a ban on the use of such seed-dressings on cereals, except in the case of autumn sown wheat, where there was danger of attack from wheat bulb fly. ABMAC insisted that it should be implemented through the formal machinery of the Notification Scheme, so as to emphasise that 'the voluntary ban' arose from independent scientific assessment, rather than giving way to public clamour. For the Ministry, the most urgent task was to educate farmers as to the precautions to be taken, with the secondary aim of dispelling the idea, so assiduously cultivated in some quarters, that the Ministry was indifferent to the risks to wildlife.

On more than one thousand visits to warehouses in January 1962, Ministry field-staff found only a few cases of seedsmen unaware of which proprietary dressings might be safely used, and when. Despite continued criticism of the detail of labelling and leaflets, it seemed that little seed of the wrong kind was sown that spring. There were considerably fewer reports of large-scale bird deaths (PRO, MAF 284, 246–7 and 250).

As Christopher Soames remarked at a departmental meeting, the Ministry's position was 'suspect', in the sense that it had allowed dieldrin-dressed seed to be used before its full effects were known. Although manufacturers were very worried about recent adverse publicity, and the prospect of more to come, the main stumbling block remained the dependence of farmers on what Claude H.M. Wilcox (an Under Secretary) called 'the black three', namely aldrin, dieldrin and heptachlor. Soames was especially concerned about the suspicions of both the Nature Conservancy and voluntary conservation bodies as to the sub-lethal effects of these persistent pesticides, namely their impact on the fertility and breeding behaviour of birds of prey and other groups at the end of 'the food chain'. Soames decided, on the basis of the accumulating evidence, and the obviously considerable role of such chemicals in farming, that the Advisory Committee should undertake a more strategic view of the question.

What began as an attempt to assuage wildlife interests came increasingly to encompass the well-being of *Homo sapiens*. President Kennedy had recently accepted a report of his Scientific Advisory Committee, recommending the orderly reduction in the use of such chemicals as dieldrin and other chlorinated hydrocarbons, with a view to their eventual elimination. Although the residue levels in human fat in North America were thought likely to be higher than in Britain, the Ministry expected the President's report to strengthen pressure for a complete withdrawal. In the course of the Advisory Committee's investigation, as ordered by Soames, its Scientific Sub Committee was also deeply concerned as to the pervasiveness of such organo-chlorine residues. A Residues Panel, appointed under the Ministry's Chief Scientific Adviser (covering the Food sector), found residues not only in mutton fat (as possibly derived from dieldrin sheep dips) but also in beef products and butter. Such a build-up of residue through the food chain would undermine the whole assumption that a chemical was safe if used in the recommended way. Although it was generally difficult, if not impossible, to demonstrate a causal link between any particular formulation or use of a chemical and its actual impact on wildlife or, for that matter, the human condition, members of the Scientific Sub Committee believed every effort should be made to arrest, if not reverse, the build-up of such residues through selective controls. Their two main recommendations were a ban on the use of dieldrin in sheep dips and in insecticidal fertiliser mixtures. As officials noted, such an approach had 'a family resemblance' to the American solution, but without any goal of eventual elimination made explicit (PRO, MAF 284, 354).

The Advisory Committee considered such recommendations at its meeting in December 1963. The Assistant Secretary in charge of the Ministry's Animal Health Division protested that there was no scientific proof that sheep dips were the source of dieldrin residues found in human fat. The Sub Committee had been unduly influenced by the alleged threat to carrion-eating birds, which were themselves enemies of the sheep farmer. Whilst dieldrin was so effective as to require only one dip a year, substitute chemicals were so weak as to need several. Not only was there extra cost in rounding up the sheep, but there was bound to be a greater incidence of fly-strike. The Ministry's responsibilities for animal welfare could not be ignored. The Advisory Committee sought compromise through the more gradual phasing-out of dieldrin dips, or their restriction, say, to upland holdings (PRO, MAF 284, 355).

At a further meeting of the Sub Committee in January 1964, L.J. Smith, the Assistant Secretary in charge of the Ministry's Labour, Safety and Seeds Division, complained of the considerable gap in the draft report to the Minister, between its account of the facts known and the recommendations for further restriction. If the report was to hang together, the concept of a progressive, and possibly dangerous, contamination of the environment had to be brought out more explicitly as the major factor causing the Advisory Committee to come to its conclusions. By doing so, it became possible to claim that although the direct evidence against dieldrin in sheep dip was not very strong, it was at least a contributory factor to such contamination. As Smith conceded, it remained open to debate as to whether such reasoning justified the agricultural cost of abandoning such dips. His personal view was that such usage could not survive long the publication of evidence of significant residues in home-produced meat, such as the Pesticides Panel had already found. Although the Advisory Committee was obviously impressed by the wildlife arguments, they were now also seriously concerned about the effect on human beings. The case against organo-chlorine pesticides had become much wider and, therefore, stronger.

The point for political decision had been reached. On the one hand, the Chairman of the Advisory Committee, Sir James Cook (an organic scientist and Vice-Chancellor of Exeter University), had assumed ministers would want it to take 'a very conservative view'. It had accordingly recommended that the Government should take out 'an insurance policy, at a substantial premium, against the possibility of future damage to human life and wild life'. Its recommendations sought to create a safeguard against any insidious effects that might arise and take time to reveal themselves. On the other hand, as Soames warned in a paper to the Cabinet's Home Affairs Committee, the introduction of such a concept might be 'the last straw that broke the back of the Notification Scheme'. In as much as industry, and particularly Shell, might refuse to co-operate, Soames wanted to know, prior to any negotiation, how far he might have the backing of ministers in threatening legislation, if 'they won't come quietly under the voluntary scheme' (PRO, MAF 284, 355, 359 and 376).

Soames's paper to the Home Affairs Committee recommended that the Minister for Science, in association with Agriculture Ministers and the Minister of Health, should assume responsibility for the Notification Scheme (now called the Pesticides Safety

Precautions Scheme) and therefore receive such reports as prepared by the Advisory Committee. Not only was this necessary if the Scheme was to be extended to non-agricultural types of pesticide, but also it overcame the presentational difficulties of explaining the merits and disadvantages of an agricultural chemical. The public invariably regarded Agriculture Ministers as interested parties. Such a transfer of responsibility to the Minister for Science would reflect the more strategic role the Advisory Committee was coming to assume. Since the Committee had previously been concerned only with the routine, yet vital, assessment of new pesticides, general principles had emerged more as a by-product than from any basic study of the situation. Soames's reference to the Advisory Committee of the organo-chlorine issue had set a precedent for its looking at general questions of policy. The Home Affairs Committee agreed that the Advisory Committee should be reconstituted under an obviously more 'impartial umpire', the Minister for Science (PRO, MAF 284, 354–5, 370 and 376).

Having obtained the support of ministers, Soames instructed officials to hold confidential talks with industry, with a view to seeing what progress could be made in achieving consensus. Shell was the key to whether the Committee's recommendations would be implemented without resort to compulsion. 'A pretty broad hint' had been given during informal discussions that the company would reject the recommendations. Although it regarded the greater part of the draft report as fair and balanced, Shell strongly objected to the arbitrary and unscientific way its products had been singled out for regulation. Lord Shawcross, a Director of Shell, followed up a private talk with Soames with a a formal request to meet him, accompanied by Lord Rothschild, the Head of Shell Research. It was known that Rothschild, a Fellow of the Royal Society and one-time Chairman of the Agricultural Research Council, had been doing 'a certain amount of lobbying in scientific circles'. Claude Wilcox, the Under Secretary in the Ministry, recommended a firm line. The Minister should emphasise how neither himself, nor other ministers, could agree to any watering down of the Committee's recommendations. Soames should press for a definite commitment of the company's support, warning of how it would be tragic for all concerned if he had to announce legislation to force Shell to comply with the Committee's recommendations (PRO, MAF 284, 376).

Officials acknowledged that Shell, as the holder of world patents for aldrin and dieldrin, must be concerned as to the impact of the recommendations on the attitude of overseas governments. It was not just sales of the pesticides. The main board of Shell was anxious that if, say, cotton production fell as a consequence of greater pest damage, there would be less revenue to spend on the company's main oil-based products. But as Wilcox argued, Shell must also be aware of its very weak position. If it came to public disagreement over the findings of a government committee that sought to protect public health, to say nothing of wildlife, the name of Shell would 'stink in every nostril'. Beyond a public display of unity, the Association of British Manufacturers of Agricultural Chemicals (ABMAC) was clearly worried that if a lot of mud was thrown much of it would stick to manufacturers generally. Lord Shawcross used the further meeting with Soames, on 12 March 1964, to present what he described as new and very significant information. The Advisory Committee found nothing in that evidence to justify modifying its recommendations. There had never been any dispute as to the company's data regarding the mammalian toxicity of its chemicals. Where the Committee parted company was in the interpretation of the significance of those facts (PRO, MAF 284, 370).

As Soames announced to parliament and at a press conference in March 1964, the Advisory Committee had found no evidence of any immediate hazard to human health, or to wildlife apart from certain species of predatory birds. It was however worried by the growing contamination of the environment, and had recommended that the use of aldrin, dieldrin and heptachlor should cease, except where there was no effective substitute. The fact that ICI had already ceased manufacture of heptachlor indicated that industry also subscribed to the maxim 'Better to be sure today than, possibly, sorry tomorrow'. Although Shell continued to dispute the scientific evidence, Soames spoke of how, with commendable public spirit, the company had indicated its preparedness to co-operate in following the Committee's recommendations. Much to the annoyance of the Ministry, Shell placed large advertisements in the principal newspapers reporting the news conference, highlighting its continued misgivings (PRO, MAF 284, 370).

In a briefing paper prepared for the Minister of Agriculture in the new Labour Government of October 1964, Wilcox wrote that 'one of the most complex and difficult, if relatively minor, questions' was how to deal with potentially dangerous agricultural chemicals. There was always the risk of an unexpected incident, which led to a lot of public and parliamentary fuss. In that respect the Ministry's lot was similar to that of 'inhabitants on the side of a dormant volcano' (PRO, MAF 284, 377). Yet the dialogue outlined in this section might also indicate some progress towards managing that uncertainty. Although the term 'the precautionary principle' was not used, elements of that principle may be discerned in the debates and courses of action taken both before and during the furore created by the publication of *Silent Spring* in the United States. Where the Permanent Secretary was critical of how 'we were caught napping' over the bird deaths caused by the dieldrin seed-dressings (PRO, MAF 284, 246), all parties came to perceive the need to err on the side of caution rather than wait for definite evidence to emerge of a potential risk - by which time it might be too late to remedy such damage as was being caused. Insights were gained into both the advocacy required and the frustrations likely to be incurred in developing the safeguards required for an uncertain future. There began the longest running and most extensive ecological experiment in the UK. Through the Predatory Birds Monitoring Scheme, the Institute of Terrestrial Ecology was able to relate the progressive phasing out of organo-chlorine pesticides to the recovery of such birds of prey as the Sparrowhawk as breeding species (Newton 1988).

Air Quality

In his *Politics in Industrial Society*, Keith Middlemas illustrated the importance of a three-way relationship between government, business and, for the purpose of his study of labour relations, the trade unions. A key player among business interest was the employers' umbrella-body, the Federation of British Industries (FBI), founded in 1916, and its successor body, the Confederation of British Industry. A triangular relationship might also be perceived in an environmental context, namely government, business and amenity bodies. It was pressure from that third set of interests that required the FBI's Production Committee to consider, from its first meeting, the issue of air pollution. Heavy industries made up the bulk of FBI membership. Although they caused considerable pollution, their leaders insisted that any tighter regulation would reduce competitiveness and, therefore, the prosperity of those dependent on the industry (Sheail 1997e).

By the inter-war years, the question for both government and amenity interests was not whether, but how, pollution should be curbed, if not eliminated. The Minister of Health appointed a Committee in January 1920, under Lord Newton. The description of noxious gases and smoke, in its terms of reference, as an 'evil' to be eradicated, indicated that air pollution was no longer regarded as an inevitable consequence of industrialisation. The onus was on the polluter to justify such emissions, or to eliminate them (Ashby and Anderson 1981). The Minister of Health, Alfred Mond (himself a leading industrialist), assured a deputation from the Coal Smoke Abatement Society in March 1922 that the Government was anxious to implement the findings of the Committee (Ministry of Health 1921; PD, Lords, 50, 371–4). It was within such an evolving relationship between the Government and smoke-abatement bodies that the FBI sought to identify the most effective strategy for business. Its Fuel Economy Committee argued that legislation could do no more than encourage a reduction in emissions. There was no standard means of measuring levels of emission. Smoke could not be eliminated from ordinary boiler furnaces.

The Production Committee acknowledged that there were formidable obstacles to closer regulation, but concluded, after 'a very long and serious discussion' in July 1922, that a 'non-possumus' attitude carried with it 'grave dangers'. However much the FBI held aloof, pressures for closer regulation would grow. Smoke abatement was a popular topic with the press. Public sentiment was strong. The Production Committee resolved that it should take up the Minister's invitation to join the Council of the Coal Smoke Abatement Society in pressing for legislation (CBI archives, University of Warwick, MSS 200, F1/1/142).

But how should support be given? The Production Committee decided there should be no public statement prior to a Bill being published. The interim period should be used instead to lobby the Minister and officials directly as to the shortcomings of drafts of the Bill, as they appeared. Everything should be done to ensure a manufacturer was required simply to prove that the best practicable methods were being used, within a reasonable cost, to avoid any nuisance. The rewards of that more active and constructive approach, which included four deputations to Ministers and frequent consultation with officials, soon became evident. The Bill published in October 1923 made it additionally possible, for the first time, to cite cost as a defence, whether in terms of fuel or the functioning and design of the plant. There were now problems of another kind. The Production Committee became increasingly alarmed by criticism from the Federation's own members that took no account of the major concessions wrung from the smoke abatement lobby. In a hastily drafted 'epitome of action', the Production Committee described how, once it became clear that the Government was determined to introduce a Bill, the FBI had concentrated on rendering the measure as innocuous for business as possible. To that extent, it had succeeded (CBI MSS, 200, F1/1/142–3).

There had long been demand for large-scale, co-ordinated action, in order to reduce the incidence of urban 'smog' (a combination of natural fog and solid and gaseous pollutants). It was 'the Great Smog' of December 1952 that brought matters to a head. The smog that enveloped London for five days was of exceptional density and duration. Newspapers carried accounts of a performance at Sadlers Wells being abandoned because the audience could not see the stage. Some 4,000 deaths in the Greater London area were attributed to circulatory or respiratory disorders brought about by the smog. Ministers appointed an independent committee in July 1953 'to examine the nature, causes and effects of air pollution, and the efficacy of present preventive measures', and to put forward recommendations as to what further measures might be practicable. Sir Hugh Beaver, a civil engineer, was appointed Chairman. The Committee's final report, of November 1954, was emphatic in its declaration that

> we wish to state our emphatic belief that air pollution on the scale with which we are familiar in this country today is a social and economic evil which should no longer be tolerated, and that it needs to be combated with the same conviction and energy as were applied one hundred years ago in securing pure water. We are convinced that given the will it can be prevented. To do this will require a national effort and will entail sacrifices.

The Government was urged to introduce a Clean Air Bill which, by its title and general purpose, would highlight public concern as to the costs, in human and material terms, of air pollution. The Bill should be so drafted as to enable more stringent controls to be applied as circumstances demanded and technology made possible (PRO, POWE 14, 123 and 138; PP 1953–54b).

There have been many instances of a major reform being promoted first as a Private Member's Bill. Whilst there may have been little chance of its becoming law, such a Bill, moved by an individual member of either the House of Commons or Lords, might both prod ministers and provide opportunity for assessing how a government measure might fare (Ashby and Anderson 1981). Such a course was followed when Gerald Nabarro met with success in the ballot for Private Member's Bills. He chose a Clean Air Bill, based almost entirely on the Beaver report. The debate on the Second Reading in February 1955 was generally favourable. As the

Minister of Housing and Local Government, Duncan Sandys, remarked, there was no difference of opinion in the House and 'very little outside' as to the intention of the proposals. Upon receiving a promise of a Government Bill, Nabarro withdrew his own measure. Following agreement among officials at inter-departmental level, Duncan Sandys circulated a paper to the Cabinet's Home Affairs Committee in June 1955, outlining a draft Bill whereby local authorities, with the consent of the Minister, could prescribe Smoke Control Areas, where the emission of smoke would be an offence (Scottish Record Office (SRO), DD 13, 2689; PRO, POWE 14, 682 ; PD, Commons, 545, 1221–333).

Ministers were most concerned as to the particularly heavy cost of adapting the fireplaces to burn smokeless fuels in the older properties and, in many cases, the poorer households. As drafted, the Bill provided for only half the cost being met by public funds, namely 37.5 per cent from the Exchequer and 12.5 per cent from the relevant local authority. Such was the level of misgiving that two alternatives were put to the full Cabinet. One was to confine such regulation to new properties. As the formal minutes expressed it, there was 'some measure of support for this view'. Duncan Sandys warned, however, that the Government was not only committed to implementing the main recommendations of the Beaver Committee, but there would be risk of the industrial organisations withdrawing from a clean-air policy. In as much as nearly half of atmospheric pollution was caused by domestic chimneys, business would be justified in protesting if it alone was singled out for costly regulation. Duncan Sandys accordingly recommended adoption of the second alternative, namely for 75 per cent of approved expenditure on the adaptation of domestic fireplaces being met by public funds – 50 per cent by the Exchequer and 25 per cent by local authorities. By way of compromise, the Chancellor of the Exchequer agreed to the Exchequer meeting 40 per cent of the costs, with not less than 30 per cent being met by the relevant local authority. The Bill received the Royal Assent in July 1956 (SRO, DD 13, 2688).

An essential factor in the promotion of the Clean Air Bill was the increasing availability of other forms of energy, and most obviously electricity. It was not only much cleaner, but its generation had become more efficient and therefore cheaper. The great drawback was that it could not be stored. The generating capacity of the earliest power-stations had to be far in excess of normal need, so as to cope with both peak demand and the breakdown and servicing of the generating plant. The purpose of the grid system, operating at 132,000 volts, under the Electricity (Supply) Act of 1926, was to interconnect the power stations of each part of the country in order to make more efficient use of such plant. Although close integration was achieved in coping with wartime dislocation, it was not until the installation of a supergrid, of 275,000 volts, from the 1950s onwards, that a truly national grid operated. Such an infrastructure was required both to meet the rising demand for electricity, and to enable the many small stations to be replaced by a comparatively few, large power stations on the coalfields and at the ports, as well as the nuclear power stations being built in the remoter parts of the country (Sheail 1991a).

The electricity industry was, right from the start, one of the most closely regulated of industries. It had been illegal since 1909 to build or extend a power station without the Minister's consent. In terms of air pollution, such consent resolved itself into three issues: the elimination of smoke, and of grit and dust, and thirdly of sulphur dioxide fumes. Experience indicated that hardly any nuisance would arise if mechanical grit arrestors were installed in the flues, and chimneys were built at least two-and-a-half times the height of surrounding buildings. Sulphur emissions proved less tractable. To secure consent for further phases of the Battersea power station in south-west London during the 1930s, the London Power Company developed a flue-gas washing process from the laboratory to working-plant stage within five years. The sulphur was removed by sprays of river water mixed with chalk. An improved process was installed a few years later at the Fulham power station. Further major advances were made at the Bankside power station, built immediately after the war. Although 'a notable achievement' in research and development, it was also a blind alley, in as much as there would never be enough river-water to clean the gases and remove the effluent from the power stations of the size being developed in the 1950s and 60s. Furthermore, the washing process cooled the boiler gases to such an extent that the plume descended more quickly to the ground, causing any residual sulphur dioxide to be concentrated in the vicinity of the plant (Luckin 1990).

An alternative approach was advocated by the industry's expert witnesses, who appeared before a succession of public inquiries in considering applications for the construction of power stations in the early 1960s. It was contended that if the chimneys could be built to as great a height as possible, and the (unwashed) gases were discharged at as high a temperature as possible, the plumes would rise quickly to a level where there was adequate dispersion before descending to the ground. As in the early 1930s, once the need for research and development was recognised, results came quickly. The monitoring studies showed that even the most optimistic predictions of the Central Electricity Generating Board (CEGB) were realised. The daily average sulphur dioxide concentrations recorded at six 2000 MW power stations indicated that each had a negligible effect on local concentrations. The key to such success was dispersal through a single, multi-flue chimney. The structure represented less than 1 per cent of the total capital costs of a modern coal-fired power station (CEGB 1981).

The United Nations Conference on the Human Environment, held in Stockholm in 1972, was significant in two senses. Never before had there been demands from so many different quarters for *scientific* evidence to support the political argument for improving the quality of the environment. And secondly, the main concern for the Swedish hosts was to obtain publicity for a report on the way rainfall acidity, caused by sulphur dioxide from the UK and other industrialised countries, was destroying Scandinavian lakes and forests (Royal Ministry 1971). The findings were presented not so much as a working hypothesis as a 'conclusion', thereby encouraging an almost evangelical stance on the part of the Scandinavians and a defensive posture on the part of Britain. A

Norwegian study of the impact of acid precipitation on forest and freshwater systems, covering the years 1972–75, supported the 'conclusion'. There followed a report from the Organisation for Economic Cooperation and Development (OECD) on long-range transport of air pollutants, which attempted for the first time to quantify 'who was doing what to whom'. The report's principal conclusion was that most of the sulphur deposited in Norway was derived from emissions elsewhere in Europe, and from the UK in particular (OECD 1977).

How far had the protection of the UK been at the expense of the natural environments of other countries? The financial implications were so substantial for the CEGB that a research programme was rapidly mounted, encompassing dispersal processes and atmospheric chemistry, pathways through terrestrial ecosystems, and effects on freshwater chemistry and fisheries. Whilst the challenge, as presented by the Scandinavian 'conclusions', caused the scientific debate to become dogged by antagonistic views, it also meant consensus was imperative. There were significant advances in fundamental knowledge of many aspects of atmospheric chemistry and ecological processes. Several studies in south Scotland, Wales and Norway showed that acidification had been taking place at different rates since the beginning of the Industrial Revolution, as a result of the accumulation of acid deposition. The rates reflected such variables as vegetation type, soil buffering capacity, geology and hydrology (Roberts and Sheail 1993).

The debate brought into sharp focus the practical implications of the 'polluter pays' principle. The UK Government and electricity industry regarded a further conference at Stockholm in July 1982 as an attempt by the Swedish Government to apply further pressure for a reduction in sulphur deposition to a level no greater than that in northern Scandinavia, where fisheries still flourished. Such an adjustment would have required a 75 per cent reduction in emissions from much of Europe, including the UK. Was it better to impose a cost of over £10 billion on Europe as a whole, than to introduce comparatively inexpensive 'palliatives', such as liming to protect the relatively small fishery in southern Scandinavia? Most countries represented at the Stockholm Conference temporised by affirming their support for the Convention on Long-Range Transboundary Air Pollution, drawn up by UN Economic Commission for Europe (UNECE) in 1979. They undertook specifically 'to limit and, as far as possible, gradually reduce and prevent long-range transboundary air pollution'. The UK fully recognised the political advantages of being supported by a scientific consensus. The Department of the Environment (DOE) stepped up its programme of commissioned research on the scale and extent of acid deposition, and the processes by which emissions brought about atmospheric reactions, deposition and impacts. Long-term monitoring programmes were devised, covering air pollutants, soils, waters, trees, buildings and materials (Department of the Environment 1983). With much media attention, scientists funded by the DOE and the Natural Environment Research Council demonstrated how the 'Scandinavian' problem of acid deposition and acid lakes was also occurring in the high-rainfall areas of south-west Scotland, the Lake District and upland Wales.

The attitude of the West German Government changed dramatically, following extensive forest-health surveys in 1983 that indicated some 35 per cent of the forest area was suffering excessive foliage loss. Confronted by the spectre of acute forest damage through Central and Eastern Europe, a programme was announced to reduce sulphur emissions by half within ten years, and to reduce nitrogen oxides and hydrocarbon emissions from vehicles by a gradual introduction of catalytic converters. Such a complete reversal of the West German position, the second largest exporter of sulphur dioxide in Europe, left the UK even more exposed. The DOE and Department of Energy became convinced of the need to demonstrate active exploration of ways to achieve reasonable reductions of emissions. The Inspectorate of Industrial Air Pollution notified the CEGB that flue gas desulphurisation would be regarded as the 'best practicable means' for controlling sulphur emissions at any *new* plant that might be built.

The CEGB approach was described as one of 'visible movement with minimum penalty'. Research focused on emission-control technology and assessment of the different environmental impacts. In addition to its expanding in-house programme, the CEGB invited the Royal Society of London, and the Norwegian and Swedish Academies of Science, to organise an independent 5-year programme of research on Surface Water Acidification (SWAP). The CEGB and British Coal established a £5 million fund to support the research. Industry regarded such investment as evidence of its determination to find effective solutions, as opposed to 'a crippling burden on electricity consumers'. Critics saw it as a further attempt to buy time. Although UK emissions of sulphur dioxide had fallen by 40 per cent since 1970, they remained the highest in Western Europe. There continued to be no obvious way of rebutting the charge 'the dirty man of Europe' (Elsworth 1984; Pearce 1987).

There seemed until the mid-1980s little possibility of emission levels rising. The country was in economic recession. The nuclear sector would provide any additional generating capacity required. However, the position changed as a rise in electricity demand was forecast, and nuclear-power development was further delayed. Far from declining, CEGB predictions warned of a likely increase in emissions during the 1990s. If that were to be avoided, there had to be limits on the emissions from both new and existing plant. The CEGB announced in March 1986 that flue gas desulphurisation would be fitted to new coal-fired stations, thereby ensuring a steep decline in emissions beyond the year 2000. The decision was also taken internally to embark on a retrofit programme. Some 6 months of intense discussion followed, in which the scientific evidence of environmental impacts played a crucial part in justifying to the Treasury the large-scale expenditure required, in terms of capital and running costs to the industry and therefore to the consumers of electricity (Sheail 1991a).

The pieces of the scientific jigsaw puzzle had begun to fall into place. The long-standing scepticism of the CEGB had been amply borne out, namely that there was no simple correlation between the emissions from power stations and the changes taking place in the fisheries and forests of other parts of Europe. Recent increases in acid deposition were significant, but some lakes had been acidifying for nearly 200 years. Although acute acid-episodes could cause fish mortality, surface water chemistry was considerably affected by catchment processes. Forest decline was similarly a complex process, with no single cause-and-effect relationship with acid deposition. Yet whilst the findings from the various research programmes were very different from those so confidently proclaimed by pressure groups and some sectors of the scientific community, any further increase in emission levels was unacceptable. From the models constructed of surface water acidification, it was clear any further increase in surface deposition would both extend and prolong acidification.

The DOE announced in September 1986 that it had authorised the CEGB to implement its proposals to retrofit 6000 MW of high-merit plant between 1988 and 1997, at a cost of nearly £800 million. In May 1987, the Government endorsed plans by the CEGB to instal low-NOx burners at the 12 largest stations at a cost of £170 million over 10 years, with the aim of reducing emissions by 30 per cent per station. Such moves anticipated the European Community's Directive on Large Combustion Plant, which emerged in its final, agreed form in June 1988. The emissions of sulphur dioxide from new plant were to be reduced by 80–95 per cent, and by up to 50 per cent for NOx. For existing plant in the UK, the Directive required phased reduction of sulphur dioxide from 1980 levels by 20, 40 and 60 per cent by 1993, 1998 and 2003. NOx emissions were to be reduced by 15 and 30 per cent by 1993 and 1998 respectively.

Air pollution has remained high on the political agenda, most obviously for its bearing on climate change. Some 30 years after the signing of the Nuclear Test Ban Treaty in 1963, an important goal for the United Nations' Conference at Rio in June 1992, was an international agreement to limit carbon dioxide emissions. Where the earlier treaty was essentially achieved by representatives of the two superpowers, an Earth Summit was required to instigate the political thinking, as underpinned by scientific knowledge, as to how the vastly more diffuse sources of atmospheric pollution might be regulated. The difficulties of matching scientific knowledge with policy need, which had characterised the acid-rain issue, were encountered in even starker form at Rio and subsequently at the Kyoto conference on ways of curbing the production of 'greenhouse gases', held in Japan in 1997. Whilst the scientific complexity of the acid-rain processes emphasised the need for what became known as 'integrated pollution control', the more global approach consciously sought by the Kyoto Framework Convention relied even more heavily upon an ability to compare and evaluate the impacts and demands made on individual lifestyles, cultures and political outlook.

CHAPTER 9

The Century of the Environment

Introduction

Much of this book has been concerned with thought, communication and action as they affected human relationships with the environment over a wide range of temporal and geographical scales. Scientific discovery and technological development promised to free humanity from much of the disease, hunger and poverty that had previously made human life so miserable. But such advances were not cost-free. That rapid change of fortune for an increasing proportion of the human population pressed against 'the finite resources' of the natural environment. It seemed to threaten social structures and time-honoured values (Howard and Louis 1998).

A century of writing and publication sought to identify the mechanisms by which such new-won freedoms from want and suffering could be reconciled with the need for self-restraint and responsibility in their use. The world of human experience must have seemed very small to readers of *The Times*, when that newspaper commissioned in the early 1930s oblique photographs taken of southern England from as high as 20,000 feet, using for the first time infra-red photography to obtain remarkable clarity (Rawling 1933). For many people the most beautiful, yet awesome, image of the twentieth century was the photograph of the Earth as a heavenly body, taken from space. That single image encompassed all animate life. Life itself appeared so fragile and finite (Watson 2000). Yet if the vantage points for viewing the world were novel, there was nothing new in the way such perceptions were interpreted and applied. As Michael Redclift remarked of the late-twentieth-century concept of 'sustainable development', it was as much a prisoner of the past as a harbinger of an alternative future. Not only were we profoundly influenced by the knowledge and experience of the past, but we consciously sought out such guidance in determining what would work well or, more usually, could go so badly wrong (Redclift 1994). There was therefore a practical purpose in identifying the most formative influences on twentieth-century environmental history.

Historians have already detected a common bond between the opening and close of the twentieth century, namely the striking combination of hope and fear. Despite the pomp and circumstance that are now so closely associated with the final years of Queen Victoria's reign, late-nineteenth-century Britain was an anxiety-ridden nation. Its eminence as 'the workshop of the world' was faltering. The abject state of farming and forestry was seen as proof of how the countryside was becoming marginalised. There was no staunching the flow of people to the towns (Cannadine 1995). How could responsibility for the largest Empire ever known be reconciled with tolerance of such appalling conditions in 'the urban backyards'? In reporting the jubilee celebrations of the Manchester and Salford Sanitary Association in 1902, *The Manchester Guardian* commented on how personal pride in the Empire, on which the sun never set, was also 'tempered by the reflection that there were courtyards and slums at home on which the sun never rose'. It was absurd to use the word 'Imperial' only in an overseas context. The role of the city's scavenging department was also a 'truly Imperialist' function, and one probably of far greater benefit to mankind as a whole.

This present book has sought to follow the consequences of such unease and frustration into the twentieth century, as they manifested themselves in the extraordinarily wide spectrum of activities that impacted on the physical environment of town and countryside. As David Cannadine wrote, in his 'contextual history' of the founding of the National Trust for Places of Historic Interest or Natural Beauty, such anxiety and mistrust encouraged appraisal, celebration and conscious preservation of what was gauged to be meritorious of the past. Fresh forms of enterprise were called for. By a private Act of 1907, the National Trust was empowered to declare its properties inalienable as a further guarantee to intending donors of property. A Housing Act of 1909 included the words 'town planning' in its title. As their name implied, the first concern of 'town planners' was to improve the urban environment. Although it was the dynamic qualities of towns and cities that excited most comment, history was consciously used both as an inspiration and as a warning of what to avoid. The first major project of the journal *Town Planning Review*, launched in 1911, was a history of the capital cities of continental Europe. For Patrick Abercrombie, the author of the series, history offered 'the strongest argument for bold foresight and drastic action' (Abercrombie 1912).

Contributors to a volume entitled, *Science in Public Affairs*, published in 1906, sought to prove that almost any problem could be overcome through the resourceful application of what was perceived to be 'the scientific method' (Hand 1906). It offered a system, a way of looking at the world, that imposed values, ideas and programmes. 'The scientific method' created order out of chaos, an order clearly defined, measured and demonstrable. It had an obvious centralising tendency. But how far might such a system change the course of political and social life? Charles H. Pearson, the author of an earlier volume, *National Life and Character: A Forecast* (1893), was extremely sceptical. Even if it were possible to forecast the future with any accuracy, it did not follow that the knowledge and understanding derived from such investigation would have any practical value. As Pearson wrote, it was inevitable that the English coal measures would be exhausted, but no generation would 'stay its hand from using them in order to cheapen the fires of the next'. Although statesmen would much prefer 'a spreading population', most growth would continue to be in the great cities.

And yet the doggedness of individual personalities was not to be underrated. However hazardous the making of predictions, and the probability of their being ignored, some took up and pursued the challenge. The distinguished chemist, Sir William Crookes, warned, in his Presidential Address to the British Association for the Advancement of Science in September 1898, of how the world was 'in deadly peril of not having enough to eat'. Although the population grew, there was not only a limited supply of land, but the wheat lands were so 'absolutely dependent on difficult and capricious phenomena' that their productivity was bound to decline. Whilst protesting it was never his intention to create a sensation, nor 'to indulge in a "cosmic scare"', Crookes wrote in July 1899 that the 'hard and formidable *facts*' should be put before the public (Crookes 1899).

Such instances of assertiveness may provide as much commentary on society as on the tenacity of the individual. Sir Henry Rew, the statistician to the Board of Agriculture, recalled, in the third edition of Crookes's (1917) book *The Wheat Problem*, how Crookes had been vilified as trying 'to make our flesh creep'. His vision of a scarcity of food was treated as if a bad dream. Now, as Britain was threatened with military surrender through the starvation caused by a German naval blockade, the dream had become 'a grim reality'. As Rew wrote, the British people had come at last to realise that the question of food supply was among the most vital of national interests. The agricultural chemist had also begun to prove the accuracy of Crookes's expectation that it was through 'the laboratory that starvation may ultimately be turned into plenty'. It would be 'the agricultural chemist who must come to the rescue of the threatened communities'. Where there might be a limit to the land suitable for growing wheat, and also to the quantity of stored-up natural fertilisers, there was practically no limit to the resources of nitrogen which science could place at the service of agriculture (Crookes 1917).

A Royal Commission on Population debated, in the aftermath of a second world war, the optimal level of population. War had again shown how easily trade in the basic commodities could be disrupted. Britain might continue to lose, even in peacetime, its pre-eminence and ability to import its needs. Yet against such uncertainties, the Royal Commission drew encouragement from one of the most positive aspects of the inter-war years, namely the higher productivity in farming and, indeed, the glut of food. Mechanisation and improved strains of seed, livestock husbandry, and use of fertilisers, meant world supplies had outstripped demand. There should however be no complacency. Food surpluses might rapidly disappear as the population and industrial strength of parts of Asia grew. Soil erosion, so devastating in the Mid-West of North America and parts of Africa in the 1930s, might require more conservationist forms of husbandry and therefore less immediately productive methods (PP 1948–49).

How might one interpret the scale of change that far exceeded that of all previous centuries? The driving force for such an advance in human aspiration and experience was commonly seen in political, economic and social terms, with science and technology providing 'the stage props'. Robert May (at that time Chief Scientific Adviser to the UK Government) insisted that, for the twentieth century, this was the wrong way round. Science was both the stage-manager and the playwright. Social and political changes had followed, often in ways unintended or hardly guessed at. In operating the supermarket check-out, the operator read a bar code on each item, the customer handed over a piece of plastic, and the stock manager was alerted to what needed replacing. Behind it all was a host of applications-driven research in disciplines as diverse as solid state physics, optics and, in terms of computer software, topology and abstract algebra. Where the stimulus for such innovation came from economic and social circumstances, it was ultimately made possible by the further advances in the methods and techniques of the relevant science and technology (May 1995).

As the twenty-first century approached, each profession and discipline strove to assess its position in a fast-changing world. The distinguished American biologist, Jane Lubchenco, used her Presidential Address to the American Association of the Advancement of Science in February 1997 to assess how far ecologists were prepared for the further challenge of what Edward O. Wilson had already called the new 'Century of the Environment'.

If that seemed overdrawn, Lubchenco (1998) recalled how a central finding of research and development in the twentieth century had been the interrelatedness of issues previously thought to be independent of one another. Whether the issue was national security, economic prosperity, social justice or human health, each had an important environmental dimension, in as much as it depended to some degree on the structure, functioning and resilience of ecological systems. A new Social Contract for Science was needed, that encompassed not only research and training, but the scope to communicate 'the certainties and uncertainties and seriousness of different environmental or social problems'. As Lubchenco complained, far too many policies were still based on the science of the post-war decades, rather than the scientific thinking of the 1990s.

Where none would disparage such preparation on the part of scientists for the next millennium, Richard Easterlin was highly sceptical as to whether the substantial resources being invested in tackling air and water pollution and the depletion of natural resources would make the twenty-first century so very different (Easterlin 1996). If the past was any guide, the main obstacle to achieving both economic growth and social wellbeing was not the efficacy of the environmental strategies adopted, or indeed economic growth *per se*, but rather the political and military power bestowed by such knowledge and understanding Given their pervasive influence over the twentieth century, Peter Mangold warned of how the end of the Cold War and such spectacles as the world's statesmen attending an Earth Summit, might prove a false dawn. Power politics might again seep into the mainstream of international diplomacy, with potentially catastrophic results – not least for the environment (Mangold 1998; Lowi and Shaw 2000).

Raising Awareness

In his study of twentieth-century Europe, entitled *The Dark Continent*, Mark Mazower drew particular attention to the quarter century of prosperity and social cohesion in Britain after the

Second World War. Not only was government given an enhanced role, but full employment meant there were the tax revenues to support government expenditure at previously unthinkable levels. It enabled higher standards of living to be shared more widely. Such a sense of wellbeing was eroded during the 1970s. The disruption caused by the sudden rise in oil prices highlighted the fragility of Western economies. Unemployment rose. Neo-liberal economics were again fashionable. Science and technology, which had been so generously funded by business and government, became increasingly associated with pollution, discomfort and death (Mazower 1998).

Social scientists have drawn heavily on such contextual history in discerning trends in attitude towards the environment . The most long-standing and pervasive concern was to preserve the environment as 'a stock of assets'. Thus, the multiple use of watercourses in the nineteenth century had to be protected from domestic and industrial pollution, and the urban commons protected as open spaces for public recreation (Newby 1990). A second movement centred on the moral and aesthetic qualities ascribed to the countryside and coast, which were eloquently promoted by men of science and letters and given powerful institutional force by such bodies as the National Trust and Council for the Preservation of Rural England (CPRE) between the wars. For the biologist Julian S. Huxley, people did not live by bread alone. Some at least required 'the beauty of nature, the interest in nature, even the wildness of nature and the contact with wild animals living their own lives in their own surroundings' (Huxley 1931). The historian and benefactor to the National Trust, George M. Trevelyan, believed that such feelings, far from diminishing, became stronger as more and more people were able to seek the wildness and quietness of vitalised, aboriginal nature (Trevelyan 1929 and 1931). A third strand dealt not only with 'stocks' of material and aesthetic assets for mankind, but with environmental and social relationships. The environment had to be protected not only for the sake of human beings, but on behalf of the whole, living and natural, world. Using concepts and terms coined from the science of ecology, and frequently changing their meaning, the various schools of 'green' and 'deep ecological' thinking endeavoured to prescribe how environmental catastrophe might be averted by changes to human lifestyle (Healey and Shaw 1994).

As the second and third approaches developed, so the respective professions, interest groups and government itself had to adjust. Barry Cullingworth, in the first edition of his book *Town and Country Planning*, published in 1963, said that it was relatively easy to define the British style of town and country planning. By the time he came to prepare the eleventh edition in 1994, that simplicity had gone. It was not only a question of institutional change and structural upheaval. The whole concept of land-use planning had become blurred by such notions as sustainable development (Cullingworth and Nadin 1994). Those in central and local government had been swept along by the seemingly positive aspects of 'the environmental euphoria'. Their goal remained the same, namely that of conflict resolution. There remained abundant scope for using the skills of elected members and their officials in accommodating shifts in policy, as familiar protocols and procedures became infused with a genuinely heightened awareness of environmental considerations. It was an incremental approach, one of evolution rather than revolution, that had brought twentieth-century Britain through war and large-scale unemployment, as well as times of prosperity and social wellbeing.

Those chronicling the environmental movement have emphasised the role of a small number of scholars in warning of the consequences of allowing affluence and freedom of choice to overexploit and devastate the natural world. As the American critic and social commentator, Lewis Mumford, asked in 1962, 'What is the use of conquering nature if we fall prey to nature in the form of unbridled man?' Perhaps the most alarming aspect was not the degradation caused, say, by some military conflict, but that which stemmed from meeting such basic human requirements as food, drink, clothing and warmth. The American biologist, socialist and political activist, Barry Commoner, had for many years acted as a 'Cassandra of environmental disasters'. His bestselling book, *The Closing Circle*, warned of how humans had 'broken out of the circle of nature'. They had to learn 'to restore wealth to nature' as well as 'borrowing from it' (Commoner 1971).

An obvious difficulty of that learning process was that the world could not simply stop and take stock of the situation. In Philip Shabecoff's words, 'we cannot step out of the speeding jet aircraft'. The science of ecology, with its assumption that all parts of 'the community of life' were interdependent, seemed inevitably to point to a merger with human ethics (Shabecoff 1996). Aldo Leopold developed such an ecological view of the world in his book *Sand County Almanac*, written at his weekend refuge in Wisconsin shortly before his death in 1948. To Leopold, the sight of geese was more important than television; the chance to find a pasque flower was as much an inalienable right as free speech. As he readily conceded, the assurance of such spectacles would have 'little human value until mechanisation assured us of a good breakfast, and until science disclosed the drama of where they came from and how they live'. Once achieved, there was even greater need for a new 'land ethic', based on love and reverence for the natural world. Rather than perceiving the world as 'a commodity belonging to us', it should be seen as 'a commodity to which we belong'. Although the book made little immediate impression, the editor of an enlarged edition of his writings, in the 1960s, was encouraged by the more rebellious attitude of the generation of Leopold's grandchildren. That same youth was maturing at a time of pivotal importance for the preservation of 'things wild and free' (Leopold 1966).

Donald Worster and others have written of how self-conscious environmental history was itself a product of that same search for knowledge and understanding of the relationship of the natural world with human ethics. European Conservation Year in 1970 had confounded sceptics by its success in becoming a benchmark from which to measure further growth in the environmental movement. Whilst no one denied the inhibiting effect of the economic recession of the 1970s and, at times, in the 1980s, the hostility of government to anything construed as deflecting effort from greater productive effort, Hal Rothman discerned 'a resilience and an ability to reach into a deep well of public support to combat powerful adversaries'. That evidence of maturity may provide further explanation as to why conservation and environmentalism have become such widely investigated aspects of historical writing. A constellation of ideas and sentiments had emerged in the early twentieth century as to inequity and waste in the use and management of natural resources (Rothman 2000). It was a belief system that, by evoking the past as an inspiration for the future, in the guise of sustainability, both in terms of the 'quality of life' and a more secure economic future, made positive assumptions for the present-day wellbeing. By tying the future so closely to the past, in the moral guise of not cheating on our children and their children, there was a further and urgent reason for improving the environment of the present generation.

In a stimulating volume, *Costing the Earth*, Frances Cairncross cited 'an intriguing analogy' drawn by the head of a Swedish engineering firm, as to how 'we treat nature like we treated workers a hundred years ago'. In the same way as no cost was included for the health and social security of workers, so today 'we include no cost for the health and security of nature'. Looking ahead, that Swedish businessman speculated on how environmental protection might come to be perceived in the same light as the rise of the welfare state over the past fifty years – as a drag on growth and a burden to corporate costs, but also a huge, hard-to-quantify source of increased human wellbeing (Cairncross 1991). Such reflective thought had to be nurtured. Where leading figures in the various conservation bodies might have an important catalytic role, the most significant advances were likely to come through self-enlightenment on the part of business and industry. The various trade associations or 'peak' bodies had an important part to play. The Confederation of British Industry (CBI) had acquired considerable expertise and experience in mitigating the effects of industrial activity (Sheail 1997e). None was better briefed than CBI members and officers as to the impacts of different forms of regulation on business.

It was in the spring of 1991 that officers first canvassed the idea of the CBI carrying out its own thorough review of the UK planning system. Planning was perceived as an essential part of what was now described as the environmental movement. It bore heavily on industrial costs and therefore the competitiveness of British goods and services. Planning was too important to be left entirely to the planning profession. The relevant files of the CBI make it possible to reconstruct the steps by which a Task Force came to be appointed, and the manner in which its report, *Shaping the Nation*, was received.

Crucially, the essential prerequisites for such an enquiry were in place. First, it would be incremental in the sense that the CBI had recently published a report, *Trade Routes to the Future. Meeting the Transport Infrastructure Needs of the 1990s*. It suggested ways by which the planning system could be made more responsive to the pressing needs of industry. Secondly, it was timely, in the sense that there was expected to be a debate on the 'environment' at the annual conference of the CBI, in November 1991. Thirdly, there was the mechanism for such an enquiry. A Task Force was appointed each year to investigate a topic of relevance. And fourthly, there was willing collaboration from a professional body, whose expertise and experience provided much-needed credibility. The President-elect of the Royal Institution of Chartered Surveyors (RICS), Christopher Jonas, reacted enthusiastically to the suggestion first broached by the Director-General of the CBI, Sir John Banham, that the next Task Force should focus on the planning system. Jonas wrote that, if it included members of the RICS, its report

> would create a single voice to articulate the land use needs of industry and provide a focus for contact with planning policy-makers. In the longer term, it could be used to exert a powerful lobbying influence on government land use policy.

For the CBI, such a venture served to publicise the recent appointment of John Cridland as its first Director of Environmental Affairs. It was Cridland who secured the final agreement to the terms of reference being to 'consider the land use needs of the business community, especially for infrastructure projects and other works of major importance'. The Task Force of 21 members appointed in January 1992 was made up of senior business executives and chartered surveyors, and an Assistant County Planning Officer. The RSPB turned down an invitation for its Chief Executive to serve as a member. The Chairman of the Task Force was Ian Prosser, the Chairman and Chief Executive of Bass PLC.

The purpose of the introductory chapter of the eventual report was to establish a 'natural' authority for its conclusions. It therefore highlighted the CBI's ability to canvass the views of its 3,000 UK members, as well as its regional councils, local authority associations, the planning profession and environmental groups. Whilst business was responsible for only 15 per cent of the 500,000 planning applications made each year, construction costs made up a third of total investment in the English economy. The Task Force believed it was both essential and possible to modify the planning system so as to reduce that level of expenditure, without sacrifice to social and environmental conditions. There would, however, be no 'big bang' solution. Even if the planning regimes of international competitors were found to be better, the cost of completely replacing the existing system of planning control would be prohibitive. Improvement had to come through evolution (Confederation of British Industry 1992).

Of the report's 28 recommendations, most publicity was given to the need for a more integrated planning framework. The Task Force found that most frustration, conflict and uncertainty arose not from the individual procedures of the system, but from the lack of any firm or comprehensive direction by government. It was not simply poor communication. There was 'a strategic policy vacuum'. In as much as most development proposals were first considered at a local level, it was hardly surprising that so many became bogged down by NIMBYism (the Not In My Back Yard mentality). A more top-down approach was needed, where policies were interpreted and implemented at the local level, rather than the other way round.

The Task Force proposed a new policy mechanism, namely an annual national-policy paper that, from the combined perspective of government departments, would set out a national framework for land use and infrastructure, together with a core-funding commitment by the Treasury. As the report was at pains to stress, the purpose was not to extend central planning. Rather, an enabling strategy was sought, whereby it was no longer necessary to second-guess the decisions that were most properly taken at a higher level in government. Far from eliminating local democracy and accountability, there would be a more integrated approach, focused on longer-term considerations. There would be greater consistency in interpreting and implementing policy in every part of the country and at all levels of central and local planning.

The report of the Task Force, published as *Shaping the Nation*, was unanimously approved by the annual conference at Harrogate, and formally accepted as CBI policy in January 1993. The Government was publicly challenged to react. In his speech to the Harrogate conference, the Secretary of State for the Environment, Michael Howard, commended the report for its timeliness. The Government had anticipated many of its recommendations. It had published three-year public-expenditure totals and an annual road programme. It had done much to streamline the work of the local planning authorities, which took 98 per cent of the planning decisions required. It was not, however, in Howard's gift to meet the recommendation of an annual planning statement, linked with 5-year core funding for infrastructure development. All governments needed the flexibility to respond to changes in economic circumstances. An annual statement would in any case be contrary to the Government's policy of extending competition and market discipline. There was now so much private investment in all aspects of the infrastructure and services that it would be entirely inappropriate for the Government to intervene.

Here, a distinction has to be drawn between the different audiences addressed by the report. John Cridland and others of the CBI had anticipated the rebuff. In its public statement, the CBI noted how the Task Force had always assumed it would take time for the more strategic recommendations to be implemented. The CBI was in fact playing a long-game at two levels, the more important being the raising of awareness of environmental issues among its own membership. The deliberately assertive tone of the original press release announcing the appointment of the Task Force must have caused members to think the outcome was entirely predictable. The press release emphasised the major deficiencies of the present planning system and the urgent need to address them. Having won the confidence of the membership for its initial position, there was soon evidence of greater open-mindedness. As Ian Prosser wrote, in the Foreword to *Shaping the Nation*, 'Our perception of the problem has changed as we have conducted our work.' Whilst the many concerns of business were strongly felt and had to be taken seriously, it was apparent that the planning system worked quite well for much of the time. There were 'good reasons for many of the elaborate checks and balances'. For the Task Force, the inquiry was a chance to break new ground by gathering real evidence of how the system might be made more accommodating of business needs and, at the same time, an opportunity to demonstrate the commitment of industry to sustainable development.

It was in the chapter that dealt with 'hearing the voice of business' that the CBI's more pressing concerns came to the fore. As the Task Force emphasised, local businesses had to become key actors in the planning system. Not only did they have a responsibility to the wider community but their discharging of such responsibility was an extremely sound, long-term business investment. Typically, business executives were only interested in planning when an application for development consent ran into trouble (and then only to complain of blinkered and irrational attitudes). Over half the local authorities canvassed by the CBI survey felt a greater input could be made. Although custom required the Task Force to stand down, the regional CBI councils were urged, as a matter of priority, to audit their existing inputs to Local Development Plans, and to put forward proposals of their own for strengthening and widening the business contribution.

In pressing for that greater involvement in the planning process, the CBI derived both further locus and encouragement from the favourable reception given to the report by both the media and planning profession. According to a leader in *The Planner*, it was both intriguing and gratifying that the planning system should receive such endorsement from the Task Force. Of course the report had expressed serious misgivings but, for the most part, these were shared by the Royal Town Planning Institute itself. In winning such respect from the planning profession and apparently moving ahead of government in its prescription for meeting infrastructural needs, the CBI Task Force had achieved its more immediate educative role of encouraging a more constructive relationship with the wider planning and environmental movement.

'Movers and Shakers'

As the impacts of human activity gained global significance, politicians and statesmen strove both to demonstrate their awareness of what was happening, and to compete with one another in voicing such concerns. As the American ambassador to the United Nations, Adlai Stevenson, reminded its Economic and Social Council, in July 1965,

> we travel, passengers on a little spaceship, dependent on its vulnerable reserves of air and soil, committed for our safety to its security and peace, preserved from annihilation only by the care, the work, and, I will say, the love we give our fragile craft.

As major users of those reserves of air, soil and the oceans, governments had a vested interest in minimising the extent of their guilt, and in asserting their credentials for protecting such a 'fragile craft'.

Within Britain, the first White Paper to deal explicitly with 'man's impact on his environment', *The Protection of the Environment. The Fight Against Pollution*, was published in May 1970. Where as in the early 1960s the power of science and technology had been invoked as the key to modernising industry, there was now political capital to be made from invoking those same forces in protecting the environment from its worst excesses. At the Labour Party Conference in September 1969, the Prime Minister, Harold Wilson, identified the environment as an issue moving to the centre of the political stage. As well as removing 'the scars of nineteenth century capitalism', every effort had to be made to ensure the 'second industrial revolution' did not bequeath 'a similar legacy to future generations' (Wilson 1971).

A survey conducted following the *Torrey Canyon* disaster found that 10 government departments, plus a wide range of local authorities and other agencies, had some responsibility for controlling pollution. Although it was neither necessary nor practicable to bring such regulation under a single executive department, some oversight was needed. Through the lobbying of the Chief Scientific Adviser, Sir Solly Zuckerman, and personal interest of Harold Wilson, approval was given in the autumn of 1969 for establishing a Central Scientific Unit on Environmental Pollution in the Cabinet Office and a standing Royal Commission on Environmental Pollution. One would be a facilitator, and the other a watchdog. As well as 1970 being European Conservation Year, governments and agencies were beginning to prepare for the United Nations' Conference on the Human Environment in 1972 (PRO, CAB 168, 190–2).

A general election was called before work on a promised White Paper on the environment could be completed. Harold Wilson pressed for publication. Lord Kennet, the Parliamentary Under Secretary in the Ministry of Housing and Local Government (and himself a distinguished author), wrote a summary version over a weekend, with officials at the end of the telephone. Dubbed by one Deputy Secretary as something of 'a political manifesto' (PRO, CAB 168, 202), it recounted how the UK was pursuing an active course in preparatory discussions at an international level and in attending to 'its own environmental defences'. Although the most important reason for intervention continued to be public health, the White Paper emphasised how pollution had to be tackled wherever it impaired the ordinary pleasures derived from the enjoyment of amenity and, therefore, the 'contentment of people in the quality of their life'. Four prerequisites had to be met: better scientific and technological knowledge; agreement as to economic priorities; 'the correct legal and administrative framework'; and the fourth was the will to do the job (PP 1969–70).

There was movement too on the international front. Following warnings from the Swedish delegation of its being marginalised, the General Assembly of the United Nations resolved to convene a major conference on the Human Environment, in Stockholm. An official secretariat was appointed under a Canadian industrialist, Maurice Strong, who invited the biologist Rene Dubos in May 1971 to act as Chairman of a distinguished group of experts in preparing an 'unofficial report'. Written with the economist, Barbara Ward, it identified the two foremost tasks as those of formulating 'the problems inherent in the limitations of the Spaceship Earth' and secondly of devising 'patterns of collective behaviour compatible with the continued flowering of civilisations'. Since 'a dourly materialistic approach' was unlikely to win hearts and minds, Ward and Dubos (1972) saw the overriding need as one of honouring and cherishing both the natural and the cultural diversity of the world. The Stockholm Conference called for a United Nations Environmental Programme which, following its eventual ratification by governments, was set up in Nairobi, Kenya, in 1974.

The earlier exalted tone faded; stridency took over. A new British journal, *The Ecologist*, published 'A blueprint for survival'. In calling for 'a new philosophy of life', it warned of how current trends would inevitably lead to

> the breakdown of society and the irreversible disruption of the life-support systems on this planet, possibly by the end of the century, certainly within the lifetimes of our children. (Goldsmith *et al.* 1972)

The warning was endorsed by 36 largely academic figures. It drew heavily on a report, *Man's Impact on the Global Environment. Report of the Study of Critical Environmental Problems*, sponsored by the Massachusetts Institute of Technology (1970). But where that report had been sober and imbued with humility, another leading British scientist, Lord Ashby, attacked the *The Ecologist's* 'Blueprint' for the way it 'rang the doomsday bell with frantic vigour'. Lavish with prescription as to what *must* be done, there was scarcely any reference to what *was* being done or, more important, *how* it was being done (Ashby 1978).

Amid the clamour to be heard, there was a common desire to predict what would happen. As Kenneth Hare, a British geographer and physicist in the University of Toronto, wrote, the honest answer was that no one could model the processes of man–environment interplay well enough to predict the future. It was not simply the complexity of the natural systems being modelled, or of marshalling the science in precise enough terms. It was the fact that great human decisions were *not* mass decisions. Given that it remained the public's privilege to choose politically between the options developed, only a range of *possible* futures could be specified. Much would depend on the energies and skills of the 'movers' and 'shakers', in terms of whether that choice was exercised and the use to which it was put. A key question was whether there would be the institutions capable of taking a sufficiently long-term view as to realise the environmental goals so earnestly and individually advocated (Hare 1985).

Formal conferences rarely pioneer, but they may provide a *locus* for key players to force the pace of change. Following a second Conference on the Human Environment, held in Stockholm in 1982, the United Nations established a World Commission on Environment and Development. Its Chairman was Gro Harlem Brundtland, the Norwegian Prime Minister and an environmentalist of distinction. The Commission's report, *Our Common Future*, published in 1987, proved of pivotal importance in crystallising and disseminating the concept of sustainable development. In as much as population and economic growth were putting unsustainable pressures on the natural environment, they were an obstacle to future economic and social development. The economy and ecology were so closely interwoven, whether locally, regionally or globally, as to be 'a seamless net of cause and effect' (World

Commission 1987). As Lemons and Brown (1995) recalled later, the Commission not only identified poverty and environmental degradation as one and the same problem but, more positively, promoted sustainable development as the only kind of growth that could meet the needs of the present, without compromising the wellbeing of future generations. By such a fusion of geographical and generational concerns, the Commission put the need for political transformation on 'the front burner of international governance'.

Within the British context, an obvious 'mover and shaker' was the British Prime Minister, Margaret Thatcher. As she recalled in her autobiography, *The Downing Street Years*, there was a great burst of public interest in the environment in 1988-89. As a research chemist by training, she regarded herself as obviously well placed, both among British politicians and at international meetings, to emphasise the significance of the large 'hole' that scientists of the British Antarctic Survey had measured in the ozone layer, and of the part played by CFCs (Chlorofluourocarbons) in bringing it about. Margaret Thatcher wrote of how she took a close personal interest in the scientific evidence, from the first international meeting and agreement in Montreal in 1987, to her last days in office, when addressing the Second World Climate Conference in Geneva (Thatcher 1993).

Sir Crispin Tickell, Britain's outgoing ambassador to the United Nations, had suggested the Prime Minister might make a major speech on the environment. An invitation to speak at the Royal Society of London in September 1988 was the perfect opportunity. In her words, the speech 'broke quite new political ground' (Thatcher 1993, pp. 640–1). Having cited the evidence gathered by British scientists for the increase in greenhouse gases, the size of the ozone hole, and acid deposition, Margaret Thatcher warned that mankind might have begun 'a massive experiment'. Since the health of the economy and environment depended on each other, the Government was committed to the concept of sustainable economic development. 'Protecting this balance of nature' was one of the greatest challenges of the late twentieth century. As *The Times* remarked, the speech was all the more remarkable for the fact that the Prime Minister had appeared sceptical of such issues. Although given in a scientific context, the speech was profoundly political. It acknowledged public concern and delighted those Tory backbenchers wanting a green tinge to the Government's free-enterprise policies (Harris 1997, pp. 326–33).

Environmental conservation had entered politics. The Green Party, formed in 1973, won 15 per cent of the vote in the 1989 European Parliament Election (Garner 1999). Part of Margaret Thatcher's speech to the Conservative Party Conference in October 1988 dealt with 'Protecting our world'. In an obvious allusion to Friends of the Earth, she spoke of how 'we Conservatives' were 'not only friends of the earth . . . (but) are its guardians and trustees for generations to come'. With clear Burkean overtones, she stated that

> no generation has a freehold of this earth. All we have is a life tenancy – with a full repairing lease. (Cooke 1990)

There was stimulus too from abroad. The Russian President, Mikhail Gorbachev, had referred to the twin issues of development and environment in his address to the General Assembly of the United Nations. He called for the creation of a 'centre for urgent ecological relief, which would co-ordinate and send international expert teams to regions struck by acute environmental pollution' (Gorbachev 1996). In a speech to her Party Conference in October 1989, which explicitly linked conservatism with 'conserving what is best', Margaret Thatcher gave notice that her forthcoming address to the United Nations would press for 'a sort of good-conduct guide'. Devoted entirely to 'the global environment', that address of the following month warned that though the threat of global annihilation and regional war had receded, the prospects of irretrievable damage to the atmosphere, oceans and earth itself were becoming more real. The threat was more fundamental and widespread than anything previously known. Through sound science and economics, a strong framework had to be built for international action that encompassed the effects of climate change, the thinning of the ozone layer, and loss of precious species. A realistic programme and timetable for action was required, where the industrialised nations contributed proportionately more by way of investment in the solutions required. The negotiations would be as hard as any disarmament treaty (Harris 1997, pp. 361–72).

Such obvious recognition of the value of environmental issues in promoting the Government's standing, both domestically and on the world stage, enabled Chris Patten (the Secretary of State for the Environment) to become more ambitious. A little-noticed precedent had been established in 1987, when the Secretaries of State for the Environment, Scotland and Wales had been joined by the Minister of Agriculture in contributing a 'Ministerial Foreword' to a guide, entitled *Protecting Your Environment*, published to mark the European Year of the Environment (Department of the Environment 1987). They were joined by a further seven ministers in presenting 'Britain's first comprehensive White Paper on the Environment', *This Common Inheritance*, in September 1990. With a prefatory letter from the Prime Minister, it acknowledged in the most explicit way possible the extent to which anxieties as to the use and management of the natural environment had caught the headlines and excited public concern (PP 1989–90). The names of an additional four ministers (including the Chancellor of the Exchequer) were added to the title page of *This Common Inheritance. 'The First Year Report'*, which appeared in 1991, ostensibly to indicate how far some 78 actions on the part of Government were being met. There was again a letter from the Prime Minister, now John Major, as if to indicate there had been no tailing off in Government interest (PP 1990–91).

As a direct response to the Brundtland report, the General Assembly of the United Nations had approved, in December 1989, the holding of what became the first Earth Summit, the United Nations' Conference on Environment and Development in Rio de Janeiro. The meeting of June 1992 was the largest and most ambitious summit conference ever held, in terms of the number of issues addressed and number of delegations in attendance. John Major claimed to be the first head of state of a G7 government to announce his attendance, an act which caused others to follow

(Major 1999). Conventions were signed on sustainable development and biodiversity with a seriousness previously associated with Summit Conferences on world trade and disarmament. Where a further threshold of political perception had been crossed, none doubted the scale of adjustment required. Shabecoff (1996) wrote of how the 200 heads of state and their advisers carried 'an overwhelming burden of intellectual, cultural and institutional baggage'. They were required to address the economic causes of environmental decline using the tools that had, for the most part, wreaked such devastation. Their methods of diplomacy were those more commonly associated with pressing national advantage through power and competition. Where radical solutions were sought, few had experience of working with environmental groups and other democratic institutions.

It was not only governments that had to reposition themselves. Where once a 'rumbustious campaigning style' might have been appropriate, the environmental columnist, Jonathan Porritt, writing in the *Daily Telegraph* of 14 January 1995, wondered whether ankle-biting (and much worse) were still appropriate. One in ten people now belonged to an environmental pressure group. The 15 largest groups had an estimated income of £163 million. They owned almost 3 per cent of the total land area, playing a significant part in the economy of many rural areas (Dwyer and Hodge 1996, p. 55; Rawcliffe 1998). As a mass lobby and an authoritative source of knowledge and thinking, they were well placed to lead the consensus-building now required for exploiting that raised public consciousness. Yet the conservation movement remained as diverse as ever. There were plenty of opportunities for its more radical elements to seize the initiative, if their publicity stunts were outrageous enough to attract television cameras.

The *Brent Spar* was a 14,500-tonne oil-storage buoy, located 118 miles to the north-east of Shetland. Its obsolescence and removal marked the beginning of what promised to be Britain's largest and most expensive waste-disposal operation. Over 200 gigantic offshore structures had been built in the UK sector of the North Sea since 1967. The Department of Trade and Industry approved plans by Shell UK, in November 1994 to sink the *Brent Spar* in 6,000 feet of water on the edge of the continental shelf. Greenpeace protested at both the principle of disposal at sea, and the pollution likely to arise from the toxic sludge that remained from drilling operations. About a dozen 'eco-guerillas' from different countries occupied the otherwise empty installation. Although they were dislodged, the media coverage instigated a consumers' boycott of Shell garages and 30 per cent decline in sales in Germany. Alarmed at the ambivalent stance of the German Government, Shell aborted the dumping mission a day before the *Brent Spar* was due to be scuttled. Where for Greenpeace it was 'a staggeringly welcome victory', the most discouraging aspect for industry had been the ease with which Greenpeace, by fighting a highly focused, single-issue campaign, had undermined 'the most carefully laid out and scientifically reasoned plans'. Despite the precautions taken by Shell in consulting interested parties, German members of Greenpeace had still been able to hijack the issue. In the face of 'populist sound bites', Shell's response had appeared too technical (Catterall and Preston 1997).

A *Financial Times* survey of the county of Somerset, published on 12 April 1995, focused on the tensions more typically encountered by those endeavouring to reconcile 'wealth creation' with a 'quality of living style'. The leading article stated that as the county intensified its efforts to attract more inward investment, economic growth had to be balanced with protecting the environment. Without jobs, the younger people would leave and Somerset would become socially and economically a geriatric county. Although the obvious course was to create jobs, it was bound to cause significant changes to the physical use and appearance of the county. As the Chief Executive of the Somerset Chamber of Commerce conceded, 'a very big awareness of environmental issues' did not 'always sit comfortably with business in a thriving economy'. It was something far more complex than a simple clash of interests. As the Leader of the County Council remarked, industry was attracted to Somerset *because* of the attractiveness of its environment. The environment had to be protected for the sake of job creation.

The Environment White Paper of 1990 met the political object of demonstrating that the Government, after a decade in office, had kept abreast of public concern. Where the previous White Paper of 1970 had also emphasised the 'obligation on us all' to help protect and improve the environment, the new environmental strategy was an outstanding opportunity also to emphasise how the purpose of government had shifted from one of executive action to that of facilitating and enabling the actions of others. That more humble stance was especially emphasised in a further White Paper, *Rural England. A Nation Committed to a Living Countryside*, published jointly by the Secretary of State for the Environment and Minister of Agriculture in October 1995. As they made clear, it was entirely wrong to expect assertiveness. The health of rural England did not rest in the hands of government and its agencies. As in centuries past, the countryside was the outcome of a myriad human actions. It had accordingly to be perceived through the eyes of those who lived and worked in the countryside, rather than from some administrative viewpoint in Whitehall. The reality of rural life was that it depended on lots of small-scale changes for any success to be assured. Each had to take full cognisance of the real differences that occurred, both between town and country and within the different parts of the extraordinarily diverse rural environment (PP 1994–95).

Such reasoning, developed in the context of English rural life, sought further to explain the move of governments generally away from rationality, modelling and systems towards what Blowers and Evans (1997) called 'a softer focus on planning as an enabling activity facilitating change'. An essentially practical activity, planning was project based, drawing on past experience and assessment as to what might be possible. In the broadest sense, planning created visions of what the environment could be like, taking close account of such participatory ventures as those being promoted under Local Agenda 21, following the Rio conference. There was an affinity with what Martin Holdgate, writing in an international context, perceived as the essential ingredients of 'a sustainable world', where communities were structured and empowered to give effect to the decisions of their respective peoples. It was about achieving that common object by bringing together the intelligence, experience, self-perceived interests and willingness of such people. As Holdgate (1996) recognised, it was by no means an easy and automatic process. Conflicts would arise. Lack of knowledge and resources were obvious stumbling blocks. There was, however, no other way of achieving that more substantial and permanent progress.

As Ian Christie commented, such a deep and wide-ranging process as implied by democratic argument, trade-offs and consensus building, pointed to a truth so easily overlooked, namely that sustainable development was at root another way of describing planning for a decent society. It was with that goal in mind that the planner Thomas Sharp had written, two generations previously, of how the landscape was an index to civilisation. Where human survival had always depended on adaptation of town and countryside, there was, through conscious design, always the potential to satisfy an aesthetic need, so as to make them 'home' as well as a 'workplace' (Sharp 1936). As Christie (2000) remarked, there was no single 'Big Green Idea' as to how that 'home' or 'global habitat' might be achieved, but rather many 'little ideas'. These might lead to 'bigger ideas' that so caught the imagination and proved necessary that, with hindsight, they appeared blindingly obvious.

This book has sought to illustrate the range of devices used to demonstrate how, 'by doing good to the environment, we enrich our lives in quality and prosperity'. As one prominent Conservative politician, John Redwood, wrote, 'The British people are not keen on revolutions'. Most changes were achieved peaceably. As a nation, Britain had coped well with periods of explosive technical change (Redwood 1999). It was therefore entirely in character for the Prime Minister, Tony Blair, to seek consciously in the last months of the twentieth century not a revolution in attitude toward the environment but rather a reawakening of the vision of a world where

> we can be richer by being greener; and by being greener we will enrich the quality of our lives. (Blair 2000)

The appeal was made before an audience of the Confederation of British Industry and Green Alliance. However much the intention was one of incremental advance, the landscape historian, Joan Thirsk, nevertheless wondered whether the turn of the twenty-first century marked something special in the sense of there being a greater determination to secure change whilst recognising the need to conserve some memory of worlds past (Thirsk 2000). Through pursuing and expanding the modest examples developed in this book, readers may themselves find evidence of how a concern for the life-giving properties of land, air and water came to be perceived as an integral part of 'a decent and fulfilling life'.

Bibliography

Abercrombie, P. (1912) 'Paris. Some influences that have shaped its growth', *Town Planning Review*, 2, 113–23.
Abercrombie, P. (1926) 'The preservation of rural England', *Town Planning Review*, 12, 5–56.
Abercrombie, P. (1932) *Town and Country Planning* (London: Thornton Butterworth) 132–3.
Abercrombie P. and Archibald, J. (1925) *East Kent Planning Scheme*. (Liverpool and London University Presses).
Abercrombie, P. and Johnson, T.H. (1922) *The Doncaster Regional Town Planning Scheme* (Liverpool University Press).
Acland, F.D. (1918) 'The land and agriculture', in *Liberal Policy in the Task of Political and Social Reconstruction* (London: Liberal Publication Department) 96–9.
Advisory Council for Agriculture and Horticulture (1978) *Agriculture and the Countryside* (London: Ministry of Agriculture).
Anonymous (1914) 'The British Ecological Society', *Journal of Ecology*, 2, 55–6.
Anonymous (1931) 'Town planning and aviation', *Journal of the Royal Institute of British Architects*, 38, 296–300.
Anonymous (1966) *Proceedings of the Countryside in 1970. Second Conference* (London: Royal Society of Arts) 101–5.
Ashby, E. (1978) *Reconciling Man with the Environment* (London: Oxford University Press).
Ashby, E. and Anderson, M. (1981) *The Politics of Clean Air* (Oxford: Clarendon Press).
Astor, Viscount, and Rowntree, B.S. (1935) *The Agricultural Dilemma* (London: King).
Astor, Viscount, and Rowntree, B.S. (1938) *British Agriculture* (London: Longmans Green).
Atkinson-Willes, G.L. (1963) *Wildfowl in Great Britain* (London: HMSO).
Bagwell, P.S. (1988) *The Transport Revolution* (London: Routledge).
Barber, D. (1988) 'The countryside: decline and renaissance', *Journal of the Royal Agricultural Society*, 149, 81–9.

Barr, J. (1969) *Derelict Britain* (Harmondsworth: Penguin).
Beloff, M. (1975) Introduction, in *The Politics of Reappraisal 1918–1939* (eds G. Peele and C. Cook) (London: Macmillan) 1–13.
Bevin, E. (1937) 'Industry and the health resort', *Better Health*, 10, 219–21.
Blair, T. (2000) 'Richer and greener', Speech made on 24 October 2000.
Blenkinsop, A. (1975) 'National parks: the dream and the reality', *The Countryman*, 80(3), 83–90.
Blowers, A. and Evans, B. (eds) (1997) *Town Planning in the 21st Century* (London: Routledge).
Bonner, W.N. (1989) 'Seals and man – a changing relationship', *Biological Journal of the Linnean Society*, 38, 53–60.
Booth, A.E. (1978) 'An administrative experiment in unemployment policy in the thirties', *Public Administration*, 56, 139–57.
Briggs, A. (1968) *Victorian Cities* (Harmondsworth: Penguin) 311–60.
Brimblecombe, P. and Pfister, C. (eds) (1990) *The Silent Countdown: Essays in European Environmental History* (Berlin: Springer) 1–6.
British Medical Association (1902) *Handbook and Guide to Manchester* (Manchester: Ireland).
Bromhead, P. (1973) *The Great White Elephant of Maplin Sands* (London: Elek).
Brown, R. (1993) 'Cultivating a "green" image: oil companies and outdoor publicity in Britain and Europe, 1920–1936', *Journal of European Economic History*, 22, 347–65.
Bryant, B. (1996) *Twyford Down. Roads, Campaigning and Environmental Law* (London: Spon), vii–ix.
Buchanan, C. (1981) *No Way to the Airport. The Stansted Controversy* (London: Longman).
Buchanan, C.D. (1958) *Mixed Blessing. The Motor in Britain* (London: Leonard Hill).
Bunce, M. (1994) *The Countryside Ideal* (London: Routledge).
Butterfield, W.J.A. (1912) 'The relation of modern road surfacings to fish life', *Proceedings of the Institution of Municipal and County Engineers*, 38, 192–131.
Cabinet Office (1967) *Torrey Canyon* (London: HMSO).
Cabinet Office (1980) *Climatic Change. Its Potential Effects on the UK and the Implications for Research* (London: HMSO).
Cairncross, F. (1991) *Costing the Earth* (London: Economist Books).
Calder, N. (ed.) (1973) *Nature in the Round* (London: Weidenfeld & Nicolson) 3–4.

Cannadine, D. (1995) 'The first hundred years', in *The National Trust: The Next Hundred Years* (ed. H. Newby) (London: National Trust) 11–31.

Carnaghan, R.B.A. and Blaxland, J.D. (1957) 'The toxic effects of certain seed-dressings on wild and game birds', *Veterinary Record*, 69, 324–5.

Carson, R. (1963) *Silent Spring* (London: Hamish Hamilton).

Catterall, P. and Preston, V. (eds) (1997) *Contemporary Britain. An Annual Review 1996* (Aldershot: Dartmouth) 330–2.

Central Electricity Generating Board (CEGB) (1977) *Annual Report 1976–77* (London: CEGB).

CEGB (1981) *Submission to the Commission on Energy and the Environment* (London: CEGB).

CEGB (1987) *Annual Report 1986–87* (London: CEGB).

Cherry, G.E. (1974) *The Evolution of British Town Planning* (Leighton Buzzard: Leonard Hill).

Cherry, G.E. (1975) *Environmental Planning. Volume II. National Parks and Recreation in the Countryside* (London: HMSO).

Cherry, G.E. (ed.) (1981) *Pioneers in British Planning* (London: Architectural Press) 1–18.

Cherry, G.E. (1982) *The Politics of Town Planning* (London: Longman).

Cherry, G.E. (1988) *Cities and Plans. The Shaping of Urban Britain in the Nineteenth and Twentieth Centuries* (London: Arnold) 157–62.

Cherry, G.E. (1991) 'Planning history: recent developments in Britain', *Planning History*, 6, 33–45.

Cherry, G.E. (1994) *Birmingham. A Study in Geography, History and Planning* (Chichester: Wiley) 3.

Cherry, G.E. and Rogers, A. (1996) *Rural Change and Planning. England and Wales in the Twentieth Century* (London: Spon).

Christie, I. (2000) 'In search of the "Big Green Idea"', *Town and Country Planning*, 69(10), 287–90.

Clapp, B.W. (1994) *An Environmental History of Britain since the Industrial Revolution* (London: Longman) xii.

Commoner, B. (1971) *The Closing Circle* (New York: Knopf).

Confederation of British Industry (1992) *Shaping the Nation* (London: CBI).

Cooke, A.B. (ed.) (1990) *Our Threatened Environment. The Conservative Response* (London: Conservative Political Centre) 4.

Cooke, G.W., Pirie, N.W, and Bell, G.D.H. (1977) *Agricultural Efficiency* (London: Royal Society).

Cornish, C.J. (1895) *Wild England of To-day* (London: Seeley).

Cornish, C.J. (1902) *The Naturalist on the Thames* (London: Seeley).

Countryside Commission (1970) *The Coastal Heritage* (London: HMSO).
Countryside Commission (1974) *New Agricultural Landscapes* (London: HMSO).
Countryside Commission (1987) *Forestry in the Countryside* (Cheltenham: Countryside Commission).
Countryside Commission (1988) *Annual Report 1987–88* (Cheltenham: Countryside Commission).
Countryside Commission (1991) *Annual Report 1990–91* (Cheltenham: Countryside Commission).
Countryside Commission (1992) *Annual Report 1991–92* (Cheltenham: Countryside Commission).
Countryside Commission (1993) *Handbook for Countryside Stewardship* (Cheltenham: Countryside Commission).
Court, W.H.B. (1951) *Coal* (London: HMSO) 291–5.
Courthope, G.L. (1944) 'Post-War Agricultural Policy', *Journal of the Royal Agricultural Society*, 105, 70–1.
Cowan, R.J. (1961) Ironstone workings and land restoration, *Chartered Surveyor*, 94, 83–9.
Cox, G., Lowe, P. and Winter, M. (1986) *Agriculture: People and Policies* (London: Allen & Unwin).
Cronon, W. (1990) 'Modes of prophecy and production: placing nature in history', *Journal of American History*, 76, 1122–31.
Crookes, W. (1899) Address, in *Report of the Sixty-Eighth Meeting* (ed. British Association for the Advancement of Science) (London: Murray) 3–38.
Crookes, W. (1917) *The Wheat Problem* (London: Longmans Green).
Crossman, R. (1975) *The Diaries of a Cabinet Minister. Volume I. Minister of Housing 1964–66* (London: Hamish Hamilton and Cape).
Crowe, S. (1966) *Forestry in the Landscape* (London: HMSO).
Crump, W.B. (1913) 'Two nature reserves', *Country Life*, 33, 678–9.
Cullingworth, B. (1996) 'A vision lost', *Town and Country Planning*, 65(6), 172–4.
Cullingworth, B. (ed.) (1999) *British Planning* (London: Athlone Press) 276–82.
Cullingworth, J.B. (1975) *Environmental Planning. Volume I. Reconstruction and Land Use Planning 1939–1947* (London: HMSO).
Cullingworth, J.B. (1988) *Town and Country Planning in Britain* (London: Unwin Hyman) 311–13.
Cullingworth, J.B. and Nadin, V. (1994) *Town and Country Planning in Britain* (London: Routledge).

Davies, J.E.H. (1962) 'Pipelines', *Journal of the Royal Society of Arts*, 111, 166–89.
Department of the Environment (1976) *Planning Control over Mineral Working* (London, HMSO).
Department of the Environment (1977) A *Study of Exmoor* (London: HMSO).
Department of the Environment (1983) *Acid Deposition in the United Kingdom. UK Review Group on Acid Rain* (London: DOE).
Department of the Environment (1987) *Protecting your Environment. A Guide* (London: HMSO).
Department of Trade and Industry (1992) *Guidelines for the Environmental Assessment of Cross-Country Pipelines* (London: HMSO).
Dewey, P. (1997) *War and Progress. Britain 1914–1945* (London: Longman) 327.
Dix, G. (1978) 'Little plans and noble diagrams', *Town Planning Review*, 49, 329–52.
Dolbey, S. (1974) 'The politics of Manchester's water supply', in *Campaigning for the environment* (eds. R. Kimber and J.J. Richardson) (London: Routledge & Kegan Paul) 75–102.
Doos, B.R. (1994) 'Why is environmental protection so slow?', *Global Environment Change*, 4, 179–84.
Dougil, W. (1936) *The English Coast: Its Development and Preservation* (London: Council for the Protection of Rural England).
Dower, J. (1932) 'Aerodromes', *Journal of the Royal Institute of British Architects*, 39, 501–15.
Dower, J. (1942) 'Reconstruction in the Yorkshire Dales', *Yorkshire Dalesman*, 4, 44–7.
Dower, J. (1943) 'Holiday use of countryside and coastline', *Journal of the Royal Institute of British Architects*, 50, 181–4.
Dower, J. (1944) 'The landscape and planning', *Journal of the Town Planning Institute*, 30, 92–8.
Dower, M. (1965) *The Fourth Wave. The Challenge of Leisure* (London: Civic Trust).
Doyle, B.M. (2001) 'Mapping slums in a historic city', *Planning Perspectives*, 16, 47–66.
Draper, P. (1977) *Creation of the DOE,* 4 (London: HMSO, Civil Service Studies).
Dunlap, T.R. (1981) *DDT: Scientists, Citizens and Public Policy* (Princeton University Press).

Dwyer, J. and Hodge, I. (1996) *Countryside in Trust* (Chichester: John Wiley).
Earle, J.B.F. (1974) *Black Top. A History of the British Flexible Roads Industry* (Oxford: Basil Blackwell).
Easterlin, R.A. (1996) *Growth Triumphant* (Ann Arbor: University of Michigan Press).
Eden, S., Tunstall, S.M. and Tapsell, S.M. (1999) 'Environmental restoration: environmental management or environmental threat?', *Area*, 31(2), 151–9.
Elsworth, S. (1984) *Acid Rain* (London: Pluto Press).
Engholm, B. (1985) 'The Scott report – a personal perspective', *Planning History Bulletin*, 7(2), 39–43.
Everson, P. and Williamson, T. (eds) (1998) *The Archaeology of Landscape* (Manchester University Press) 1–24.
Eyler, J.M. (1997) *Sir Arthur Newsholme and State Medicine* (Cambridge University Press).
Fedden, R. (1968) *The Continuing Purpose* (London: Longmans) 45–7.
Fletcher, J.S. (1918) *The Making of Modern Yorkshire* (London: Allen & Unwin) 204.
Foot, M. (1962) *Aneurin Bevan* (London: MacGibbon & Kee) 471–4.
Forestry Commission (1955) *Agreements on Afforestation in the Lake District* (London: HMSO).
Forestry Commission (1980) *Sixtieth Annual Report* (London: HMSO).
Fraser, D. (ed.) (1982) *Municipal Reform and the Industrial City* (Leicester University Press) 7–8.
Garner, R. (1999) 'Environmental policy', in *Changing Party Policy in Britain* (ed. R. Kelly) (Oxford: Blackwell) 215–32.
Gibson, J. and Peskett, P. (1998) *Record Offices. How to Find Them* (Bury: Federation of Family History Societies).
Goldsmith, E., *et al.* (1972) 'A blueprint for survival', *The Ecologist*, 2(1).
Goose, H. (1912) *Norwich Under Water, 1876 and 1912* (Norwich: Goose).
Gorbachev, M. (1996) *Memoirs* (London: Doubleday) 460–1.
Gregory, R. (1971) *The Price of Amenity* (London: Macmillan).
Grieve, H. (1959) *The Great Tide. The Story of the 1953 Flood Disaster in Essex* (Chelmsford: Essex County Council).
Hall, P. (1996) *Cities of Tomorrow* (Oxford: Blackwell) 4.
Hall, P. *et al.* (1973) *The Containment of Urban England. Volume I* (London: Allen & Unwin).
Haller, J.C. (1921) 'Roads and road transport', *Journal of the Institute of Transport*, 2, 156–64.
Hamlin, C. (1990) *A Science of Impurity* (Bristol: Adam Hilger) 8–9.

Hand, J.E. (ed.) (1906) *Science in Public Affairs* (London: George Allen).
Hardy, D. and Ward, C. (1985) 'Shoreham Beach: a case study in the emergence of modern town planning', *Town Planning Review*, 56, 273–91.
Hare, F.K. (1985) 'Future environments: can they be predicted?', *Transactions of the Institute of British Geographers*, 10, 131–7.
Harris, R. (ed.) (1997) *Margaret Thatcher. The Collected Speeches* (London: Harper Collins).
Harrison, M. (1991) 'Thomas Coglan Horsfall and the example of Germany', *Planning Perspectives*, 6, 297–314.
Hassan, J. (1998) *A History of Water in Modern England and Wales* (Manchester University Press).
Haworth, W. and Rodgers, C.P. (eds) (1992) *Agriculture, Conservation and Land Use* (Cardiff: University of Wales Press).
Healey, P. and Shaw, T. (1994) 'Changing meanings of "environment" in the British planning system', *Transactions of the Institute of British Geographers*, 19, 425–38.
Hennock, E. P. (1973) *Fit and Proper Persons* (London: Edward Arnold).
Hennock, E.P. (1982) 'Central–local government relations in England', *Urban History Yearbook* (no volume number), 38–49.
Hiley, W.E. (1939a) Editorial, *Quarterly Journal of Forestry*, 33, 1–4.
Hiley, W.E. (1939b) 'Swiss forestry', *Quarterly Journal of Forestry*, 33, 159–63.
Holdgate, M.W. (1996) *From Care to Action. Making a Sustainable World* (London: Earthscan).
Holford, W. (1948) Obituary notice, *Journal of the Royal Institute of British Architects*, 55, 38–9.
Holford, W. (1959) 'Power production and transmission in the countryside: preserving amenities', *Journal of the Royal Society of Arts*, 108, 180–210.
Holland, W.W. and Stewart, S. (1998) *Public Health* (London: Nuffield Trust).
Hooley, E.P. (1894) *Management of Highways* (London: Biggs).
Horne, R. and Frost, S. (1991) 'Opencast mining in England and Wales: a review of legislation and policy', *Land Use Policy*, 8, 29–35.
Horsfall, T.C. (1904) *The Improvement of the Dwellings and Surroundings of the People. The Example of Germany* (Manchester University Press).
Hoskins, W.G. (1955) *The Making of the English Landscape* (London: Hodder & Stoughton).
House of Lords Record Office (1997) *Witnesses Before Parliament. A Guide to the Data of Witnesses in Committees on Opposed Private Bills* (London: House of Lords Record Office Memorandum 85).

Howard, M. and Louis, W.R. (eds) (1998) *Oxford History of the Twentieth Century* (Oxford University Press) xix–xxii.
Huxley, J. (1931) *What Dare I Think?* (London: Chatto & Windus) 20–4.
Institute of Terrestrial Ecology (1997) *Ecology and Twyford Down* (Huntingdon: Centre for Ecology and Hydrology).
Institute of Terrestrial Ecology (1998) *Scientific Report, 1997–98* (Huntingdon: ITE) 74–9.
Keeble, L. (1952) *Principles and Practice in Town and Country Planning* (London: Estates Gazette).
Kimber, R. and Richardson, J.J. (eds) (1974) *Campaigning for the Environment* (London: Routledge & Kegan Paul) 212–25.
Kirby, K.J. and Watkins, C. (eds) (1998) *The Ecological History of European Forests* (Wallingford: CAB International) 1–24.
Lamb, R. (1996) *Promising the Earth* (London: Routledge).
Laybourn, K. (ed.) (1997) *Social Conditions, Status and Community* (Stroud: Sutton) 1–8.
Lemons, J. and Brown, D.A. (eds) (1995) *Sustainable Development* (Dordrecht: Kluwer Academic).
Leopold, C.C. (ed.) (1966) *A Sand Country Almanac* (New York: Oxford University Press).
Lister-Kaye, J. (1979) *Seal Cull* (Harmondsworth: Penguin).
Long, A.P. (1926) 'Fire control', *Journal of the Forestry Commission*, 5, 39–42.
Lord, E. (1999) *Investigating the Twentieth Century* (Stroud: Tempus).
Lord President of the Council (1957) *Forestry, Agriculture and Marginal Land. A Report of the Natural Resources (Technical) Committee* (London: HMSO) 5–7.
Lowe, P. and Goyder, J. (1983) *Environmental Groups in Politics* (London: Allen & Unwin).
Lowe, R. (1997) 'Archival report. Plumbing new depths', *Twentieth Century British History*, 8, 239–65.
Lowi, M.R. and Shaw, B.R. (2000) *Environment and Security* (London: Macmillan).
Lubchenco, J. (1998) 'Entering the century of the environment', *Science*, 279, 491–7.
Luckin, B. (1990) *Questions of Power. Electricity and Environment in Inter-War Britain* (Manchester University Press).
MacEwen, A. and MacEwen, M. (1982) *National Parks: Conservation or Cosmetics?* (London: Allen & Unwin).

Major, J. (1999) John Major. The Autobiography (London: HarperCollins) 510–1.
Mangold, P. (1998) From Tirpitz to Gorbachev (London: Macmillan).
Marr, T.E. (ed.) (1904) Housing Conditions in Manchester and Salford (Manchester: Sherratt & Hughes).
Massachusetts Institute of Technology (MIT) (1970) Man's Impact on the Global Environment (Cambridge, Mass.: MIT).
Matless, D. (1998) Landscape and Englishness (London: Reaktion Books) 25–7.
Mawhinney, B. (1999) In the Firing Line (London: HarperCollins).
May, R.M. (1995) 'The force behind a dramatic century', Financial Times, 18 November 1995.
Mayne, A. (1993) The Imagined Slum (Leicester University Press).
Mazower, M. (1998) Dark Continent (London: Allen Lane).
Middlemas, K. (1970) Politics in Industrial Society (London: Deutsch).
Ministry of Health (1921) Committee on Smoke and Noxious Vapours Abatement (London: HMSO).
Ministry of Health (1935) Report on Greater London Drainage (London: HMSO).
Ministry of Housing and Local Government (1964) The South East Study, 1961–1981 (London: HMSO).
Ministry of Transport (1963) Traffic in Towns (London: HMSO).
Ministry of Transport and Ministry of Agriculture and Fisheries (1922) Joint Committee on Damage to Fisheries (London: HMSO).
Moore, N.W. (1987) The Bird of Time. The Science and Politics of Nature Conservation (Cambridge University Press).
Moore-Colyer, R. (1996) 'Ironstone people and politics', Landscape History, 18, 57–70.
Mortimer, I. (ed.) (1997) Record Repositories in Great Britain (London: PRO Publications).
Muller, J. (1999) 'Although God cannot alter the past, historians can', Planning History, 21(2), 11–19.
Murray, K.A.H. (1955) Agriculture (London: HMSO).
National Farmers' Union (1977) Caring for the Countryside (London: NFU).
Nature Conservancy (1960) Annual Report (London: Nature Conservancy) 44–7.
Nature Conservancy Council (1984) Nature Conservation in Great Britain (Peterborough: NCC).
Newby, H. (1990) 'Ecology, amenity and society: social science and environmental change', Town Planning Review, 61, 3–12.

Newsholme, A. (1936) *The Last Thirty Years in Public Health* (London: Allen & Unwin) 46–7.

Newsome, D. (1997) *The Victorian World Picture* (London: Murray).

Newton, I. (1988) 'Determination of critical pollutant levels in wild populations', *Environmental Pollution*, 79, 143–51.

Oliver, F. (1931) 'The aesthetic aspect of afforestation', *Journal of the Forestry Commission,* 10, 51–4.

Oliver, F.W. (1928) 'Nature reserves', *Transactions of the Norfolk and Norwich Naturalists' Society*, 12, 317–22.

Openshaw, S., Carver, S. and Fernie, J. (1989) *Britain's Nuclear Waste* (London: Belhaven).

OECD (Organisation for Economic Cooperation and Development) (1977) *The OECD Programme on Long Range Transport of Air Pollutants* (Paris: OECD).

O'Riordan, T. (1985) 'Halvergate Marshes', *Ecos*, 6(1), 24–31.

O'Riordan, T., Kemp, R. and Purdue, M. (1988) *Sizewell B* (London: Macmillan).

Osborn, F.J. (1942) Introduction, in *Industry and Rural Life* (ed. H.B. Newbold) (London: Faber).

Osborn, F.J. and Whittick, A. (1963) *The New Towns: The Answer to Megalopis* (London: Leonard Hill).

Parliamentary Papers (PP), (1894) XVI, Part 1. *Report of Mr R. Hunter Pringle*, 31–133, Part 2. *Minutes of Evidence*, Q. 17682 and 17689.

PP (1902a) XXV Cd 1231. Local Government Board, *Thirty-First Annual Report, 1901–2* (London: Stationery Office) cxx–cxxi.

PP (1902b) XX Cd 1319. Departmental Committee on British Forestry, *Report*.

PP (1904) XXXII Cd 2175. Inter-Departmental Committee on Physical Deterioration, *Report*.

PP (1906) XLVIII Cd 3080. Royal Commission on Motor Cars, *Report*.

PP (1909) XIV Cd 4460. Royal Commission on Coastal Erosion, *Second Report (on Afforestation)*, 4.

PP (1911) XL. Road Board, *First Report*, 6–7.

PP (1912–13) XLVI Cd 6464. Royal Commission on Sewage Disposal, *Eighth Report*.

PP (1917–18) XVIII Cd 8881. Reconstruction Committee, Forestry Sub-Committee, *Final Report*.

PP (1921) XII. Forestry Commission, *First Annual Report*.

PP (1923) XI. Forestry Commission, *Third Annual Report*, 3–5.

PP (1924–25) XII. Forestry Commission, *Fifth Annual Report*, 6
PP (1926) XXIII Cmd 2581. Minister of Agriculture and Fisheries, *Agricultural Policy*.
PP (1927) X. Forestry Commission, *Seventh Annual Report*, 6–7.
PP (1930–31) XVI Cmd 3851. Financial Secretary to the Treasury, *Report of the National Park Committee*.
PP (1936–37) XII Cmd 5303. Minister of Labour, *Third Report of the Commissioner for the Special Areas (England and Wales)*.
PP (1939–40) IV Cmd 6153. Royal Commission on the Distribution of the Industrial Population, *Report*.
PP (1941–42) IV Cmd 6386. Expert Committee on Compensation and Betterment, *Final Report*.
PP (1942–43) IV Cmd 6447. Forestry Commission, *Post-War Forest Policy*.
PP (1943–44) III Cmd 6500. Forestry Commission, *Supplementary Report on Post-War Forestry Policy*.
PP (1943–44) VIII Cmd 6537. Minister of Town and Country Planning, *The Control of Land Use*.
PP (1944–45) V Cmd 6628. Minister of Town and Country Planning, *National Parks in England and Wales*.
PP (1945–46) XIII Cmd 6906. Minister of Town and Country Planning, *Report on the Restoration Problem in the Ironstone Industry*.
PP (1944–46) XIII Cmd 6906. Minister of Town and Country Planning, *Report on the Restoration Problems in the Ironstone Industry in the Midlands*.
PP (1946–47a) XIII Cmd 7121. Minister of Town and Country Planning, *Report of the National Parks Committee*.
PP (1946–47b) XIII Cmd 7122. Minister of Town and Country Planning, *Conservation of Nature in England and Wales*.
PP (1948–49) XIX Cmd 7695. Royal Commission of Population, *Report*.
PP (1953–54a) XIII Cmd 9165. Minister of Housing and Local Government, *Report of the Departmental Committee on Coastal Flooding*.
PP (1953–54b) VIII Cmd 9322. Minister of Housing and Local Government, *Committee on Air Pollution report*.
PP (1957–58) House of Commons, Standing Committee B, Volume II, *Opencast Coal Bill 1958*, col. 589–97.
PP (1962–63) XXII Cmnd 2056. Lord President of the Council, *Noise. Final Report*.
PP (1965–66) XIII, Cmnd 2928. Minister of Land and Natural Resources, *Leisure in the Countryside: England and Wales*.

PP (1966–67) XLIX, Cmd 3246. Secretary of State for the Home Department, *The Torrey Canyon*.
PP (1969–70) XII, Cmnd 4375. Secretary of State, *Protecting the Environment. The Fight Against Pollution*.
PP (1974–75) IV, Cmnd 6020. Secretaries of State and Minister of Agriculture, *Food from Our Own Resources*.
PP (1983–84) HL-247. Select Committee on the European Committee, *Agriculture and the Environment*.
PP (1984–85) HC-6. Commons Committee on the Environment, *First Report. Operation and effectiveness of Part II of the Wildlife and Countryside Act 1981*.
PP (1989–90) Cm 1200. Secretary of State et al. *This Common Inheritance – Britain's Environmental Strategy*.
PP (1990–91) Cm 1655. Secretary of State et al. *This Common Inheritance. The First Year Report*.
PP (1993–94) Cm 2674. Royal Commission on Environmental Pollution, *Transport and the Environment*.
PP (1994–95) Cm 3016. Secretary of State for the Environment and Minister of Agriculture, *Rural England*.
Pearce, F. (1987) *Acid Rain* (London: Penguin).
Pearson, C.H. (1893) *National Life and Character* (London: Macmillan).
Pearson, R.S. (1933) Address, *Forestry*, 7, 1–3.
Pearson, S. Vere (1939) *London's Overgrowth and the Causes of Swollen Towns* (London: Daniel).
Peterson, J.A. (1979) 'The impact of sanitary reform upon American city planning', *Journal of Social History*, 13, 83–104.
Pimlott, J.A.R. (1947) *The Englishman's Holiday* (London: Faber).
Plowden, W. (1971) *The Motor Car and Politics, 1896–1970* (London: Bodley Head).
Rawcliffe, P. (1998) *Environmental Pressure Groups in Transition* (Manchester University Press).
Rawling, S.O. (1933) *Infra-Red Photography* (London: Blackie).
Read, G.F. (ed.) (1997) *Sewers – Rehabilitation and New Construction* (London: Edward Arnold) 33.
Redclift, M. (1994) 'Relections on the "sustainable development" debate', *International Journal of Sustainable Development and World Ecology*, 1, 3–21.
Redclift, M. (1995) 'In our own image. The environment and society as global discourse', *Environment and History*, 1, 111–24.
Redwood, J. (1999) *The Death of Britain?* (Basingstoke: Macmillan).

Roberts, T.M. and Sheail, J. (1993) 'Air quality', in *Environmental Dilemmas* (ed. R.J. Berry) (London: Chapman & Hall) 47–71.
Robertson, W.A. (1943) 'Post-war forest policy', *Forestry*, 17, 1–10.
Robinson, R. (1938) 'British forestry', *Scottish Forestry Journal*, 52, 26–40.
Robinson, R.L. (1952) 'The Society of Foresters of Great Britain', *Forestry*, 25, 82–4.
Rogers, A. (1999) *The Most Revolutionary Measure. A History of the Rural Development Commssion* (Salisbury: Rural Development Commission).
Rosen, C.M. and Tarr, J.A. (1994) 'The importance of an urban perspective in environmental history', *Journal of Urban History*, 20, 299–310.
Rothman, H. (2000) *Saving the Planet. The American Response to the Environment in the Twentieth Century* (Chicago: Dee).
Rothschild, M. and Marren, P. (1997) *Rothschild's Reserves* (Colchester: Harley Books).
Royal Ministry of Foreign Affairs and Royal Ministry of Agriculture (1971) *Air Pollution Across National Boundaries* (Stockholm).
Ryle, G. (1969) *Forest Service* (Newton Abbot: David & Charles).
Scarfe, N.V. (1942) 'Essex', in *The Land of Britain* (ed. L.D. Stamp) (London: Geographical Publications) Part 82.
Schaffer, F. (ed.) (1972) *The New Town Story* (London: Palladin).
Schaffer, F. (1974) 'The Town and Country Planning Act 1947', *The Planner*, 60, 690–5.
Schama, S. (1995) *Landscape and Memory* (London: HarperCollins) 12–13.
Schneer, J. (1999) *London 1900. The Imperial Metropolis* (New Haven: Yale University Press).
Scopes, F. (1968) *The Development of Corby Works* (London: Stewarts & Lloyds).
Shabecoff, P. (1996) *A New Name for Peace* (Hanover, NH: University Press of New England).
Sharp, E. (1960) 'What's wrong with local government', *Municipal Review*, 31, 712–17.
Sharp, F. (1969) *The Ministry of Housing and Local Government* (London: Allen & Unwin) 20–7.
Sharp, T. (1936) *English Panorama* (London: Dent).
Sheail, J. (1973) 'Changes in the use and management of farmland in England and Wales, 1915–19', *Transactions of the Institute of British Geographers*, 60, 17–32.
Sheail, J. (1975) 'The concept of national parks in Great Britain before 1950', *Transactions of the Institute of British Geographers*, 66, 41–56.

Sheail, J. (1976a) *Nature in Trust: A History of Nature Conservation in Britain* (Glasgow: Blackie).
Sheail, J. (1976b) 'Coasts and planning in Great Britain before 1950', *Geographical Journal*, 142, 257–73.
Sheail, J. (1977) 'The impact of recreation on the coast; the Lindsey County Council (Sandhills) Act, 1932', *Landscape Planning*, 4, 53–72.
Sheail, J. (1979a) 'The introduction of statutory planning in rural areas; the example of the North Riding of Yorkshire', *Town Planning Review*, 50, 71–83.
Sheail, J. (1979b) 'The Restriction of Ribbon Development Act: the character and perception of land-use control in inter-war Britain', *Regional Studies*, 13, 501–12.
Sheail, J. (1981) *Rural Conservation in Inter-War Britain* (Oxford University Press).
Sheail, J. (1983) '"Deserts of the moon". The Mineral Workings Act and the restoration of ironstone workings in Northamptonshire', *Town Planning Review*, 54, 405–24.
Sheail, J. (1984) 'Constraints on water-resource development in England and Wales: the concept and management of compensation flows', *Journal of Environmental Management*, 19, 351–61.
Sheail, J. (1985) *Pesticides and Nature Conservation: The British Experience 1950–1975* (Oxford: Clarendon Press).
Sheail, J. (1987) *Seventy-Five Years in Ecology. The British Ecological Society* (London: Blackwell Scientific).
Sheail, J. (1991a) *Power in Trust: An Environmental History of the Central Electricity Generating Board* (Oxford: Clarendon Press).
Sheail, J. (1991b) 'Road surfacing and the threat to inland fisheries', *Journal of Transport History*, 12, 135–47.
Sheail, J. (1991c) 'The Opencast Coal Act 1958', *Town Planning Review*, 62, 201–14.
Sheail, J. (1992) 'Opencast coal mining and the restoration of farmland', *Journal of the Royal Agricultural Society*, 152, 100–11.
Sheail, J. (1993a) 'Pollution and the protection of inland fisheries in inter-war Britain', in *Science and Nature. Essays in the History of the Environmental Sciences* (ed. M. Shortland) (London: British Society for the History of Science) 41–56.
Sheail, J. (1993b) 'The agricultural pollution of watercourses: the precedents set by the beet-sugar and milk industries', *Agricultural History Review*, 41, 31–43.

Sheail, J. (1993c) 'Sewering the English suburbs', *Journal of Historical Geography*, 19, 433–47.
Sheail, J. (1993d) '"Taken for granted" – the inter-war West Middlesex drainage scheme', *London Journal*, 18, 143–56.
Sheail, J. (1995a) 'New Towns, sewerage, and the allocation of financial responsibility: the post-war UK experience', *Town Planning Review*, 66, 371–87.
Sheail, J. (1995b) 'John Dower, national parks, and town and country planning in Britain', *Planning Perspectives*, 10, 1–16.
Sheail, J. (1995c) 'War and the development of nature conservation in Britain', *Journal of Environmental Management*, 44, 267–83.
Sheail, J. (1995d) 'Nature protection, ecologists and the farming context', *Journal of Rural Studies*, 11, 79–88.
Sheail, J. (1996) 'Town wastes, agricultural sustainability and Victorian sewage farms', *Urban History*, 23, 189–210.
Sheail, J. (1997a) 'The sustainable management of industrial watercourses – an English perspective', *Environmental History*, 2, 197–215.
Sheail, J. (1997b) 'Scott revisited: post-war agriculture, planning and the British countryside', *Journal of Rural Studies*, 13, 387–98.
Sheail, J. (1997c) 'The new National Forest', *Town Planning Review*, 68, 305–23.
Sheail, J. (1997d) 'The National Forest of the English Midlands – a local government perspective', *Local Government Studies*, 23, 1–16.
Sheail, J. (1997e) 'Business and the environment: an inter-war perspective on the Federation of British Industries', *Contemporary British History*, 11, 21–41.
Sheail, J. (1998) *Nature Conservation in Britain: The Formative Years* (London: Stationery Office).
Sheail, J. (2000) 'The Countryside (Scotland) Act of 1967 revisited', *Scottish Geographical Journal*, 116, 25–40.
Sheail, J. (2001) 'Leisure in the English countryside: policy making in the 1960s', *Planning Perspectives*, 16, 67–84.
Sheail, J. and Mountford, J.O. (1984) 'Changes in the perception and impact of agricultural improvement: post-war trends in the Romney Marsh', *Journal of the Royal Agricultural Society*, 145, 43–56.
Shoard, M. (1980) *Theft of the Countryside* (Aldershot: Temple Smith).
Short, B. (1997) *The Benefit of State Surveillance in Twentieth-Century Britain* (University of Cambridge, Board of Continuing Education, Occasional Papers 2).

Sidwick, J.M. (1976) 'A brief history of sewage treatment', *Effluent Water Treatment Journal*, 16, 193–9.
Silkin, Lord (1972) Foreword, in *The New Town Story* (ed. F. Shaffer) (London: Paladin) 11–13.
Simmons, I.G. (1993) *Environmental History. A Concise Introduction* (Oxford: Blackwell).
Smith, A.E. (1970) *Nature Conservation in Lincolnshire* (Lincoln: Lincolnshire Naturalists' Union).
Smith, E.G. (1989) 'Environmentally Sensitive Areas: a successful UK initiative', *Journal of the Royal Agricultural Society*, 150, 30–43.
Smout, T.C. (ed.) (1993) Introduction, in *Scotland since Prehistory: Natural Change and Human Impact* (Aberdeen: Scottish Cultural Press) xiii–xx.
Smout, T.C. (2000) *Nature Contested. Environmental History in Scotland and Northern England since 1600* (Edinburgh University Press).
Stamp, L.D. (1946) 'The place of science in town and country planning', *Advancement of Science*, 3, 337–48.
Stamp, L.D. (1948) *The Land of Britain: Its Use and Misuse* (London: Longmans Green).
Steers, J.A. (1944) 'Coastal preservation and planning', *Geographical Journal*, 104, 9–27.
Steers, J.A. (1948) *The Coastline of England and Wales* (Cambridge University Press).
Steers, J.A. (1973) *The Coastline of Scotland* (Cambridge University Press).
Steinberg, T. (1991) *Nature Incorporated* (Cambridge University Press).
Steven, H.M. (1952) 'The progress of technical forestry in Britain, 1926–51', *Forestry*, 25, 85–91.
Summers, C. (1978) 'Grey seals', *New Scientist*, 80 (1131), 694–5.
Sutcliffe, A. (1981a) 'Why planning history?', *Built Environment*, 7, 65–7.
Sutcliffe, A. (1981b) 'Britain, public health, suburbanization and the example of Germany', in *Towards the Planned City: Germany, Britain, the United States and France, 1780–1914* (ed. A.R. Sutcliffe) (Oxford: Blackwell) 47–87.
Sutcliffe, A. (1988) 'Britain's first town planning act', *Town Planning Review*, 59, 289–303.
Sutcliffe, A. (1999) 'Twenty-five years of planning history', *Planning History*, 21(2), 9–10.
Tarr, J. (1996) *The Search for the Ultimate Sink – Urban Pollution in Historical Perspective* (Akron: University of Akron Press).

Tarr, J. et al. (1984) 'Water wastes: a retrospective assessment', *Technology and culture*, 25, 226–63.
Taylor, W.L. (1930) 'The problem of fire in British forests', *Forestry*, 4, 78–92.
Taylor, W.L. (1939) 'Forestry, foresters and forestry policy in Great Britain', *Forestry*, 13, 99–104.
Thatcher, M. (1993) *The Downing Street Years* (London: HarperCollins) 638–41.
Thirsk, J. (ed.) (2000) *The English Rural Landscape* (Oxford University Press) 9–14.
Tomlinson, P. (1982) 'The environmental impact of opencast coal mining', *Town Planning Review*, 53, 5–28.
Trafford, B. (1978) 'Recent progress in field drainage', *Journal of the Royal Agricultural Society*, 139, 139–40.
Trevelyan, G.M. (1929) *Must England's Beauty Perish?* (London: Faber).
Trevelyan, G.M. (1931) *The Call and Claim of Natural Beauty* (London: University College).
Troup, R.S. (1938) *Forestry and State Control* (Oxford: Clarendon Press).
Vincent, D. (1998) *The Culture of Secrecy. Britain, 1832–1998* (Oxford University Press) 141–2.
Wade, P.M., Sheail, J. and Child, L. (eds) (1998) 'The National Forest; from vision to reality', *East Midland Geographer*, 21(1).
Walker, P. (1977) *The Ascent of Britain* (London: Sidgwick & Jackson) 181–2.
Ward, B. and Dubos, R. (1972) *Only One Earth* (London: Deutsch).
Ward, S.V. (1988) *The Geography of Interwar Britain: The State and Uneven Development* (London: Routledge) 211–27.
Ward, S.V. (ed.) (1992) *The Garden City: Past, Present and Future* (London: Spon).
Warde Fowler, W. (1893) 'Gilbert White of Selborne', *Macmillan's Magazine*, 68, 182–9.
Watson, P. (2000) *A Terrible Beauty* (London: Weidenfeld & Nicolson) 580–1.
Webb, S. and Webb, B. (1920) *A Contribution for the Socialist Commonwealth of Great Britain* (Cambridge University reprint 1975).
Wells, T.C.E. and Sheail, J. (1988) 'The effects of agricultural change on the wildlife interest of lowland grasslands', in: *Environmental Management in Agriculture* (ed. J.R. Park) (London: Belhaven Press) 186–201.
Whitby, M. (ed.) (1996) *The European Environment and CAP Reform Policies and Prospects for Conservation* (Wallingford: CAB International).
Williams, M. (1998) 'The end of modern history', *Geographical Review*, 88, 275–300.

Williamson, P. (1999) *Stanley Baldwin* (Cambridge University Press) 12–18.
Wilson, H. (1971) *The Labour Government* (London: Weidenfeld and Nicolson) 706 and 732–3.
Winegarten, A. and Acland-Hood, M. (1978) 'British agriculture and the 1947 Agricultural Act', *Journal of the Royal Agricultural Society*, 139, 74–82.
Winter, J. (1999) *Secure from Rash Assault* (Berkeley: University of California).
Winter, M. (1996) *Rural Politics* (London: Routledge).
Wise, M.J. (1962) 'The Midland Reafforesting Association and the reclamation of derelict land in the Black Country', *Landscape Design*, 57, 13–18.
Wood, F. (1912) *Modern Road Construction* (London: Griffin).
World Commission on Environment and Development (1987) *Our Common Future* (London: Oxford University Press).
Worster, D. (ed.) (1988) *The Ends of the Earth. Perspectives on Modern Environmental History* (Cambridge University Press) 289–308.
Worster, D. (1990) 'Transformations of the earth: toward an agroecological perspective in history', *Journal of American History*, 76, 1087–106.
Yelling, J.A. (1986) *Slums and Slum Clearance in Victorian London* (London: Allen & Unwin).
Young, K. and Garside, P. (1982) *Metropolitan London. Politics and Urban Change, 1837–1981* (London: Arnold) 165–6.

Index

Abercrombie, P. 23, 24–5, 28, 30, 105–6, 108, 259
acid rain 190, 251–6, 275
Acland, Francis Dyke 83, 86, 87, 88, 89
aerodrome (airfield, airport) 116, 191–6, 198, 199, 200, 208
afforestation 84, 85, 87–8, 89, 90–6
agriculture (farming) 7, 10, 54, 109–15, 119, 151–7, 158–65, 173, 220, 231, 232, 233, 235–45, 260, 261
Agriculture Act
 1947 151
 1986 167, 168–9
airfield *see* aerodrome
airport *see* aerodrome
amenity 78–9, 94–8, 99–100, 104, 110, 115, 118–20, 133, 158, 184, 228, 233
archaeology 2, 189, 215, 217
archives 7, 11
Areas of Outstanding Natural Beauty 122, 133, 134, 136, 189, 216
Association of British Manufacturers of Agricultural Chemicals 237, 239, 244
Association for the Preservation of Rural Scotland 106, 108

Barber, D. 164, 165, 174
Basildon New Town 63–72
Bevan, A. 33
Bevin, E. 35–6
Birmingham 18, 58, 76, 188, 207
Board of Agriculture 82, 83, 85, 87, 88, 110, 260
Board of Agriculture for Scotland 86, 87
Board of Trade 28, 194, 204, 207
Boer War 13, 15
Brighton 49
Brighton Corporation Act 1931 35

British Coal (National Coal Board) 234, 235, 254
British Ecological Society 125, 128
British Petroleum 198, 201, 214
Buchanan, C.D. 182, 185, 191–4
Buchanan Report 185–7
Burns, J. 19, 21, 219

Cabinet 8, 30, 33, 68, 69, 74–5, 151, 230, 233, 249
 Home Affairs Committee 139, 142, 144, 200, 201, 204, 205, 206, 242, 249
 Natural Resources (Technical) Committee 98
 Reconstruction Committee 120, 121
Callaghan, J. 134, 225
car ownership 1, 37, 45, 95, 123, 139, 140, 142, 178, 182, 185
carbon dioxide emissions 255–6
Carson, R. 222, 235–6, 245
Central Electricity Generating Board 132–3, 214, 223–6, 251, 252, 253, 254, 255
Chamberlain, N. 107, 109, 125, 184
chemical industry/works 53–4, 199–200, 235–45
Chernobyl 226–7
Clean Air Act 1956 248–50
climate change 255–6, 275, 276
coal industry 24, 55–6, 137, 218, 227, 231–5, 247, 250, 254, 259
coast 36, 41, 124, 131–7, 140, 148
compensation and betterment 23, 32, 38, 40, 43, 44, 161, 162, 164, 183–5, 200
Confederation of British Industry 188, 214, 246, 266–71, 282
Cornwall 133, 221, 222
Council for the Preservation of Rural Wales 106, 108

301

Council for the Preservation (Protection) of Rural England 96–7, 106–8, 116, 131, 162, 163, 164, 182, 229, 263
Country Landowners' Association 166, 169, 175, 202, 203, 210, 211
Countryside Act 1968 100, 122, 145
Countryside (Scotland) Act 1967 99–100, 145
Countryside Commissions 122, 139, 141, 143, 144–5, 154, 159, 161, 163, 164, 165, 166, 168–75, 216
'Countryside in 1970' Conferences 138–9, 140, 142
Crosland, A. 134, 146, 193, 195
Crossman, R.H.S. 8, 74, 135, 136
Crouch, river 64–72
Crowe, S. 78–9, 100–1
Cumberland (Cumbria) 28, 97, 105, 224, 227

Dalton, H. 66, 68, 70, 230–1
Dent, G. 127, 129
Department of Agriculture and Fisheries for Scotland 149, 150, 158, 164, 167
Department of Energy 207, 208, 209, 224, 225, 226, 253
Department of the Environment 146, 147, 155, 156, 157, 161–4, 169, 174–6, 188, 195, 208, 209, 214, 224, 253, 255, 269, 277, 280
Department of Trade and Industry 146, 194, 195, 197, 207, 278
Doncaster 22, 23, 24, 191
Dower, John 96, 116–22, 128, 140, 191
Dower, Michael 140, 165
Durham 28, 29
Duke of Edinburgh 135, 138, 235

East Coast Flood Disaster 219–21
ecology 2, 78, 79–80, 215, 261–2, 264
electricity industry 191, 203, 223–7, 250–5
empire 12, 15, 83, 127, 258
Enterprise Neptune 134–7
environmental assessment 214–6

environmental history 1, 2, 3, 4, 9, 10, 265–6
environmental movement 6, 11, 17, 147, 263–4, 265, 278, 279
Essex 59–61, 64–73, 110, 111, 192, 196, 219–20
Esso 197, 198, 199, 200, 201, 207–17
Esso Petroleum Act 1961 197–203, 204
Europe 2–3, 82, 93, 127, 130, 159, 196, 252, 253, 262
European Conservation Year 1970 146, 147, 265, 272
European Economic Community 197, 212, 214
  Common Agricultural Policy 167–8
Exmoor 154–7, 159, 160

farming see agriculture
Federation of British Industries 50, 246, 247
fisheries 50, 64–71, 73, 79, 104, 148–50, 180–1, 252
Forest Parks 81, 94–8
Forestry Act 1919 83, 92
Forestry Commission 10, 83, 84, 87, 90, 92, 93, 94–7, 98–102, 171, 175, 234
Forestry Sub-Committee of Reconstruction Committee 83, 84, 86, 87, 88
Foulness (Maplin Sands) 193–6
Friends of the Earth 147, 148, 162, 163, 164, 190, 276

Garden Cities see New Towns
gas industry 16, 53
Gatwick 192, 208
Geddes 'axe' 84, 90
government, central 7–8, 27–33, 34, 41, 42, 43–5, 49–50, 72, 89, 107–8, 109, 114, 135, 137, 151, 158, 173–6, 200–3, 212, 221, 223–7, 246, 255, 264, 269, 272, 280
government, local 21, 22, 23–6, 31, 32, 33–41, 42, 43–5, 49–50, 108–9, 122, 141–2, 172–3, 177–8, 203, 228, 264, 270, 279
Graffham Water 75, 79

Index

green belt 44, 131
Greenpeace 148, 149, 279
Greenwood, A 9, 108
Grieve, R. 142–3
Gummer, J. 167, 176

Hampshire 91, 104, 180, 181, 189–91, 198, 200, 203, 217
Heathrow 192, 198, 199, 200, 208
Hertfordshire 59–61, 192
Highlands 86, 95–7, 141, 143, 144
Holford, W. 120, 133
holidays 35–8
Holidays with Pay Act 1938 35
Home Counties 28, 30, 44, 57
Home Office 37, 219–20
Horsfall, T.C. 17, 18, 19
House of Commons 33, 34, 76–8, 80, 90, 97, 135, 164, 202, 203, 206, 219–20, 221, 230, 248–9
House of Lords 29, 34, 39–41, 80, 96, 114, 167–8, 182–3, 205–6
housing 13–14, 19–20, 39–40, 44, 56, 57, 69, 131, 182–4, 233
Housing, Town Planning, &c., Act 1909 19–20, 21, 27, 259
Howard, E. 10, 42, 62
Hudson, R.S. 112, 114

Imperial Chemical Industries (ICI) 79, 244
iron-ore industry 228–31

Keilder Water 79–81, 101
Kent 106, 152–3, 180, 217, 238

Lake District 73–5, 95–7, 101, 105, 108, 114, 139, 172, 253
Lancashire 73, 232, 234
land drainage 57, 111, 152, 154, 160, 161–2, 218–9
Layfield Enquiry 225–6
Lee, river 59, 60, 61, 63
Leeds 47, 48, 186
Leicestershire 79, 171, 172, 174–5
Letchworth Garden City 19, 62
Lincolnshire 130–1

Lindsey County Council (Sandhills Act) 1932, 36–8
Local Acts 33–41, 72
Local Government Act
  1894 177
  1929 22
Local Government Board 19, 21, 47, 49, 50, 219
local history 1–2
London 12, 14, 15, 30, 49, 57–61, 63, 76, 104, 125, 186, 188, 189, 191, 192, 193, 194, 196, 198, 208, 248

MacDonald, J.R.L 91, 107, 108, 183, 184
Manchester 13, 14, 16, 17, 18, 19, 47, 73–5, 207, 209
Manchester and Salford Sanitary Association 13, 14, 15, 16, 17, 18, 258
Maplin Sands *see* Foulness
Marples, E. 200, 205
Middlesex County Council Acts 58, 184
Middlesex East Drainage Scheme 59–61
Middlesex West Drainage Scheme 58–9, 60
Midland Reafforesting Association 227–8
Midlands 28, 207, 209, 228
Midlands Forest *see* National Forest
Milford Haven 207, 209
Minister for Science 242–3
Ministry of Agriculture, Fisheries and Food 50, 64–71, 92, 111, 112, 122, 151, 152, 154, 155, 156, 159, 161, 162, 164, 166, 167–8, 169, 176, 180, 181, 211, 233, 234, 235–45, 277, 280
Ministry of Health 9, 21, 22, 23, 24, 26, 31, 34–5, 37, 43, 57, 59, 61, 64, 65, 68, 69, 106, 107, 108, 109, 183–4, 229, 232, 242, 246
Ministry of Housing and Local Government 68, 74–5, 100, 135–6, 138, 146, 220, 221, 249, 272
Ministry of Land and Natural Resources 135, 137, 139

Ministry of Local Government and Planning 68, 69, 70
Ministry of (Fuel and) Power 197, 199, 200, 201, 204, 205, 206, 207, 223, 232, 233, 235
Ministry of Town and Country Planning 31, 39–41, 62–7, 119, 120–2, 229, 233
Ministry of Transport 146, 180, 181–2, 183–4, 185, 189, 190, 200, 205
Moorhouse, J. 14, 15
Morrison, W.S. 67, 120
motorways 143, 186, 188–90

National Coal Board *see* British Coal
National Farmers' Union 156, 166, 200, 202, 203, 210, 211
National Forest (Midlands Forest) 170–6
National Park Committee 1929–31 107–8
National Parks 96, 98, 107–9, 114, 115–22, 133, 134, 136, 137, 141, 155–6, 158–9, 165
National Parks and Access to the Countryside Act 1949 122, 154
National Parks Commission 27, 121, 122, 136, 139, 141
National Parks Committee 1945–47 122, 128
National Trust 96, 102, 104–5, 124–7, 133–7, 156, 258–9, 263
National Trust for Scotland 143
Natural Environment Research Council 147, 148, 149, 190, 253
Naturalists' (Wildlife) Trusts 127, 130–1, 147, 191
Nature Conservancy 128–30, 133, 138, 147, 154, 155, 195, 222, 238, 240
Nature Conservancy Council 147, 149, 159, 160, 161, 168, 216
nature reserves 2, 119, 122–30, 161, 216
Nettlefold, J.C. 18, 19, 20
New Forest 92, 104, 170, 172, 176, 210
New Towns (Garden Cities) 9, 10, 27, 42, 62–72, 143, 172
New Towns Act 1946 62
Newbury 186, 189

Newsholme, A. 49–50
Nicholson, M. 129, 138
nitrogen oxides emissions 253, 255
Norfolk 91, 124, 126, 218
Norfolk Broads 161, 163, 164, 168
Norfolk Naturalists' Trust 126–7
North-East 12, 28, 79–81
North-West 28, 209
Northamptonshire 228–31
Northumberland 80–1, 101, 116, 131, 235
Norwich 14, 186, 218–19
Nottinghamshire 14, 50–6, 171, 172, 177–8, 179
nuclear power industry 222–7
nuclear power stations 133, 134, 223–7, 250

oil industry 197–217, 278–9
oil refineries 134, 197–8, 201, 207, 221–2
  Fawley 198, 199, 207, 208, 209, 210
Oliver, F. 124, 125–6, 127
Opencast Coal Act 1958 234–5
Osborn, F. 63, 112
outdoor recreation 16, 35–8, 94–8, 101–2, 108, 118–19, 137, 139–45, 158, 165, 169, 170–6, 263
oyster fishery 62–73

Patten C. 174, 277
Pembrokeshire 134, 139
Pennines 12, 114, 191
Pepler, G. 24, 106–7, 109
personal health 12, 13, 14, 15, 18, 35
pesticides 11, 222, 235–45
Pipe-lines Act 1962 197, 204–7, 213
pipelines 10, 196–217
  mainline 207, 209
  midline 209, 212, 215, 216, 217
  South-East 208–9, 210–12, 213, 215, 216, 217
Pipelines Inspectorate 200, 205, 206, 207, 211, 213
planning history 4–5, 10, 17, 62, 82
pollution 271–3
  air 11, 16, 17, 177–8, 246–56, 262

Index

pollution – *continued*
   water   46–56, 57–61, 63–72, 213, 262
population   12–13, 30, 45, 57, 62, 259
Porchester, Lord   155, 156, 157, 158
power stations   250–1, 254, 255
Private Bills   72, 104–5, 197, 199, 202, 203
public health   12, 13, 14, 37, 48–56, 258

radioactivity   222–7
Ramblers' Association   102, 175
record offices   *see* archives
Reith, Lord   31, 32, 112, 132
reservoirs   73–81, 197
Restriction of Ribbon Development Act 1935   182–5
ribbon development   62, 107, 182–5
roads   105, 177–81, 182–91
   dust   178–9
   surfacing   178–82
Robinson, R.   92, 96–8, 99
Romney Marsh   152
Roskill Commission   193, 196
Royal Commission on Coastal Erosion   85
Royal Commission on the Distribution of Industrial Population   30, 112
Royal Commission on Environmental Pollution   177, 272
Royal Commission on Population   260–1
Royal Commission on Sewage Disposal   47, 48, 49, 51
Royal Society of London   254, 275
Rutland Water   75–9

Scandinavia   82, 251, 252, 253, 254, 266, 273
science and technology   48, 259, 260, 261–2, 263, 271, 273, 274, 275
Scotland   28, 29, 30, 44, 132, 141–2, 143, 144–5, 149, 191, 198, 227, 252, 253
Scott, Lord Justice, 112, 113, 115, 118
Scottish Office   90, 141, 142, 143, 144
Seals   148–50

Secretary of State for Scotland   31, 92, 99, 101, 142, 144–5, 149, 151, 236, 277
Selborne, Lord   88–90
sewerage   46–8, 49–56, 57–61, 63–73
Shell   210, 279
Shell Chemicals   237, 239, 242, 243, 244, 245
Silkin, L.   39, 41, 62, 67, 230
Site of Special Scientific Interest   154, 159, 161, 189, 196, 216
Sizewell B   225–6
slums   13–14, 18, 19, 20, 62, 76
smog   247–8
smoke abatement   246, 247, 249
Soames, C.   235, 240, 242, 243, 244, 245
Society for the Promotion of Nature Reserves   123, 125, 127, 130
Somerset   25, 116, 160, 161, 279
South-East   29, 44–5, 64, 75, 193, 194, 196, 208
South-West   116, 188
Special Areas   29 97
Stamp, L.D.   26–7, 113, 114
Standing Committee on National Parks   108–9, 118
Stansted   192, 196, 208
suburbs   18, 19, 22, 41, 56–61, 62, 182–5, 186
sulphur emissions   250–6
surface water acidification   251–5
Surrey   91, 184
sustainable development   258, 264, 266, 274, 278, 280–1

Teesdale   78–80
Thames, river   64–72, 104, 131, 198, 216, 220
Thatcher, M.   163, 225, 275–6
timber industry   82, 91, 98, 170, 171, 173, 175
Torrey Canyon   221–2, 272
tourism   94–5, 142, 143, 221
Town and Country Planning Act 1932   22, 27, 43, 108
Town and Country Planning Act 1947   27, 32–3, 41, 43, 122, 185, 230

town planning 20–6, 32–3, 40–1, 42–5, 48, 59, 62–4, 106, 108–9, 112, 116, 118, 160, 162–3, 164, 191, 193, 225, 228, 230–1, 235, 259, 264, 267–71
Treasury 9, 32, 63, 64, 83, 92, 94, 97, 100, 108, 109, 122, 132, 134–5, 144, 145, 164, 175, 206, 220, 231, 249, 254, 269, 277
Tyne, river 79–81
Tyneside 28, 29

United Nations General Assembly 276
  Conference on the Human Environment 1972 251, 272, 273
  Conference on the Human Environment 1982 252–3, 274
  Earth Summit at Rio 1992 11, 255–6, 277–8, 280
United States 2, 4, 5, 46, 121, 127, 128, 138, 140, 186, 200, 201, 214, 315, 222, 224–5, 227, 240, 245, 261, 264–5, 271

Vincent, H.G. 112, 117, 132

Waldegrave, W.M. 162, 164
Wales 28, 29, 30, 44, 136, 209, 235, 252, 253, 277
  North 98, 101, 106, 131, 227
  South 28, 207, 218, 232

Walker P. 146, 188, 226
War, First World 20, 21, 83, 980–9, 110, 151, 260
War, Second World 26, 31–2, 84, 98–9, 111, 116, 117, 120, 127–8, 152, 232
waste disposal 10, 14, 46–8, 49–56, 57–61, 63–72, 278–9
Water Resources Board 75, 77, 79
water supply 10, 13, 46, 47, 60, 63, 72–81, 213, 232
Watson, J.D. 58–61
Welwyn Garden City 62, 63
West Sussex County Council (Lancing and Shoreham Beaches) Bill 39–41
Wicken Fen 105, 124–5, 126
wild life 104, 110, 115, 123–31, 137, 158, 160, 190–1, 236, 237–45, 263
Wild Life Conservation Special Committee 128, 129
Wildlife and Countryside Act 1981 158, 161, 167
Willey, F. 135, 137, 139, 140, 141, 142
Wilson, H. 221, 272

Yorkshire 21, 22, 24–6, 36, 104, 123, 127, 160
Yorkshire Dales 117–18

Zuckerman, S. 221–2, 236, 272